A Selectional Theory of Adjunct Control

Linguistic Inquiry Monographs
Samuel Jay Keyser, general editor

A complete list of books published in the Linguistic Inquiry Monographs series appears at the back of this book.

A Selectional Theory of Adjunct Control

Idan Landau

The MIT Press
Cambridge, Massachusetts
London, England

The MIT Press would like to thank the anonymous peer reviewers who provided comments on drafts of this book. The generous work of academic experts is essential for establishing the authority and quality of our publications. We acknowledge with gratitude the contributions of these otherwise uncredited readers.

This book was set in Times New Roman by Westchester Publishing Services. Printed and bound in the United States of America.

Library of Congress Cataloging-in-Publication

Names: Landau, Idan, author.
Title: A selectional theory of adjunct control / Idan Landau.
Description: Cambridge : The MIT Press, 2021. | Series: Linguistic inquiry monographs | Includes bibliographical references and index.
Identifiers: LCCN 2020044364 | ISBN 9780262542852 (paperback)
Subjects: LCSH: Control (Linguistics) | Grammar, Comparative and general--Syntax.
Classification: LCC P299.C596 L37 2021 | DDC 415--dc23
LC record available at https://lccn.loc.gov/2020044364

10 9 8 7 6 5 4 3 2 1

Contents

Series Foreword

We are pleased to present the eighty-fourth volume in the series *Linguistic Inquiry Monographs*. These monographs present new and original research beyond the scope of the article. We hope they will benefit our field by bringing to it perspectives that will stimulate further research and insight.

Originally published in limited edition, the *Linguistic Inquiry Monographs* are now more widely available. This change is due to the great interest engendered by the series and by the needs of a growing readership. The editors thank the readers for their support and welcome suggestions about future directions for the series.

Samuel Jay Keyser
for the Editorial Board

Preface

In March 2019, I attended a workshop organized under the auspices of DGFS (Deutsche Gesellschaft für Sprachwissenschaft) 41 at Universität Bremen, titled "Crosslinguistic Variation in Control Phenomena." The organizers of the workshop urged participants to explore "noncanonical control phenomena" in a comparative perspective. While I chose to present work on noncanonical nonobligatory control (NOC) in *complements*, a number of the other presentations were concerned with *adjunct* control. These presentations discussed fascinating and recalcitrant data that challenged conventional wisdom in the field (see the papers from this workshop collected in Mucha, Hartmann, and Trawiński to appear). To me, they acted like a wake-up call to tackle this topic, which, quite frankly, I have worked my way around for many years. It always seemed too difficult.

Nonetheless, in 2017 I wrote a short article on adjunct control (Landau 2017). That article contained the seed of the present work: the idea that nonfinite adjuncts are structurally ambiguous between property-denoting and proposition-denoting clauses, responsible for obligatory control (OC) and NOC, respectively (ultimately, an adaptation of the proposal in Williams 1992). What happened next was that the empirical basis for this idea was much expanded by Jeffrey Green (2018, 2019), who nonetheless offered an alternative theoretical treatment, within the movement theory of control. It was only natural for me to consider whether the crude proposal in Landau 2017 could be developed into a full-fledged theory of adjunct control, taking into account *all* the known facts. Spurred by the challenging discussions at the Bremen workshop and the emerging implications of my own work and Green's, I embarked on the present study.

One thing that was clear from the outset was that the theory of adjunct control to be developed must be continuous with—indeed, a natural outgrowth of—the two-tiered theory of control (TTC) developed in Landau 2015. Adjuncts are only mentioned fleetingly in that work, on its very last pages (pp. 84–85), where I suggest that right-edge adjuncts fall under (predicative) OC and left-edge ones fall under (logophoric) NOC. In fact, I have since come to realize that *both* positions can host *either* type of adjunct; but the fundamental distinction between the two types was just right. What was needed then, and is provided here, is a compositional account of how either predicative or logophoric adjuncts combine with the main predicate—wherever they occur.

The continuity with the TTC goes further. The same machinery used in Landau 2015 to account for OC in complements is used here to account for the OC/NOC alternation in adjuncts. Strikingly, this idea turns out to hold the key to why OC appears to be the default choice between the two options—language-internally, typologically, and in acquisition (see chapter 13). Thus, the fundamental building blocks of the TTC receive corroboration from various domains of syntactic inquiry.

The study of control, I believe, has reached an impressive level of maturity—and, as the saying goes, with great power comes great responsibility. Theories of control can no longer content themselves with accounting for a narrow set of data, confined to one language, or one syntactic configuration, or one grammatical module. Indeed, they must be accountable to as many sources of (dis)confirming evidence and as many theoretical considerations as are practically available.

In this spirit, the present work integrates findings and insights from a variety of linguistic subfields: the syntactic decomposition of VPs into event-related layers; the formal semantic treatment of subordination and adjunction; the pragmatics of topicality and logophoricity as it affects NOC; and the acquisition profile of adjunct control, an area of extensive psycholinguistic inquiry, whose findings I reinterpret in light of the present theory (see chapter 12). Such strong ties between the theory of control and independently established bodies of knowledge are to be expected if the proposals made within this theory have a kernel of truth to them. The bigger the kernel is, the stronger the ties will be. Thus, this work goes some way toward fulfilling the promissory statement with which Landau 2015 ended: "[T]he TTC may form the basis of a truly comprehensive theory of control" (p. 85).

Parts of this work were presented in linguistics colloquia at Georg August Universität Göttingen and Universität Leipzig; I thank the audiences for their feedback. I was also fortunate to have drafts read by a number of smart and generous people, who made numerous comments that no doubt improved the end result. It is a pleasure to acknowledge and thank them for their contributions: Stefanie Bode, Silke Fischer, Inghild Flaate Høyem, Juliana Gerard, Vikki Janke, Victoria Mateu, and Gillian Ramchand. Special thanks to Jeffrey Green and Alexander Williams for their careful commentary on virtually every aspect of this work. While we remain in disagreement on some issues, their input has been priceless. I am also indebted to Anne Mark from the MIT Press for her meticulous editorial work on the manuscript. I dedicate this work to my dearest, beloved ones—Shira, Elya, and Nimrode. You are my light and comfort.

1 Introduction

Theories of control have been continually challenged by the vexed relationship between complement control and adjunct control. Strategic responses widely differ, from full assimilation of the two types to total separation. These responses reflect different empirical descriptions. On certain theories, adjuncts display obligatory control (OC) just like complements (Williams 1980, Mohanan 1983, Clark 1990, Hornstein 1999, 2003, Pires 2007, Witkoś and Żychliński 2014, McFadden and Sundaresan 2018), drawing on a single underlying grammatical mechanism: functional control, predication, movement, or Agree. At the other extreme there are theories explicitly restricted to complement control, positing mechanisms that cannot extend to adjuncts (Chierchia 1984, Landau 2000, Jackendoff and Culicover 2003) and thus leaving the relationship between the two types unclear. Finally, some theories acknowledge that adjunct control may display either OC or nonobligatory control (NOC), yet attempt to unify NOC with OC in complement control at the theoretical level (Williams 1992, Español-Echevarría 2000, Landau 2013, 2015, 2017, Green 2018, 2019). The present study is a further step in the latter direction.

It seems to me that the time is ripe for a genuine theory of adjunct control. Recent years have seen considerable advances on two fronts. First, the theory of control itself has come to maturity, integrating syntactic and semantic insights too long unrelated. It now enables informed inferences from the better-understood area of complement control to the area of adjunct control. Second, the complex empirical terrain of adjunct control is gradually taking precise shape, setting clear empirical boundary conditions on potential theories in this area. These two strands will also be reflected in the present work: the theoretical proposal will be based on finer-grained descriptions of the patterns of control attested in English adjuncts.

1.1 Why Do We Need a Theory of Adjunct Control?

There can be little doubt that a theory of adjunct control is badly needed. Here are a number of reasons why.

At a very basic descriptive level, there are many misconceptions about control into adjuncts. Possibly the most common one, and the one most harmful to ongoing research, is the belief that all or most adjuncts fall under OC.[1] This is plainly false.

It is an old observation that at least absolutive adjuncts (sometimes called "free adjuncts") allow NOC in a variety of circumstances. Most often, NOC is observed when the matrix subject is an expletive (1a) or an inanimate DP (1b–c), but crucially, this is not required (1d). Note that the controller is some previously mentioned individual in (1a,c), arbitrary in (1b), and the speaker in (1d). (Examples (1a–d) are from Jespersen 1954:409, Friedrich 1978:240, Williams 1992:300, and Jespersen 1954:408, respectively.)

(1)   a.   Looking out of the window, there were the flower beds in the front garden.
       b.   Motoring down the road to New York, numerous signs read "Visit Our Snake Farm."
       c.   Having just arrived in town, the main hotel was a vision indeed.
       d.   Having communicated my wishes to my wife, the next morning the poor girl entered my apartment.

It is true that subject control is the default reading, when possible, although how strong a default it is, is not yet settled. Kortmann's (1991) corpus study revealed only 8.5% nonsubject-control readings out of more than 1,400 sentences with "free adjuncts." However, Duffley and Dion-Girardeau's (2015) corpus study, encompassing 3,161 sentences with free adjuncts, revealed a significantly higher 29% nonsubject control for gerundive free adjuncts and 24% for infinitival ones. Finally, in Herbeck's (2020) study of the distribution and interpretation of five different nonfinite adjuncts in two corpora of spoken Spanish, out of 2,215 sentences with null-subject adjuncts 28% displayed nonsubject control (20% extrasentential and 8% object control).

The factors behind the preference for local subject control have been discussed fairly extensively in the literature on NOC, and I address some of them in chapters 3, 11, and 13.[2] One point that deserves emphasis (see Green 2018, 2019) emerges from examples like (1d). Strictly speaking, *OC never blocks NOC*. At most, OC masks NOC. Hence, "competition"-based theories of the interplay between OC and NOC should be properly understood as theories of performance, not competence. The grammar always makes the two derivations available for those adjuncts that support them; however, an array of other factors—parsing preferences (proximity, linear order), pragmatic notions (logophoricity and topicality), and s(emantic)-selectional requirements (±animate) of the main and embedded predicates—conspire to either increase or decrease the accessibility of each reading.

Two types of examples show this most vividly. First, in the right circumstances a local human subject need not be the controller. This is visible not only in absolute adjuncts like (1d) but elsewhere as well. (Examples are from Español-Echevarría 2000:101 and Green 2018:36, respectively.)

(2) a. $Bill_i$ will introduce the ambassador to the president [in order PRO to give him_i the opportunity to observe their reactions].

    b. Strangely, the candidates talked avidly when we_i asked them where they were from, but they hesitated [after PRO_i asking them about their work].[3]

Similar facts obtain outside English. ((3a) is from Witkoś and Żychliński 2014: ex. (40)); (3b) is from Georgieva 2018:180, a spontaneous example.)

(3) a. *Polish*

    $Chłpcy_i$ wiedzą,   że Jan_j modli   się
    boys   know   that   Jan   prays   REFL
    [żeby $PRO_{i/arb/*j}$ nie   robić mu_j krzywdy].
    so.that   not   do.INF   him   harm
    'The boys know that Jan prays not to be harmed.'

    b. *Umdurk* (Uralic; Permic) (SIM = simultaneous temporal adjunct)

    [Granica-jez ortći-ku]   pasport-e   pećat'   ug   pukto.
    border-ACC   cross-CVB.SIM   passport-ILL   stamp   NEG   put.PRS.3PL
    '[PRO_i when crossing the border], $they_j$ don't put a stamp in the passport.'

I believe that such examples are in principle available with all NOC adjuncts, although they are quite uncommon (for reasons to be discussed in section 14.2). Out of the blue, they are normally judged anomalous (leading to the false impression that OC is the only option), but spontaneous speech attests them. They support the general point that this study shares with Green 2018: OC and NOC are not in complementary distribution, and furthermore, NOC may obtain even if OC does not lead to semantic anomaly.

The second type of example that makes this point very clearly involves adjuncts that *simultaneously* alternate between the local (OC) and nonlocal (NOC) readings (example from Green 2018:40).

(4) The $pool_i$ was the perfect temperature [after $PRO_{i/arb}$ being in the hot sun all day].

This point has broader implications for studies of child language that focus on the development of adjunct control. These studies have consistently assumed that examples like those in (2)–(4) are impossible in the adult language. Here is a representative quote: "In the adult grammar an arbitrary reading can be assigned to the subject of a temporal where there is no suitable controller in the main clauses (as in *After skiing quickly, hot chocolate tastes good*). However, where the surface subject is a suitable controller, control by the subject has the force of a rule, not simply a preference" (Goodluck and Behne 1992:167n10). In fact, it *is* a (strong) preference, not a rule, in the adult grammar; nonlocal control is allowed in (2)–(4) despite the presence of a suitable local subject controller. This understanding of the true scope of NOC throws an entirely new light on so-called errors by children, specifically on nonsubject-control interpretations that they assign to temporal adjuncts, a classic finding in the field. Indeed, it demands that we reinterpret these findings as overgeneralization from, rather than violations of, the target grammar. I undertake this task in chapter 12.

Indeed, if NOC in absolutive adjuncts is at least recognized in older studies, NOC in temporal clauses is virtually unknown, if not simply denied, as in Culicover and Jackendoff 2005:426 (although see Jones 1992 for an early classification of temporal adjuncts under NOC). Yet Landau 2013, 2017 and Green 2018 document many such examples.

(5) a. The meeting was canceled without knowing the reasons.
  b. The night sky can be an unforgettable spectacle while/when camping in the desert.
  c. Potatoes are tastier after boiling them.
  d. This happens especially frequently when trying to reach numbers in New York.[4]

Contrary to standard descriptions, object control into temporal adjuncts is sometimes acceptable, as in this example from the internet (via Paz 2019:7).

(6) Woman's$_i$ family beats abusive husband$_j$ with sticks [after PRO$_j$ leaving her$_i$ with black eye].

A recent experimental study with 70 native speakers of English revealed that contextual priming significantly shifts speakers away from local subject control to object control with temporal adjuncts (Janke and Bailey 2017). While sentences of type (7a) elicited on average only 4% object control judgments, the rate increased to 11% in weakly primed examples like (7b) and to 51% in strongly primed examples like (7c). (Examples are from Janke and Bailey 2017:545.)

(7) a. Ron tapped Hermione while feeding the owl.
  b. I'm going to tell you something about Hermione. Ron tapped Hermione while feeding the owl.
  c. Hermione is looking after the birds. Hermione takes out the food. Ron tapped Hermione while feeding the owl.

This sensitivity to the topic-salience of antecedents is a hallmark of NOC. Janke and Bailey explain object control into these adjuncts as arising from ambiguous attachment possibilities, essentially reducing it to OC. This is incorrect, I believe, for the construction shows great susceptibility to extrasentential control in any event; see sections 5.3 and 11.3 for further discussion of these matters.

Quite generally, alongside OC, NOC is attested in *most* types of adjuncts, once the proper conditions are attended to; this is documented extensively for English in chapter 5. Moreover, there is reason to believe that the actual scope of NOC has been seriously underestimated in other languages as well (see section 11.1). Correcting the false impression that adjuncts fall under OC *as a matter of grammatical necessity* is another important goal of this study. Instead, I will describe many adjuncts as alternating between OC and NOC.

Why assume an "alternation"? Why can OC readings not be simply subsumed under NOC, harboring a single mechanism? The [±human] effect already suggests this is not feasible ([−human] OC readings cannot be subsumed under NOC). In fact, arguments in favor of the fundamental OC-NOC distinction will recur throughout this work. Here, I will briefly mention two novel observations (see sections 5.1, 5.3, 14.2, and 14.5 for the full discussion).

Consider rationale clauses and their paraphrases as "remote control" (a term coined in Williams 2015).

(8) a. Martha wrote this book in order to get rich.
    b. Martha wrote this book for a reason. The reason was to get rich.
    c. This book was written in order to be sold to Hollywood.
    d. *This book was written for a reason. The reason was to be sold to Hollywood.

While remote control proceeds unhindered with a human controller (8b), it breaks down with an inanimate controller (8d). This points to a duality of mechanism, masked in the pair (8a–b) but nonetheless real.

Next, consider the familiar ellipsis test, where OC requires a sloppy reading and NOC allows a strict reading. Contrary to the common view, temporal adjuncts do allow a strict reading of PRO, but crucially, only when it is human.

(9) a. Bill felt much better after quitting his heavy drinking. His family did too.
      [*His family felt much better after he quit his heavy drinking.*]
    b. The storm was over. Water was cut off for 16 hours, but returned after electricity had been cut off for 11 hours.
    c. The storm was over. Electricity returned after being cut off for 11 hours. Water did too.
      [*Water returned after being cut off for 11 hours.*]

The subject of the antecedent clause in (9a), *Bill*, can control the PRO subject of the elided adjunct, producing the strict reading. The subject of the antecedent clause in (9c), *electricity*, cannot control the PRO subject of the elided adjunct; thus, *Water did too* entails that water, not electricity, had also been cut off for 11 hours.[5] The intended strict reading, shown in (9b) to be perfectly sensible, is not available in (9c). The difference has to do with the [±human] feature, again pointing to two distinct grammatical mechanisms, which stand in an overlap rather than inclusion relation.

So far, I have focused on adjuncts displaying an OC/NOC alternation. Yet this is only part of the picture. The central observation addressed in this work is different and little-known (Green 2018, 2019, which directly tackles it, is an exception). It is the fact that controlled adjuncts fall into two basic categories. In the *strict OC* category we find adjuncts that always display OC, regardless of context. In the *alternating OC/NOC* category we find adjuncts that display either OC or NOC, depending on context (such as the temporal and absolutive adjuncts illustrated above). The very distinction is rarely noticed. Most accounts of adjunct control either assume that all adjuncts fall under OC or assume that they all allow NOC. Indeed, the very idea of an *alternation* between OC and NOC would strike some authors as bizarre, assuming as they do that the OC reading is just a special case of the NOC reading, demanding no duality of analysis. For others, the idea is incoherent, as NOC can only emerge when OC cannot.

However, by now there is extensive evidence that adjuncts, sometimes the very same adjunct, may display either OC or NOC (as in (4)). The following examples involve rationale clauses, but the point holds true for a number of other adjuncts.

(10) a. Flowers$_i$ produce pollen [(in order) PRO$_i$ to reproduce].
    b. The door is open [(in order) PRO to greet passing neighbors].

The control relation in (10a) must be OC because NOC is restricted to human antecedents. The control relation in (10b) must be NOC because OC is restricted to local, sentence-internal antecedents. These characteristic properties are established in Landau 2013, 2017 and reviewed here in chapter 3. As I will show in chapter 5, there are at least six types of adjuncts in English that display a similar OC/NOC alternation. At the same time, at least four different types of adjuncts display strict OC, as in the result clause in (11).

(11) a. [Meghan Markle's accent]$_i$ has changed [PRO$_i$ to become more British].
    b. *Meghan Markle$_i$ regretted that her accent had changed [PRO$_i$ to become less sure of herself].

Even though in (11b), just as in (10b), the local subject (*her accent*) is inanimate, and even though the attempted human controller, *Meghan Markle*, is both explicitly referenced in the main clause (as a possessive pronoun) and highlighted as a discourse topic in the preceding text, that human antecedent cannot control PRO in the adjunct clause. In other words, even the conditions most favorable to NOC cannot overrule OC when the latter is forced. This situation is, of course, familiar from complement control. Yet the fact that adjuncts split into two categories along these lines is barely known. In Landau 2013:chaps. 6–7, I tacitly acknowledged this split in choosing to discuss certain types of adjuncts under adjunct control and others under NOC. Green (2018, 2019) upholds this split and attempts to derive it under the movement theory of control. A further major empirical goal of this study, therefore, is to firmly establish the empirical distinction between strict OC and OC/NOC adjuncts. As we will see, the line can be elusive at times.

Two immediate questions arise: (i) why do complements not display a similar alternation? and (ii) how can we account for this alternation? Question (i) is, in fact, a misconception. Some complements *do* display NOC, specifically with verbs of communication (Landau 2020). Yet it is true that by and large, complement control is obligatory. The reason is ultimately selectional (Williams 1994, Jackendoff and Culicover 2003). In the two-tiered theory of control (TTC), selection is reflected in the contextual coordinates made available on the C head of the controlled clause: if these coordinates are locked to the participants of the reported speech/thought act, OC will ensue.

Question (ii) is the focus of the present study, offering a specific incarnation of a classical question: what determines the distribution of OC? The rich history of research on this topic has really produced only two candidate answers: (i) the internal makeup of the controlled clause, and/or (ii) the structural position (attachment site) of the controlled clause. Answer (i) has been extremely fruitful in exploring how finiteness and nominalization interact with control across different languages (see the survey in Landau 2013:secs. 4.1, 5.6). It also informs a long research tradition that distinguishes between "small" and "big" infinitives, each with its own distribution and interpretation, going back to the founding work by Rosenbaum (1967) (see Bouchard 1984, Koster 1984, Rochette 1988, Wurmbrand 2003, 2004, Grano 2015, Landau 2015, 2017, Wurmbrand and Lohninger to appear). Answer (ii) has usually taken the form of linking OC to VP-internal position (of the controlled clause) and NOC to VP-external position (Manzini 1983, Landau 2001, Fischer 2018, Green 2018, 2019).

The present study develops an account that combines the insights of both traditions, applying them to adjuncts, while grounding them semantically in the basic toolkit of the TTC. In the TTC, the fundamental distinction between predicative and logophoric control in complements turns on the semantic type of the complement: property or proposition. The semantic type correlates with syntactic size, the smaller clause (FinP) denoting a predicate and the larger one (CP) a proposition. Nonfinite adjuncts too, I argue, come in these two formats. They may denote either properties or propositions. The choice is dictated by the prepositional (P) head of the adjunct, which introduces the nonfinite clause. Heads that strictly s-select predicative clauses produce strict OC; heads that s-select predicative or propositional clauses produce alternating OC/NOC adjuncts.[6] These semantic types constrain, in part, the adjunction possibilities open to the two categories of adjuncts. A fully compositional analysis of the two categories of adjuncts, and their integration with the main clause, is developed in chapter 6.

The empirical content of the proposal derives from a novel correlation between the type of adjunct (OC/NOC or OC) and whether or not it has a variant with a lexical subject, that is, an overtly propositional variant. Concerning the examples above, we find a propositional variant for rationale clauses but not for result clauses (see section 2.2 for further nuances, such as the possibility of shifting finiteness between the two variants).

(12) a. The door is open (in order) for us to greet passing neighbors.
      b. *Meghan Markle's accent has changed for her to become less sure
          of herself.

This correlation—which I call the *Propositional Variant Criterion*—provides, for the first time, a solid distributional diagnostic for *any* theory of control to work with. It is also bolstered by typological evidence, and raises fundamental questions about default settings in grammar construction (see chapter 13).

The compositional analysis introduces strict OC and OC/NOC adjuncts at different attachment sites in the clause. It thus generates a number of syntactic predictions—for example, whether the adjunct will *necessarily* or *optionally* be included in VP-targeting operations. These predictions are all tested in chapter 7. Importantly, they contrast with the predictions of the common approaches to adjunct control, which attempt to *deduce* the type of control from the attachment site. "Binary configurational" theories derive entailments like "Position X → OC" or "Position Y → NOC." But these entailments are systematically falsified. For example, a popular idea is that whenever the matrix subject c-commands the adjunct, OC is forced and NOC excluded. But it is not difficult to find examples of low NOC adjuncts. In (13a), the embedded negative polarity item (NPI) is licensed by the matrix negation under c-command, yet NOC is possible. In (13b), the matrix subject must c-command the embedded pronoun for variable binding to be possible, and still NOC is allowed.

(13) a. The door isn't open in order to greet anyone, I just needed some fresh air.
     b. Every road$_i$ in this area is dangerous when driving on it$_i$ during the rainy season.

In fact, as chapter 10 shows, VP-targeting tests are not refined enough to differentiate the attachment sites of OC and NOC variants of alternating adjuncts. The OC-NOC distinction does interact with syntactic hierarchy, but in a more intricate way. Therefore, yet another major goal of this study is to sort out the syntax-semantics correlations in the realm of adjunct control: which syntactic consequences follow from which modification relation, and how semantic and syntactic aspects of adjunct control may converge to support a unified analysis.

The last chapters of this work take a closer look at NOC. Rather than dismissing it as the dull "elsewhere" case, I investigate NOC in its full internal richness. Previous research has left many questions unsettled: Is NOC conditioned by logophoricity, topicality, or both? Are NOC interpretations disjoint from OC interpretations or do they subsume them as a special case? Precisely where in the grammar do OC and NOC compete? Is the choice between them resolved in the syntax or in the pragmatics, or is it a processing matter altogether? We will see that there is, in fact, much evidence bearing on these questions. The evidence has been accumulated in several subfields (occasionally unaware of each other): theoretical syntax, acquisition studies, and processing studies. Synthesizing the results of these different research strands under a unified explanatory model is one last goal of this work.

In short, then, there are six answers to the question "Why do we need a theory of adjunct control?":

1. To establish the true (and wider) range of NOC possibilities with adjuncts;

2. To establish the fundamental distinction between strict OC adjuncts and alternating OC/NOC adjuncts;

3. To understand this distinction in terms of a general theory of control and the property-proposition divide that lies at its core;

4. To provide an explicit compositional analysis (so far lacking) of clausal adjunction, from which control behavior will naturally follow;

5. To tie together the syntax and semantics of controlled adjuncts by showing their predictions to be aligned; and

6. To flesh out the analysis of NOC and demonstrate its consequences for processing and child data.

These are the goals. They may well be too ambitious, but at least they strike me as the right ones to pursue.

1.2 Controlled Adjuncts: Basic Properties

The fundamental cut between strict OC adjuncts and OC/NOC adjuncts produces two main categories; the former category is further divided into strict subject OC and strict object OC. Table (14) specifies the members of these categories in English. It is important to bear in mind that the inventory of adjuncts, as well as their specific semantic nuances, varies from one language to another. The universal claim embodied in table (14) is that the categories themselves are invariant, although *which* adjuncts populate them in particular languages is subject to variation.

(14) *Controlled adjuncts in English*

Strict OC		Alternating OC/NOC
Subject control	Object control	
Goal clause	Result clause	Rationale clause
Stimulus clause	Subject purpose clause	Object purpose clause
		Justification clause
		Temporal clause
		Absolutive clause
		Telic clause

Two clarifications are in order. First, result clauses modify unaccusative verbs; they are controlled by the *deep* object, hence classified under object control. Independently in English, the object must raise to become a subject, but this is not necessary in all languages. Second, my focus on English is largely dictated by the rich and fine-grained level of descriptive and analytic accounts of adjunct control in English, compared with the scarcity of such accounts for other languages. Ultimately, the theory to be developed here should generalize to adjunct control in any possible language. As it happens, the choice of English in this particular case seems relatively harmless because the language harbors a fairly extensive system of nonfinite, controlled adjuncts, with each of the three universal categories in (14) represented by *some* members. Still, I will occasionally refer to other languages when the relevant evidence exists.

The ten types of adjuncts in table (14) are illustrated in (15). More varieties and options are provided in the specific sections dedicated to each type, in chapters 4 and 5.

(15) a. *Goal clause*
We traveled to visit family relatives in Ireland.
b. *Stimulus clause*
He shuddered to remember the boy he'd been back then.
c. *Result clause*
Groundwater has seeped in to create a small labyrinth of canals.
d. *Subject purpose clause*
Jane bought this nightstand to fit between the bed and the cupboard.
e. *Rationale clause*
They only started dating (in order) to prove me wrong.
f. *Object purpose clause*
Mozart wrote this sonata to play with a flute.
g. *Justification clause*
She dumped him for cheating on her.
h. *Temporal clause*
The kids started fighting after getting along nicely for two hours.
i. *Absolutive clause*
Looking outside the window, Bill sighed in despair.
j. *Telic clause*
This masterpiece was rediscovered in the Renaissance, only to be forgotten again.

I assume that adjunct clauses are always introduced by some subordinating head, distinct from their own C head. Often, the adjunct's head is overt and mandatory: *before, after, despite, without, for, only,* and so on. At other times, it is optional, like *in order* in rationale clauses or *with* in absolutive clauses. The null hypothesis is that the head is syntactically and semantically present, but simply not parsed at PF. Finally, some adjuncts never occur with an overt head, yet clearly their semantic relation to the main clause is not arbitrary, and often it is very specific (e.g., result or stimulus clauses).[7] Again, it would not seem reasonable to locate that meaning in the complementizer of such adjuncts (itself usually null). Uniformity and standard compositionality require that we assume a distinct null head that mediates the modification relation between the two clauses and contributes its specific flavor. Since most overt adjunct heads are prepositions, I assume that the null ones are too, but this assumption is not crucial (e.g., there may be null Adv heads). In short, the adjuncts discussed in this work all have the form $[_{PP}$ P CP$]$.[8]

Following Haider (2000, 2004), Ernst (2002, 2007, 2014), and Nilsen (2004), in this study I accept the idea that the hierarchical distribution of adjuncts is largely derivable from their meaning. This is particularly natural for adjunction within the extended VP (which does not involve Cinque's (1999) adverb hierarchy). Outside VP, as we will see, more variability is found, in that the same adjunct (e.g., a temporal clause) can attach at any point between VP and TP. Actual linearization will depend on prosodic factors; clausal adjuncts are typically sentence-initial or sentence-final, and can occur sentence-medially only if set off by prosodic pauses (commas).

Studies of adverbial syntax typically focus on nonclausal adverbials. Thus, one finds elaborate classifications of adverbs into categories such as *speaker-oriented, evaluative, epistemic, subject-oriented, quantity, manner*, and so on. At a deeper level, the fine-grained multitude of adverbials cluster in a few supercategories: modification of process, event, proposition, or speech act. These types correspond to hierarchical organization, the first being projected the lowest and the last the highest. The clausal adjuncts in (15) do not easily fit the fine-grained classes. The supercategories are slightly more relevant: strict OC adjuncts are all process modifiers, while alternating OC/NOC adjuncts instantiate event and proposition modification.

These labels, however, do not translate into any substantive theory of adjunct *control*. To this end, in chapter 6 I will construct general semantic templates for the three categories of adjuncts in (14); these templates will entail specific compositional results for syntactic organization, which I will then explore in chapter 7. In its general spirit, then, the present study harmonizes with the ultimate goal of selectional/scopal theories of adverbial syntax. In its details, however, it goes far beyond what they have to offer.

The intrinsic semantics of each clausal adjunct, its specific flavor and conditions of verification, will be of little concern in this study. I will typically use intuitive concepts like *result* or *goal* to talk about the meaning of result or goal clauses, not mistaking this quasi-circular talk for true explication. This strategy will be seen to be harmless insofar as one focuses on *compositional* properties of the adjuncts (i.e., how they are integrated with the main clause) rather than on their *denotational* properties. Although much can and should be said about the subtle distinctions between, for example, stimulus clauses and clauses specifying just any general cause, or between goal clauses and rationale clauses, those discussions have little bearing on how the three *categories* of adjuncts represented in table (14), abstracted away from specific tokens, are semantically integrated, and how their control profile is determined. Any semantic distinctions among the ten types of adjuncts that do not bear on their attachment site will have no consequences for the OC/NOC distribution, and so will not concern us here.

One striking distinction between strict OC and OC/NOC adjuncts that *is* of key significance is the semantic selectivity of the former. Each of the strict

OC adjuncts places heavy semantic restrictions on the range of predicates it may combine with (see chapter 4 for data and discussion). Goal clauses are only compatible with goal-oriented unergative verbs; result clauses are only compatible with unaccusative verbs; stimulus clauses are only compatible with unergative verbs that convey an emotional response; and subject purpose clauses are only compatible with a small class of verbs whose theme object "becomes available" for further manipulation. In fact, as we will see, strict OC adjuncts occasionally "blend into" selected complement clauses, in the sense that their semantic contribution is remarkably close to that of such complements. This close similarity is naturally explained if, like complements, these adjuncts merge with the verbal root and "augment" its core meaning.

In contrast, alternating OC/NOC adjuncts are rarely selective. Rationale, temporal absolute, and justification clauses can modify pretty much any type of matrix predicate: stative or eventive, telic or atelic, unaccusative or unergative, and so on. Object purpose clauses do exhibit high selectivity for the matrix theme, of the same nature seen with subject purpose clauses, but this is only because of their *object* gap—an operator trace—and not because of any requirement imposed by the control relation itself (which, in fact, admits NOC). Finally, telic clauses select eventive (nonstative) matrix predicates, but this requirement is structurally neutral and may operate at any level of the clausal spine in which the event argument is still accessible.

The high semantic selectivity of strict OC adjuncts, as opposed to the non-selectivity of OC/NOC adjuncts, ought to be reflected in their attachment sites. Indeed, the proposal to be developed places strict OC adjuncts as adjuncts to the lowest projection in the VP, namely, the root (see section 6.3.1). At that level, they are in a proper position to s-select the right kind of root, and possibly to c-select the right kind of light v that combines with the root's projection. This low position also accounts for the peculiar immobility of these adjuncts and their inseparability from the VP. This is the first sense in which the present theory is *selectional*: the adjunct PP selects the kinds of roots and light v heads that it modifies.[9] The second sense in which selection plays a key role is in pairing the P head of the adjunct either with a property-denoting clausal complement or with a proposition-denoting one (see section 2.1).

This way of ensuring OC indicates that the "limitations" of the TTC, discussed in Green 2019, are not real. Green's point is that the TTC (as formulated in Landau 2015) has no natural account for OC adjuncts. Because adjuncts are not selected, they should always be able to project the full logophoric structure that produces NOC. The point missed here is that while adjuncts are unselected, they are *selectors* themselves. Furthermore, P heads of adjuncts are also selectors. By taking into account what semantic type is selected as the nonfinite complement of the P head, and what type of matrix eventuality is selected by the entire adjunct, we can naturally account for strict OC adjuncts within the TTC.

In contrast to strict OC adjuncts, OC/NOC adjuncts are attached at the highest projection within the VP, namely, at VoiceP. Specifically, in their OC guise they combine with the predicative node Voice′, and in their propositional guise they combine with VoiceP (see section 6.3.2). This high position does not let them select for any particular root or light v, and simultaneously accounts for their syntactic independence from the main VP.

2 Capturing the Fundamental Cut: Predicative vs. Propositional Adjuncts

In this chapter, I will briefly describe the property-proposition divide in the analysis of clauses and how it plays out within the general framework of the TTC assumed here (section 2.1). Then I will spell out how this well-established distinction holds the key to a genuine understanding of the cut between strict OC and OC/NOC adjuncts (section 2.2). After providing empirical descriptions in chapters 4 and 5, in chapter 6 I will present a fully explicit analysis of how each category of adjuncts is integrated with the main clause, syntactically and semantically.

2.1 Mapping Nonfinite Clauses to Semantic Types

A simple and elegant theory of the relation between the syntax and the semantics of nonfinite clauses, in the complement domain, was developed by Chierchia (1984). The theory starts from the observation that some nonfinite complements allow a lexical subject while others do not, a distinction that cuts across the infinitive-gerund divide. Below I mark the subject of controlled complements as PRO, although Chierchia (1984) expressly denied the existence of a null syntactic subject and took control clauses to be bare VPs (he later recognized PRO in Chierchia 1989).

(16) a. I tried [PRO/*him/*me to play sonatas].
    b. I practiced [PRO/*his/*my playing sonatas].

(17) a. I wanted [PRO/him to play sonatas].
    b. I like [PRO/John playing sonatas].

For Chierchia (1984), a controlled clause, being subjectless, was just a VP. Trivially, it could only denote a property. This straightforwardly divided OC verbs into two types: (i) *Type I*: V s-selects a property, and (ii) *Type II*: V s-selects either a property or a proposition. Thus, for Chierchia, the existence of a propositional complement did not rule out a predicative complement. In fact, the majority of control verbs pattern with *want* and not with *try* in allowing a propositional complement.[1] The implication was that most control verbs are systematically ambiguous in their s-selectional profile.

The latter implication was seen as disturbing to later accounts, which therefore try to avoid it. Analyzing infinitival complements of adjectives, in Landau 1999 I propose a sharper dichotomy between control predicates, which select a propositional argument, and noncontrol predicates, which may take a predicative modifier. Wurmbrand (2002) cleans up the ambiguity in Chierchia's system by reanalyzing type II verbs as only selecting propositions (OC, then, is dissociated from predication). Finally, in the TTC, control complements fall into two types: predicative and logophoric, the latter being propositional. On this theory, there are two routes to OC: one via predication, the other via variable binding, each with its own characteristic empirical profile.

Under the TTC, predicative control clauses are formed by moving PRO to Spec,FinP, creating a chain that is interpreted as λ-abstraction; the resulting FinP denotes a property, type <e,<s,t>>. Logophoric control clauses are formed by projecting a CP layer on top of this FinP, in which the derived predicate is saturated by a null nominal (*pro*), associated with a coordinate of the context of evaluation (AUTHOR or ADDRESSEE); the resulting CP denotes a proposition, type <κ,t> (κ = the semantic type of context tuples). The coordinate *pro* is bound by the matrix controller, accounting for the φ-agreement between the controller and PRO.

The two clausal structures are schematized in (18) .

(18) a. *Predicative clause:* [$_{\text{FinP}}$ PRO$_i$ Fin [$_{\text{TP}}$ ~~PRO$_i$~~ . . .]]
    b. *Propositional clause:* [$_{\text{CP}}$ *pro* C$_{[+\text{log}]}$ [$_{\text{FinP}}$ PRO$_i$ Fin [$_{\text{TP}}$ ~~PRO$_i$~~ . . .]]]

In this work, I keep to the traditional propositional type <s,t> and the property type <e,<s,t>> (see section 6.1 for elaboration).

Importantly, both mechanisms in (18a–b) end up in OC with complement clauses. Predicative control establishes OC by predicating the complement of the controller. Logophoric control establishes OC by associating the embedded *pro* with the doxastic counterpart of (the referent of) a matrix argument. In contrast, as we will see, they part ways in adjunct clauses, where only the predicative route results in OC. The different interpretations of logophoric clauses in complement vs. adjunct positions follow from s-selection. Only in complement clauses (of attitude predicates) is the context of evaluation, encoded on C, locked by selection to the reported (matrix) context; hence, only in complements will the AUTHOR or ADDRESSEE coordinate of that context correspond to a matrix participant. Adjuncts being unselected, their C head is free to pick out any salient context of evaluation and, consequently, associate *pro* with a coordinate of that context (= a NOC controller).

2.2   The Propositional Variant Criterion

Although the property of having a propositional variant is not explicitly discussed in Landau 2015, it is taken up by Grano (2015:17–19). Grano observes that verbs of predicative control (consisting of aspectual, modal, and implicative verbs) cannot take complements with lexical subjects, while verbs of logophoric control (consisting of the subclasses of desiderative, propositional, factive, and interrogative verbs) can. Grano discusses English alone, but I believe the crosslinguistic generalization is robust. Within his theory, the distinction is related to the fact that the former class consists of raising verbs and the latter, of control verbs. However, for Grano the distinction is semantically inert (both types are propositional). Within the present framework, it can readily be translated into a Chierchia-style distinction in semantic types.

This is indeed the path I will take here. Specifically, I will assume that nonfinite adjunct clauses, just like complements, come in two types: predicative or propositional. Following Grano's method (but not his reasoning), I will use the propositional variant test to establish which is which. The results will be seen to correlate perfectly with the control profile of each adjunct.

(19) *The Propositional Variant Criterion (PVC)*
      For a clausal adjunct [P [PRO . . .]]$_W$:
      a. W has no propositional variant ⇔ W is predicative ⇔ W displays strict OC
      b. W has a propositional variant ⇔ W is either predicative or propositional ⇔ W displays OC or NOC

Several comments are in order. First, the PVC is asymmetric: a predicative variant guarantees a propositional one, but not vice versa. The asymmetry, in fact, extends beyond English and is manifested in other typological patterns. I will return to this asymmetry in chapter 13, where I derive it from general principles of syntactic economy.

Second, the system implies that nonfinite clauses with a PRO subject may, in fact, map either to a property or to a proposition. This is indeed a core ingredient of the TTC, as depicted in (18). The only difference between complements and adjuncts is the appearance of a P head in the latter case, whose function is to introduce the modification relation (more on that below). As mentioned in chapter 1, this is the second sense in which the present theory is *selectional*: the P head selects the semantic type of its complement, the clausal adjunct (property or proposition). The first sense involves the entire PP adjunct selecting the right kind of root and light v to merge with (with strict OC adjuncts).

(20) a. *Predicative adjunct:* $[_{PP}$ P $[_{FinP}$ PRO$_i$ Fin $[_{TP}$ ~~PRO$_i$~~ . . .]]]
  b. *Propositional adjunct:* $[_{PP}$ P $[_{CP}$ *pro* C$_{[+log]}$ $[_{FinP}$ PRO$_i$ Fin $[_{TP}$ ~~PRO$_i$~~ . . .]]]]

Third, I should be explicit about the content of the term "propositional variant," specifically the "variant" part. Clearly, I do not mean that the propositional variant—a clause with a lexical subject—should have the same denotation as the predicative variant. Rather, the idea is that the semantic relation denoted by the adjunct's P head should be *invariant* across the predicative-propositional divide. That is, the modifying function of the adjunct relative to the main clause should be the same.

How close must the variant be to the original adjunct to still count as a variant? To understand this issue, consider the following examples.

(21) a. Jane stepped back [in order to get a better view].
  b. Jane stepped back [in order for Bill to get a better view].

(22) a. Some things are better not said [when (*your mom) sitting at the table].
  b. Some things are better not said [when your mom is sitting at the table].

(23) a. The earth's crust melted (*for the rocks) to form magma.
  b. The earth's crust melted so that the rocks formed magma.

The adjuncts in (21) are rationale clauses; the ones in (22) are temporal clauses; the one in (23a) is a result clause; and the one in (23b) has no designated label, but it also expresses some effect causally linked to the main clause—call it an "effect clause."

There is little reason to doubt that the adjunct in (21b) is a propositional variant of the one in (21a): save for the overtness of their subjects, they are indistinguishable. In particular, the semantic contribution of *in order* is identical in both. (22a) has no *nonfinite* propositional variant; however, (22b) seems to be an adequate finite propositional variant. Once again, whatever temporal relation *when* denotes in (22a) is also denoted by *when* in (22b).[2] Things are different, however, when we compare (23a) and (23b). The result clause in (23a) is headed by a null P whose meaning is not equivalent to *so*, the head of the effect clause in (23b). Thus, result clauses can only modify unaccusative verbs, whereas effect clauses are not so restricted (24a–b). Moreover, effect clauses can be dissociated in time from their cause, unlike result clauses (24c–d).

(24) a. *The leaves trembled in the wind to fall down.
     b. The leaves trembled in the wind so that all the snowflakes fell down.
     c. For ten years, the roots spread underground to finally form a wide base (*this spring).
     d. For ten years, the roots spread underground so that a wide base was finally formed (this spring).

These differences are sufficient to secure the claim that effect clauses do not count as propositional variants of result clauses. The latter, in fact, are predicative, and indeed, as the PVC predicts, they only display OC (see section 4.2). In what follows, then, I will use the term "propositional variant" in the sense defined in (25).

(25) *Propositional variant*
     $[P_i \ XP]$ is a propositional variant of an adjunct $[P_j \ [PRO \ldots]]$ iff
     a. $P_i = P_j$
     b. $[\![XP]\!]$ is of type <s,t>.

     Note: XP may be a finite or nominalized clause, as long as the modification relation contributed by P is identical.

Note that the PVC is reminiscent of the earliest criterion offered in the literature to distinguish OC from NOC, in Williams 1980. Discussing *complement* clauses in English, Williams classifies those that may occur with a lexical subject (in a *for*-infinitive) under NOC, and those that may not under OC. However, in the domain of complements this distinction creates much confusion, as even the so-called NOC complements display characteristic OC properties (locality, bound variable interpretation of PRO, etc.); see Landau 2000:32–33 for empirical arguments against Williams's criterion. At the deeper level of grammatical mechanism, however, Williams's intuition is on the right track: antecedent retrieval is a different process in OC and in NOC, and nowhere is this more visible than in the domain of adjuncts. Unlike Williams's system, which uniquely classifies as NOC even PRO clauses that permit a lexical subject, the PVC states that such clauses genuinely alternate between OC and NOC, each associated with its semantic type (property or proposition); yet the latter is available precisely in virtue of the possibility of a lexical subject, as in Williams 1980 (on the history of the idea that even complement control conceals a duality of mechanism, see Landau 2015:2–3).

The structures in (20) have one final implication: propositional adjuncts project a complementizer, whereas predicative ones do not. In principle, this distinction should be morphologically visible. Unfortunately, many languages never lexicalize nonfinite complementizers. Others, like English, prohibit the overt sequence P^0-C^0 in any context and reanalyze some prepositions as complementizers (see footnote 8 in chapter 1). Finally, careful studies that distinguish strict OC from OC/NOC adjuncts hardly exist outside English. All these factors conspire to make direct morphological evidence for the correlation between the type of adjunct and the presence or absence of C rather scarce. Nevertheless, some supporting evidence does exist.

Circumstantial adjuncts in Lebanese Arabic appear either with the complementizer *w-* 'while' or without it. Haddad (2017) observes that only the former type allows a subject disjoint from the matrix subject, while the latter exhibits OC. Notice that other than the occurrence of a complementizer and a possibly disjoint subject, the adjuncts in (26)–(27) are identical, thus counting as variants for the PVC. (Examples are from Haddad 2017:211.)

(26) l-wleːdi$_i$ feːto: ʕa-l-beːt   [PRO$_{i/*j}$ ʕam-biɣanno:
    the-children   enter.PERF.3.PL   to-the-house   PROG-sing.IMPERF.3.PL
    ɣinniye   la-Naːnsi   ʕaʒram]
    song   by-Nancy   Ajram
    'The children walked into the house singing a song by Nancy Ajram.'

(27) l-wleːdi$_i$ feːto: ʕa-l-beːt   [**w**-hinne$_{i/j}$/ʔana:
    the-children   enter.PERF.3.PL   to-the-house   COMP-they/I
    ʕam-biɣanno: ɣinniyela-Naːnsi   ʕaʒram]
    PROG-sing.IMPERF.3.PL   song   by-Nancy   Ajram
    'The children walked into the house while they were / I was singing a song by Nancy Ajram.'

Although the Comp-less adjuncts cannot host a disjoint subject, they can host a pronominal subject, as long as it is coindexed with the matrix subject. Such "controlled pronouns" are crosslinguistically attested in predicative complement control as well (Landau 2015:80–81) and fall together with obligatorily bound pronouns in a range of other predicative constructions (see (264) in chapter 13). Contrary to Haddad's conclusion, in no way do they undermine the analysis of the controlled clause as a semantic predicate: the pronoun is λ-bound by a null operator at the edge of the clause, yielding a derived predicate.[3]

Haddad presents an additional contrast between two types of "purpose clauses"—one accepting a disjoint subject and a complementizer (*la-* 'to'), the other rejecting both and forcing OC. That pair makes the same point, though possibly in a different way, if the propositional variant is really a rationale clause and the predicative one a goal clause; see footnote 2 in chapter 4 for exactly the same correlation among morphology, syntax, and semantics in Polish purpose clauses. Clearly, more corroborating evidence is desirable. I expect that the more we learn about adjunct control and its subcategories crosslinguistically, the more opportunities will emerge for testing the prediction about the visibility of the C head.

3 OC vs. NOC

The goal of this chapter is to provide the diagnostic tools necessary for empirically classifying adjuncts as falling under either OC or NOC, or both.[1] I will establish three diagnostic properties that distinguish OC from NOC. Two of these properties hold of the distinction in general, and the third one is specific to adjunct control.

The following two properties clearly distinguish OC from NOC.

(28) a. *Locality:* The controller in OC, but not in NOC, must be an argument of the clause immediately dominating the adjunct.
   b. *Humanness:* PRO in NOC, but not in OC, must be [+human].

The locality of OC reflects the local nature of the grammatical operation that associates PRO with the controller DP. Depending on one's favorite theory, this operation may be predication, anaphoric binding, A-movement, Agree, or a lexicalized meaning postulate. None of these applies in NOC. On the other hand, the [+human] restriction follows from the logophoric nature of PRO in NOC. To the extent that analogous selectional restrictions on the DP controller can be factored out by a suitable choice of matrix predicate, no [+human] interpretation is forced on PRO in OC.

To see how locality works in this context, consider the following examples. OC dependencies are strictly local and reject generic/pragmatic control.

(29) a. Mary$_i$ realized that John$_j$ wished [PRO$_{j/*i}$ to work by himself$_j$/*herself$_i$].
   b. *My neighbors$_i$ planned [PRO$_{arb}$ to pay them$_i$ for all the hard work].
   c. *Listen, Peter will never agree [PRO to add myself to the list].

In contrast, the controller in NOC may be arbitrarily remote or embedded (30a–b), generic (30c), or pragmatically identified (30d), with no local relation to PRO.

(30) a. Sam$_i$ claimed that it was clear that it had turned out that it seemed likely that it would be impossible [PRO$_i$ to prepare himself for the exam in time].

b. [PRO$_i$ washing his car regularly] is just the sort of thing that shows how meticulous Bill$_i$ is.

c. It is dangerous for babies$_i$ [PRO$_{arb}$ to smoke around them$_i$].

d. [After PRO pitching the tents], darkness fell quickly.

As to the humanness property, notice that quite a few OC predicates do not require a [+human] PRO (31a–c).[2] Adjunct control can even obtain with weather-*it* (31d).

(31) a. This key$_i$ will serve/do [PRO$_i$ to open the door].

b. The accident$_i$ is responsible [for PRO$_i$ causing the ship to sink].

c. The transmission problem forced the car$_i$ [PRO$_i$ to stop].

d. Around here, it$_i$ always snows [before PRO$_i$ raining].

NOC is different. When the pragmatics favors a [–human] PRO, the intrinsic [+human] restriction prevails, resulting in semantic anomaly (32a–b). NOC by weather-*it* is strictly excluded (32c).

(32) a. #It is possible [PRO to dissolve in cold water].
(cf. *It is possible for this material to dissolve in cold water.*)

b. #[After PRO being spoiled in a refrigerator], there is nothing even a good cook can do.

c. *[PRO to snow all day] would be a nuisance.
(cf. *For it to snow all day would be a nuisance.*)

Let us turn now to what is known as "implicit control"—a misnomer as far as adjuncts are concerned, as we will see shortly. Since the 1980s, a consensus has emerged that the implicit agent of passives participates in OC just like any other overt argument. The textbook example (33a) was taken to illustrate this effect with rationale clause (RatC) adjuncts (see Manzini 1983, Chomsky 1986b, Jaeggli 1986, Roeper 1987, Baker, Johnson, and Roberts 1989). Indeed, some authors took this example as evidence for the syntactic presence of the implicit agent, in the form of the -*en* suffix or *pro* (see also Collins 2005). This also explained the ungrammaticality of (33b), in which the matrix unaccusative verb provides no implicit agent. Relatedly, the external argument of a middle construction was said to project only morphologically, hence to be syntactically invisible to control (33c) (from Keyser and Roeper 1984:407).

(33) a. The ship was sunk to collect the insurance.

b. *The ship sank to collect the insurance.

c. *Bureaucrats bribe easily to keep them happy.

However, subsequent consideration revealed that none of these facts bear on the syntactic visibility of external arguments, or more importantly in the present context, on whether implicit arguments participate in OC. RatC adjuncts involve subtle semantic and pragmatic felicity conditions, and these are simply not satisfied in (33b–c). Unaccusative verbs rarely denote events for which a purposeful (or design-oriented) rationale can be offered; this is visible independently of control (34a). In carefully tailored scenarios (such as a playwright rationalizing the design of a play), such predicates *can* be modified by a RatC, and the presence of control is no hindrance (34b); see Landau 2000:179–183 for detailed discussion. Finally, middles place their adverbial modification in focus, and the explanation offered by the RatC is associated with it (Williams and Green 2017); thus, (33c) implies that the reason for the ease with which bureaucrats bribe is for people to make them happy—hardly a sensible interpretation. In fact, free of the specific interpretive conditions on RatC, the implicit agent of a middle can "control" into other adjuncts (34c). The scare quotes here anticipate my claim below that implicit arguments in fact do not participate in adjunct OC, only in NOC. ((34a–c) are from Kawasaki 1993:204, Williams 1985:311, and Vinet 1987:430, respectively.)

(34) a. #The ship sank (in order) for the owner to collect the insurance.
　　 b. The boat sank in order to impress the queen and move her to murder her husband by the end of act III.
　　 c. These books sell easily without putting them in the window.

Explicitly rejecting control by implicit agents into RatCs, Williams (1985) and Lasnik (1988) instead advocate "event control," where the entire matrix event is understood as the antecedent of PRO in such examples. This proposal does not sit comfortably with the observation that events cannot normally "collect insurance." Surveying this debate, in Landau 2013:224–225 I concluded that neither camp can adequately explain the entire range of control facts associated with RatCs. Nevertheless, I believe that Williams's (1985) insight that implicit arguments cannot control adjuncts is essentially correct, and that what we see in (33a)—as well as in (34b–c)—is a form of NOC. The confusion surrounding control into RatCs (and certain other adjuncts) is rooted in their dual character: they truly display either OC or NOC. This conclusion will be established in section 5.1.

But *why* is implicit OC not an option with adjuncts? The explanation is straightforward if OC into adjuncts is a form of predication (Williams 1992, Landau 2013). Then it would fail with implicit controllers because, as is well-known, grammatical predication is contingent on syntactic visibility: implicit arguments cannot saturate predicates (Rizzi 1986, Landau 2010a). This outcome emerges immediately on the predicational account of adjunct OC but remains a puzzle for alternative theories (see chapter 10).

The implication is that implicit agents, goals, or benefactives are only able to control *adjuncts* via the NOC route. Let me reiterate the stress on *adjuncts*: implicit arguments may perfectly exercise OC into *complements*, specifically attitude complements, because OC into such complements is based on variable binding and not predication (see Landau 2007, 2015:68–75, Pitteroff and Schäfer 2019).

Returning to (33a), I now claim that contrary to appearances, it involves NOC rather than OC by the implicit agent. The crucial observation was made by Manzini (1986): an implicit external argument must be interpreted as human when it controls the PRO subject of a temporal adjunct.

(35) a. The avalanche$_i$ hit the house [before PRO$_i$ rolling down the hill].
      b. The house was hit.
      c. Mary said that the house was hit [before PRO rolling down the hill].

(35a) reconfirms (28b): there is no intrinsic [+human] restriction on OC PRO. Neither is the implicit external argument of the passive *was hit* necessarily human ((35b) can be continued with *by the avalanche*). Still, on the reading where the implicit hitter (rather than *the house*) in (35c) controls PRO (admittedly a marginal reading, for reasons to become clear), that hitter must be human and cannot be understood to be the avalanche.

Manzini interpreted these facts as an indication that PRO in (35c) is really PRO$_{arb}$, which is intrinsically specified as [+human]. The linking to the matrix implicit agent is thus pragmatic, not syntactic; both PRO and the implicit agent pick out the current sentence topic. The following pair makes the same point.

(36) a. The rain$_i$ washed the stairs [before PRO$_i$ entering the basement].
      b. The stairs were washed [before PRO$_{arb}$ entering the basement].

On the salient reading of (36a), PRO is controlled by the matrix external argument, *the rain*. In (36b), subject control is pragmatically excluded; "control" by the implicit washer is possible but it must be a human participant, not *the rain*.[3] The emergence of the [+human] restriction in situations of "implicit agent control" reveals that this is a misnomer (hence the constant scare quotes). The implicit external argument does not form a direct OC relation with PRO. Rather, as stated in (28b), these are instances of NOC, as Kawasaki (1993:169) argues. That "implicit agent control" falls under NOC is also what Español-Echevarría (2000) concludes after studying the interaction of voice and control into RatCs (see section 14.3). In line with Williams (1992), Español-Echevarría recognizes the fundamental duality of control into adjuncts.

Not only external arguments but also internal arguments (goal, benefactive, or experiencer) participate in what may seem to be "implicit control."

(37) a. Here's *Bambi* to read to your children.
  b. The university should provide a decent library to work in.

(37a–b) are taken from Bach 1982:41 and Nishigauchi 1984:223, respectively. While Nishigauchi treats such examples as OC by an implicit argument, Bach treats them as NOC. I concur with Bach. The fact that the implicit benefactive is human makes it slightly more difficult to tease apart local implicit OC from NOC. Nevertheless, in section 5.2 I return to such examples and show that they too fall under NOC.

Importantly, it is only on the predication-based theory of adjunct OC that implicit OC is excluded. Two major alternatives do not derive this result: the movement theory of control (MTC; Hornstein 1999, 2003, Boeckx, Hornstein, and Nunes 2010, Green 2019) and the Agree-based theory of control (Adler 2006, Fischer 2018, McFadden and Sundaresan 2018). On these theories, insofar as implicit arguments are viable controllers of complements, they should be viable controllers of adjuncts (see chapter 10, where the theories are compared further).

An important point of methodology, often missed, is that local control by a matrix agentive subject can *never* be taken as conclusive evidence for OC. The unavailability of any controller other than *John* in (38a) is predicted both on the OC analysis and on the NOC analysis (John being the prominent perspective holder in the given context; on the significance of prominence in logophoric binding, see Zribi-Hertz 1989). On certain accounts, OC is favored by default and yields to NOC only if the OC reading is anomalous (i.e., a selectional violation; Kawasaki 1993, Lyngfelt 1999, Landau 2017), although we have already seen some evidence in (2)–(4) that this is not always necessary (Green 2018). Either way, (38a) cannot effectively detect the presence of NOC. Indeed, once the sentence-internal logophoric antecedent is removed, NOC is available with only slight effort (38b).

(38) a. John$_i$ was nervous [while PRO$_{i/*arb}$ waiting for the bus].
  b. The sky turned dark grey [while PRO$_{arb}$ waiting for the bus].

Before I conclude this section, let me address one challenge to this line of reasoning. On the basis of a crosslinguistic study of the interaction of complement control with impersonal passives, Pitteroff and Schäfer (2019) reject the claim in Landau 2015 that implicit agents cannot function as controllers of predicative clauses. Essentially, they claim it is not the control relation in (39b) that is obstructed under passivization; rather, the problem lies in the status of the subject *it*.

(39) a. They forgot to lock the door.
     b. *It was forgotten to lock the door.

English has no true expletive *it*, Pitteroff and Schäfer argue, only an argumental, CP-placeholder *it*. This is evidenced by the fact that English lacks impersonal passives of unergative verbs (**It was danced*), where the subject *it* can only be an expletive. Because *it* in (39b) is argumental, it is forced to enter a predication relation with *forgotten*. But given that it is anaphoric to a *predicative* CP, *it* denotes a property, which cannot function as a subject of predication in Spec,TP. This state of affairs holds not only in English but also in French, Russian, and Hebrew.

In contrast, German, Dutch, Norwegian, and Icelandic do have impersonal passives of unergatives; hence, they employ true expletives that can be inserted in contexts like (39b) without invoking predication. For this reason, parallel sentences are expected to be grammatical in these languages. Pitteroff and Schäfer report that while there is "huge variation" in judgments in languages like Dutch, sentences like (40a) are generally judged acceptable, contrasting with their English counterparts. Moreover, simple secondary predication can target implicit agents as well (40b) (examples from Pitteroff and Schäfer 2019:151, 157).

(40) a. Er   werd vergeten/verzuimd (om) als   collectief te   spelen,
        there was   forgotten/missed   C   as   collective to   play
        juist wat   normaliter de   sterke kracht is   van het team.
        just   what normally   the strong power   is   of   this team
        'People forgot/failed to play as a collective, which usually is
        the strength of this team.'
     b. Er   werde naakt   gedanst.
        ther was   naked   danced
        'People danced naked.'

Consider the implications of Pitteroff and Schäfer's account for the present discussion. In particular, what would be the fate of examples like (35c) and (36b) in a language where implicit agents do, by hypothesis, exercise OC by predication? The prediction is that the NOC effect—a necessarily [+human] interpretation—will *not* arise, because the implicit external argument of the matrix verb will be able to saturate the predicative adjunct clause. The facts, however, disconfirm this prediction. The NOC effect shows up in Dutch adjuncts, under matrix passivization, no less than it does in English (examples from Marcel den Dikken, pers. comm.).

(41) a. Het onweer   terroriseerde het dorp   om   zich te ontladen.
        the thunderstorm terrorized   the village COMP SE   to discharge
        'The thunderstorm terrorized the village to discharge its fury.'

   b. Het dorp   werd geterroriseerd om   zich te ontladen.
      the village was terrorized   COMP SE   to discharge
      'The village was terrorized to discharge **one**'s fury.'   → PRO$_{[+human]}$

   c. De regen waste de straat schoon alvorens de kelder   in te lopen.
      the rain washed the street clean before the basement in to run/walk
      'The rain washed the street clean before running down into the basement.'

   d. ?De straat werd schoongewassen alvorens de kelder in te lopen.
      the street was clean.washed before the basement in to run/walk
      'The street was washed clean before **walking** into the basement.'
      → PRO$_{[+human]}$

No verb in these examples selects a [+human] subject. Passive itself does not impose this restriction either. Therefore, the restricted [+human] interpretation of PRO in (41b,d) must reflect the workings of NOC. The conjunction of these facts with the facts in (40) poses a hard problem that I leave open for future work. It seems clear that implicit agents are not equally visible to processes that have so far been grouped together under "predication," and that more fine-grained distinctions are called for. At any rate, I will continue to assume, in the present study, that adjunct OC cannot target implicit arguments and that this generalization is crosslinguistically valid.

To summarize, in the discussion to follow I will make use of these three diagnostic properties to distinguish OC from NOC in adjuncts.

(42) *Control diagnostics in adjuncts*
   a. *Explicitness:* The controller in OC, but not in NOC, must be explicit (not an implicit argument).
   b. *Locality:* The controller in OC, but not in NOC, must be an argument of the clause immediately dominating the adjunct.
   c. *Humanness:* PRO in NOC, but not in OC, must be [+human].

Not all tests will be applicable in every situation. Sometimes it is impossible to make the designated controller implicit, simply because the language or specific verbs disallow passivization or object drop. At other times a certain adjunct, by its very semantics, will require a human (or agent) controller, thereby nullifying the possibility of testing inanimate controllers. Nevertheless, we will see that in all circumstances, at least two of the tests are applicable, and significantly, their results consistently converge.[4] For further arguments in favor of the OC-NOC distinction, see sections 14.2 and 14.5.

One final conclusion, which is relevant to the overall evaluation of the present account against potential alternatives, concerns the extensional relation between OC and NOC. One often hears that OC readings are a proper subset of NOC readings—that NOC has a less restricted interpretation, and that "this less restricted interpretation in fact subsumes the one associated with OC and thus can be understood as an Elsewhere that obtains when OC fails" (McFadden and Sundaresan 2018:484). The facts, however, determine not a subset-superset but an overlap relation.

(43) *Extensional relation between OC and NOC readings*

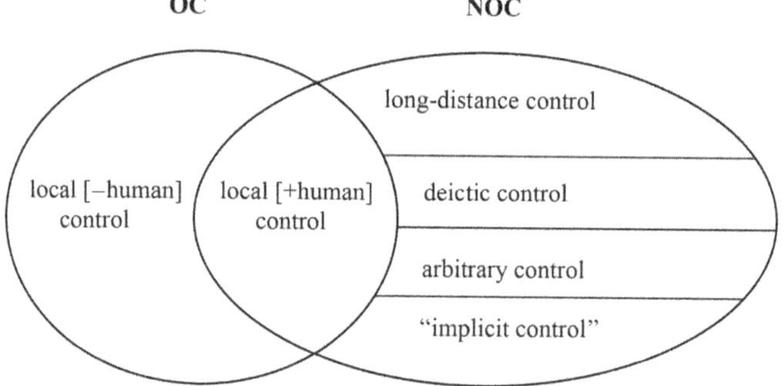

While NOC readings are indeed more diverse, they exclude [−human] control, hence do *not* subsume OC readings. As examples (5), (35c), (36b), and (38b) (and many more to come) show, NOC obtains in environments where a local antecedent is available. Even more strikingly, NOC may obtain in environments where choosing the local antecedent is semantically coherent (see (2)–(4)). The elsewhere logic is inadequate.

Does local [+human] control *really* lend itself to two derivations, OC and NOC? It is extremely difficult to answer this question, as normal circumstances do not distinguish between them. Perhaps OC prevails for some principled reason, or is just preferred for processing reasons; perhaps there is some subtle empirical way to probe this question (see section 14.2 for discussion). For now I set it aside, repeating the methodological lesson: local [+human] control is never informative regarding the OC-NOC divide. Examples with local human controllers can be used for other purposes (e.g., in testing attachment height), but they do not bear on the fundamental empirical issue that guides the present investigation—the distribution of OC vs. NOC adjuncts. This point cannot be stressed enough, for the vast majority of the data that currently informs the literature on adjunct control consists just of these systematically ambiguous examples. The conclusions drawn are accordingly ambiguous and tenuous (see chapter 10 for critical discussion). In what follows, I will base claims for OC and NOC only on data that unambiguously speak to each type.

4 Strict OC Adjuncts

In this chapter, I discuss four types of infinitival adjuncts in English: goal clauses, result clauses, stimulus clauses, and subject purpose clauses. The first three types are hardly discussed outside Huettner 1989 (briefly reviewed in Landau 2013 and Green 2018, 2019), so the discussion will heavily draw on that work. The fourth type is well-documented in various sources. For each adjunct type X, I will establish two main claims: (i) X displays OC; (ii) X has no propositional variant. Given the PVC, (ii) then derives and explains (i).

4.1 Goal Clauses

In goal constructions, "the main clause describes a kind of (possibly abstract) motion towards the goal expressed in the infinitive" (Huettner 1989:40). Only goal-oriented matrix verbs can be modified by goal clauses (examples are from Huettner 1989:38, 44).

(44) a. John went out to smoke.
    b. Max works hard to stay out of jail.
    c. *John hammered to hang the picture.

In many languages, the verbs corresponding to *go* and *come* can take non-finite complements when used as functional or semifunctional heads (Cardinaletti and Giusti 2001, Wurmbrand 2003, Cinque 2004). It is possible to view goal clauses as a natural extension of these uses to a somewhat larger class of verbs. This underscores the close affinity between strict OC adjuncts and certain complementation patterns, an affinity that will repeatedly emerge in the following sections.

Although superficially similar to rationale clauses (RatCs), goal clauses are different both in their syntax and in their semantics. Semantically, the embedded action is not separable from the matrix action; rather, it is perceived as a *realization* of the latter (in contrast to RatCs, where the two actions are clearly distinct, one serving as an instrument to bring about the other). Syntactically, goal clauses are VP-internal and unmovable. ((45a–b) are from Huettner 1989:41–42.)

(45) a. *To smoke, John went out.
     b. *What Max did to stay out of jail was work hard.
     c.   What Max does to impress the boss is work hard and stay late. *RatC*

Correspondingly, goal clauses necessarily scope under negation (46a) and do not yield the scope ambiguity typical of RatCs (46b).

(46) a. John didn't work hard to stay out of jail.
        Reading: *¬>>Adjunct, *Adjunct>>¬*
     b. John didn't work hard and stay late (in order) to impress the boss.
        Readings: *¬>>Adjunct, Adjunct>>¬*

Goal clauses require an agentive controller; hence, OC cannot be established with inanimate controllers.[1] Yet standard tests of locality and variable binding reveal that indeed goal clauses are subject to OC.

(47) a. Mary$_i$ was dying for a cigarette so John$_j$ went out [PRO$_{*i/j}$ to smoke].
     b. The doctor$_i$ fought to save the child's life and his colleagues$_j$ did ~~fight~~
        ~~[PRO$_{*i/j}$ to save the child's life]~~ too.

Significantly, goal clauses lack any propositional variant (i.e., there are no goal clauses with lexical subjects). The sentences in (48) are grammatical but do not have the goal reading. The adjunct in (48a) is interpreted as a RatC; unlike in (44a), insertion of *in order* does not alter the meaning of the sentence. The adjunct in (48b) is interpreted as an effect of the cause specified by the matrix clause. Unlike in (44b), in (48b) Max does not work hard *at* Bob's staying out of jail.[2]

(48) a. John went out (in order) for Bob to smoke.
     b. Max works hard ?(so) that Bob stays out of jail.

It is possible to bring out the uniqueness of goal clauses by attending to their temporal interpretation. A goal clause specifies an event that is contiguous in time with the matrix event. Indeed, the two clauses are perceived as describing one complex event, undivided in time. RatCs and effect clauses are clearly different in that the events they introduce are temporally independent of the matrix event. In this light, consider the following contrasts.

(49) a. *At 4 p.m., John went out to smoke at 6 p.m.
     b. *Last month, Max worked hard to stay out of jail next month.

(50) a. At 4 p.m., John went out (in order) for Bob to smoke at 6 p.m.
     b. Last month, Max worked hard so that Bob will stay out of jail next month.

The temporal separation between the matrix and embedded events is only possible under nongoal readings. The same temporal separation exists, even if implicitly, in (48).

Thus, goal clauses verify the PVC: lacking a propositional variant, they are predicative by necessity. Their OC character is explained by this fact.

4.2   Result Clauses

In result constructions, "the relationship between the main clause and the adjunct ranges from mere 'occasion' to natural causation: the infinitive expresses a non-intended sequel to the main clause action" (Huettner 1989:26). Result clauses only occur with unaccusative main verbs, or with verbs that can be coerced into a reading within the range of the unaccusative verb. ((51a–b) are from Huettner 1989:26, 32.)

(51) a.   Mary grew up to be a famous actress.
      b.   The sofa folds out to make a bed.
      c. *The leaves trembled in the wind to fall down.

Unaccusative predicates may be telic or atelic. With an atelic unaccusative, the result clause adds an endpoint to the event; with a telic one, it further specifies aspects of the lexicalized endpoint. Note that result clauses are compatible with resultative particles and predicates (*up* and *open* below; examples found on the internet[3]).

(52) a. In 2002, the southern lake shrunk and dried up to become an eastern lake and a western lake.
      b. The husk broke open to reveal a small seed that resembled an almond.

Syntactically, result clauses are VP-internal and unmovable (examples from Huettner 1989:30–31).

(53) a. *To shatter on the floor, the glass fell.
      b.   The sofa folds out to make a bed, and so does the chair (*to form a pup tent).

That result clauses support OC is demonstrated by their tolerance to inanimate controllers. That they resist NOC is demonstrated by their lack of long-distance control (54a), even when the distant potential controller is human and the local one is inanimate.

(54) a. The mayor$_i$ learned that the toxic vapors$_j$ stayed for days [PRO$_{*i/j}$ to keep the citizens indoors and complaining].
      b. The mayor$_i$ learned that the toxic vapors stayed for days so he$_j$ kept the citizens indoors and complaining.

Long-distance control is impossible even when the attempted controller is topical and human, and the local one is not.

(55) *Meghan Markle$_i$ regretted that her accent had changed [PRO$_i$ to become less sure of herself].

Discourse control, which is possible in temporal adjuncts like (56a), is not allowed in result adjuncts (56b) (examples from Green 2019:16).

(56) a. The door$_i$ opened again [PRO after trying to close it$_i$].
      b. *The door$_i$ opened again [PRO to try to close it$_i$].

Finally, only a sloppy reading shows up under VP-ellipsis.

(57) John$_i$ awoke to find the fire had gone out before Mary$_j$ did ~~awake [PRO$_{*i/j}$ to find the fire had gone out]~~.

Thus, result clauses show all the properties of OC adjuncts and none of the properties of NOC adjuncts. As we should now expect, they have no propositional variants.

(58) a. *Mary grew up [for the world to recognize her talent].
      b. *The sofa folds out [for the bed to be unnecessary].

The lack of a propositional variant explains the lack of NOC, since, by hypothesis, it reveals the predicative character of result clauses. The PVC thus correctly predicts OC behavior.

4.3 Stimulus Clauses

In stimulus constructions, "the adjuncts express not the immediate goal of the action but rather its immediate cause: roughly, the stimulus that provoked the action of the main clause" (Huettner 1989:54). Stimulus clauses must express involuntary perception and normally occur with matrix predicates that express emotional reactions (examples (59a–c) are from Huettner 1989:54–55, and (59d) is from the internet[4]).

(59) a. Mary smiled to think what a fool she had been.
      b. Max was sad to see his livelihood swept away.
      c. *Suzan frowned to look at the awful mess.
          [*Look* is voluntary.]
      d. I wept to hear about the destruction in California.

Note that (59b) may well involve a complement rather than a stimulus clause adjunct; the entire class of emotive predicates (*glad, happy, shocked, excited*, etc.) selects factive complements. Huettner's misclassification reflects the general point made above, which is that strict OC adjuncts often blend into selected complements, in the sense that they elaborate on a semantic aspect of the eventuality that is, for some predicates, a lexical entailment expressed by a complement.

Syntactically, stimulus clauses are VP-internal and unmovable (examples from Huettner 1989:55–56).

(60) a. *To see what a fool Sam was making of himself, Susan blushed.
  b. John said that Mary would tremble to hear of her father's wrath, and tremble she did (*to hear of her father's wrath).

Because the controller of stimulus clauses must be sentient, OC cannot be established using inanimate controllers. Nonetheless, it is clearly impossible to observe any NOC property with stimulus clauses: non-c-commanding control is excluded, long-distance control is excluded, and strict readings are unavailable (examples from Landau 2013:31).

(61) a. [John's$_i$ daughter]$_j$ blushed [PRO$_{*i/j}$ to see herself/*himself without the wig].
  b. Mary$_i$ giggled. Bill$_j$ blushed [PRO$_{j/*i}$ to see her$_i$/*him$_j$ in underwear]. (cf. *Mary$_i$ giggled. Bill$_j$ blushed as she$_i$ saw him$_j$ in underwear.*)
  c. Mark$_i$ trembled to hear the results of the vote, and so did Beth$_j$ ~~tremble [PRO$_{*i/j}$ to hear the results of the vote]~~.

As expected, like goal and result clauses, stimulus clauses have no propositional variant.

(62) a. Mary smiled (*for Bob) to think what a fool she had been.
  b. Bill wept (*for his wife) to hear the tragic story.

Notice that finite complements with stimulus-like meaning exist, and these of course feature lexical subjects.

(63) a. Mary smiled that/as Bob thought what a fool she had been.
  b. Bill wept that/as his wife heard the tragic story.

These sentences, however, cannot be taken as propositional variants of (62a–b), in the sense required by the PVC. Although a causal relation is expressed between the complement and matrix clauses in (63), it is not a stimulus-response relation. Temporal contiguity is not required (Mary in (63a) may have smiled days after Bill's thought), and in fact, perception itself is not required, as the complement may express nonperceptual events. Compare (59c) with (64).

(64) Suzan frowned as she looked at the awful mess.

Therefore, the same pattern found with other OC adjuncts is observed with stimulus clauses: the lack of a propositional variant indicates that the adjunct is predicative, which determines its status as an OC adjunct.

4.4   Subject Purpose Clauses

Like all purpose clauses, subject purpose clauses (SPCs) form a dependency with the matrix theme; with SPCs, the dependency is control.[5] Specifying the right type of theme for purpose clauses is an intricate matter; roughly, the theme must be made available for the action of the adjunct, by being present, created, or transferred—a global interpretation not reducible to thematic labels. *Purpose* is a broad term that covers intention, natural teleology, function, and design. Purpose clauses are distinguished from RatCs in various respects, most notably in rejecting *in order*.[6]

(65)   a.   She bought/*sold a dog$_i$ [PRO$_i$ to play with the children].
     b.   I ordered this floating shelf (*in order) to hold all my art books.
     c.   I keep this UV lamp to protect me from those dreadful mosquitos.

Syntactically, SPC clauses are VP-internal and unmovable (Faraci 1974).

(66)   a.   *To talk to them$_i$, they$_i$ brought John along.
     b.   She bought a bobcat to play with her children although I wouldn't (*to play with mine).

Evidently, the possibility of inanimate controllers indicates that SPCs support OC. NOC, however, is not available. A long-distance controller cannot override a local one even when the [+human] property is on its side.

(67)   a.   Max bought a nice shelf$_i$ [PRO$_i$ to hold my art books].
     b.   I called in Max$_i$ [PRO$_i$ to catalogue my art books].
     c.   Max$_i$ wondered where I bought that nice shelf$_j$ [PRO$_{*i/j}$ to hold/*catalogue my art books].

"Implicit control" is similarly unavailable, even when the matrix verb allows an implicit theme. This is another characteristic of OC in adjuncts (see (42a)).

(68)   a.   We're now hiring (people).
     b.   We're now hiring *(people) to manage the marketing for us.

In the case of SPCs, the lack of a propositional variant is definitional: the embedded subject must be a gap for the adjunct to qualify as an SPC. Sentences like (69) can only be interpreted (with some effort) as employing a RatC (e.g., the cat wouldn't play with the children with(out) the dog around). Crucially, adding *in order* or changing the matrix verb to one that is incompatible with SPCs has no effect on grammaticality (cf. (65)).

(69)   ?She bought/sold the dog [(in order) for the cat to play with the children].

SPCs are therefore the fourth type of adjunct that is correctly predicted by the PVC: lacking a propositional variant, an SPC must be predicative; hence, OC is the only option. Indeed, this conclusion is fully consistent with the classical literature on SPCs, in which they are viewed as null operator constructions: the controlled PRO is nothing but a trace of a null operator that moves to the edge of the adjunct (Chomsky 1980, Browning 1987, Clark 1990). As usual, operator movement creates a derived predicate by abstracting over the trace position.

(70) I ordered this floating shelf$_i$ [$_{FinP}$ Op$_i$ [$_{TP}$ t$_i$ to hold all my art books]].

Interestingly, when the abstracted position is the embedded object, as in object purpose clauses, PRO need not be subject to predication and may display a NOC character (section 5.2).

5 OC/NOC Adjuncts

Besides strict OC adjuncts, the other major category of adjuncts displays an alternation between OC and NOC.[1] Discussing temporal clauses and RatCs, I argue in Landau 2017 that this alternation reflects a genuine structural ambiguity. Here I will extend this conclusion to four more types, altogether analyzing six types of OC/NOC adjuncts: rationale clauses (RatCs), object purpose clauses (OPCs), temporal clauses, absolutive clauses, justification clauses, and telic clauses. I will adopt some of the conclusions reached by Whelpton (2001, 2002) and Green (2018) but will take issue with others. For each adjunct type X, I will establish three main claims: (i) X can display OC; (ii) X can display NOC; (iii) X has a propositional variant. Given the PVC, (iii) then derives and explains the alternation between (i) and (ii).

5.1 Rationale Clauses

The claim that RatCs exhibit either OC or NOC was first explicitly defended by Español-Echevarría (2000). In this section, I adduce further evidence in its favor.

To establish OC in RatCs, it is obviously not enough to point to standard subject control by the matrix agent (71a), nor to the impossibility of arbitrary control in such environments (71b).

(71) a. Mary$_i$ excelled in order PRO$_i$ to impress her friends.
     b. *Mary$_i$ excelled in order PRO$_{arb}$ to admire her$_i$.

The reason is that a NOC controller is typically the most salient logophoric participant. Since the agent *Mary* is just this participant, it will be picked as the NOC controller even if (71a–b) allow NOC—indeed, even if they *force* NOC (see the discussion of (43)).

However, there is a class of examples, mostly ignored in the literature, that demonstrates conclusively the availability of OC in RatCs. As observed in Landau 2013:224, 2017, these examples manifest control by an inanimate subject. (Examples (72b–c) are from Williams 1992:317 and Español-Echevarría 1998, respectively.)

(72) a. Flowers$_i$ produce pollen [in order PRO$_i$ to reproduce].
      b. This book$_i$ was written [in order PRO$_i$ to be read].
      c. The house$_i$ was emptied [(in order) PRO$_i$ to be demolished].

These OC examples are interesting for another reason: they refute the view that the controller of a RatC must be the bearer of intention—the so-called *initiator* of the matrix eventuality (see Farkas 1988, Landau 2000:181–183, Whelpton 2002). Clearly the interpretation of RatCs typically implicates such an initiator, yet under OC, that person or entity need not be the controller.

OC, however, is not the only option. NOC in RatCs can be observed whenever the controller is extrasentential, and then, indeed, it is interpreted as the initiator of the matrix eventuality. ((73a) is from Duffley 2014:204.)

(73) a. (A comment on a video demonstrating tennis techniques:)
          Note how the weight is going forwards to get power into the shot.
      b. The door is open to greet passing neighbors.
      c. The painting was on the wall in order to check how it would be received.

Under the right circumstances, even a human local subject may be "bypassed." In (74) (from Español-Echevarría 2000:101), PRO may be understood either as some third party that made Bill act or as the matrix event itself (on event control, see section 14.1).

(74) Bill$_i$ will introduce the ambassador to the president [in order PRO to give him$_i$ the opportunity to observe their reactions].

Similarly, "implicit agent control," which is an instance of NOC on the current proposal, is famously available with RatCs. ((75a–b) are from Roeper 1987:278 and Español-Echevarría 1998:131, respectively.)

(75) a. A vote was taken [PRO to elect a president].
      b. The fines were paid [(in order) PRO to avoid further complications].

According to the PVC, alternating OC/NOC adjuncts must have a propositional variant. This is indeed the case: a RatC can freely occur with a lexical subject.

(76) a. Sales would need to rise by at least 60% [in order for the company to be profitable].
      b. George bought a bigger apartment [in order for his girlfriend to move in with him].

The availability of these propositional variants, then, explains the availability of NOC in RatC.

The duality of mechanism—OC vs. NOC—in RatC adjuncts is manifested very clearly in so-called remote control constructions (Williams 2015, Williams and Green 2017). Williams observes that all the characteristic restrictions on the resolution of PRO in a RatC are preserved when the infinitival clause occurs after the copula in a specificational sentence of the form *The goal/reason/purpose was . . .* , although the controller is remote (not in the same sentence), (77a–b). Whatever control relations are not allowed intrasententially are also not allowed in remote control, (77c–d).

(77) a.   The team$_i$ traded away two outfielders [PRO$_i$ to acquire a pitcher].
 b.   The team$_i$ traded away two outfielders. The goal was [PRO$_i$ to acquire a pitcher].
 c.   *Parasites cover these sharks$_i$ [PRO$_i$ to have their gills kept clean].
 d.   *Parasites cover these sharks$_i$. The goal is [PRO$_i$ to have their gills kept clean].

Williams reasons that because remote control cannot be subsumed under any syntactic relation, it falls in the pragmatic realm. But then parsimony dictates that even intrasentential control of RatCs be handed over to the pragmatics, given that it displays the same interpretive profile.

Crucially missing from Williams 2015 and Williams and Green 2017 are RatC examples with inanimate controllers. Strikingly, this is where the parallelism between intrasentential and remote control breaks down. Compare (72b–c) with the following.

(78) a.   *This book was written for a reason. The reason was to be read.
 b.   *The house was emptied. The goal was to be demolished.

To complete the picture, observe that "implicit control" survives remoteness (as Green (2018:147) observes).

(79) a.   The ship was sunk. The goal was to collect the insurance.
 b.   The ship was sunk. The goal was to be promoted.
 c.   A vote was taken. The goal was to elect a president.

This array of data nicely comports with the thesis that RatC control is fundamentally a dual process (as adjunct control generally is). One process is strictly syntactic (Landau 2017, Green 2019, *pace* Williams 2015) and therefore cannot cross sentence boundaries; it is the only process available to inanimate controllers, hence (78). The other process, NOC, is pragmatic and is not confined to the sentence level. Tellingly, "implicit control" once again patterns with

NOC, corroborating the conclusion in chapter 3 that it is not syntactically mediated. In section 14.3, I return to examine more closely some subtle interpretive restrictions that show up in RatCs under NOC; importantly, those restrictions do not affect the present conclusions.

5.2 Object Purpose Clauses

Like SPCs (section 4.4), OPCs form a dependency with the matrix theme, which may be a subject or object, linked to an embedded object gap via a null operator. PRO is typically controlled by a goal or benefactive, if there is one, or, in their absence, by the agent.

(80) a. Carol bought Jim$_j$ a rack$_i$ [$_{CP}$ Op$_i$ [PRO$_j$ to hang coats on t$_i$]].
    b. Carol$_j$ bought a rack$_i$ [$_{CP}$ Op$_i$ [PRO$_j$ to hang coats on t$_i$]].

As noted originally in Faraci 1974, OPCs are VP-internal and cannot be fronted. In this respect, they are different from other alternating OC/NOC adjuncts (a point to which I return in section 7.2).

(81) a.   A: Alice brought a dog to play with.
       B: Jennifer did ___ too. / *Jennifer did ___ to train.
    b. *To nibble with the beer, Alice baked some nachos.

Note, though, that in this respect OPCs are just like other secondary predicates associated with the matrix object, which are also VP-internal (*Dan ate his hamburger well-done and I did ___ medium rare*).

Because the controller is nearly always human, it is difficult to tease apart OC from NOC. However, to the extent that nonhuman benefactives are tolerated in special circumstances, they are also suitable controllers for OPC.

(82) They equipped this plane$_i$ with a hose-drogue probe system [PRO$_i$ to be refuelled in flight with].

Also, due to the strong preference for OC whenever possible, we might expect OC characteristics in examples like (82). Indeed, Green (2018:173) observes that only a sloppy reading appears under VP-ellipsis in (83).

(83) Monica$_i$ bought a new frying pan to cook with, and Chandler$_j$ did ~~buy a new frying pan [PRO~~$_{*i/j}$ ~~to cook with]~~ too.

Nevertheless, OPCs are capable of supporting NOC as well. The test with "implicit argument control" yields particularly interesting results. Parallel to the paradigms in (35), (36), and (41), the attempt to target an implicit argument—here, a benefactive—as a controller gives rise to a [+human] restriction.

(84) a. They bought their bedroom this wallpaper to be decorated with.
      b. They$_i$ bought me this wallpaper to decorate their bedroom with for
          them$_i$.
      c. They$_i$ bought this wallpaper to decorate their bedroom with for
          them$_i$.
      d. *They bought this wallpaper to be decorated with.

Either a human or an inanimate benefactive may occur with *buy* and control
the OPC (84a–b). Yet when the benefactive is implicit, only the human one
may control, (84c) vs. (84d). Notice that the embedded pronoun *them*, coindexed with the matrix subject, rules out subject control in (84b–c) (by Condition B), leaving only the benefactive as a potential controller. While (84c)
requires some context (to shift control away from the matrix subject), (84d)
remains beyond redemption regardless of context. The contrast between them
indicates that in the absence of an explicit controller DP, the OPC resorts to
NOC. The search for a suitable logophoric antecedent is satisfied with a human
benefactive only.

Non-c-commanding (85a) and extrasentential (85b–c) control into OPC are
possible too, which must be due to NOC (recall that "locality" in the sense of
(42b) picks out *arguments* of the matrix clause). ((85a–b) are from Stromdahl
2018, and (85c) is adapted from Whelpton 2002:192.)

(85) a. I left it in [her$_i$ mailbox] [PRO$_i$ to look over once she returned from
          the Bahamas].
      b. They're kept in the overhead compartment [PRO$_{arb}$ to use in case of
          emergency].
      c. The car$_i$ was in the showroom [$_{CP}$ Op$_i$ [PRO to see t$_i$]].

Finally, OPCs readily accept lexical subjects.

(86) a. Check out this tennis racket. I ordered it [for you to play with].
      b. The car was in the showroom [for the crowds to see].

Strictly speaking, these are not *propositional* variants, because the embedded object position is still abstracted over, and so the OPC is a predicate.
However, we can safely disregard this aspect, as it is irrelevant to the OC/
NOC alternation, which pertains to the *subject* position. That alternation
depends on an abstracted position in OC being saturated in NOC just as it is
saturated by a lexical DP. In this sense, OPCs fall together with other alternating adjuncts, so I will continue to assume they have "propositional variants"
in the relevant (abstract) sense. The fact that they are nonetheless predicative
with respect to the object position, however, will play a role in explaining
their exceptional low attachment site (see section 7.2).

5.3   Temporal Clauses

In English, controlled temporal adjuncts are realized as gerunds. OC is clearly available, as we find such adjuncts with inanimate controllers, including weather expletives.

(87) a. That oven$_i$ worked for 25 years [before PRO$_i$ breaking down last winter].
   b. Around here, it$_i$ always snows [before PRO$_i$ raining].

At the same time, clear instances of NOC are attested with temporal adjuncts. In the following examples, PRO is controlled outside of the sentence by some prominent logophoric antecedent (often but not always the speaker(s)).[2]

(88) a. There won't be any progress [without PRO insisting on guidance from the outside].
   b. That oasis was a vision [after PRO dragging ourselves through the desert all day].

The OC/NOC alternation can be clearly observed in minimal pairs like the following, from Green 2018:277.

(89) The hamburgers$_i$ became much more popular at the school carnival . . .
   a. . . . [after PRO$_i$ cooking just a little bit longer].
   b. . . . [after PRO$_{arb}$ cooking them$_i$ just a little bit longer].

Recall also the [+human] restriction that popped up under "implicit external argument control" in (35c), (36b), and (41d)—a hallmark of NOC in these adjuncts.

   In the same vein, Green (2018) observes that the reflexive *oneself* is licensed in arbitrary control temporal adjuncts, and that long-distance control is consistent with a strict reading under ellipsis, two signatures of NOC. (Examples (90a–b) are from Green 2018:73, 74.)

(90) a. Adrenalin always kicks in [after PRO$_{arb}$ putting oneself in danger].
   b. The chef$_i$ thinks the potatoes will sell better [after PRO$_i$ adding more salt], and his wife thinks the carrots will, too. (= *will ~~sell better [after PRO$_i$ adding more salt]~~ too*)

Interestingly, as we will see in section 14.2, even local control allows a strict reading, indicating that the same string may be ambiguously parsed as OC or NOC.

   Poole (2015:2) claims that implicit agents can control *without*-adjuncts and other temporal adjuncts only in the presence of a root modal (expanding on an observation in Chomsky 1982).

(91) a. *The beer$_i$ was served without chilling it$_i$.
      b.   The beer$_i$ can be served without chilling it$_i$.

While I agree that the modal improves the sentence, I do not believe it has a dramatic effect on grammaticality. Poole presupposes that these adjuncts are subject to strict OC, hence require some matrix antecedent. The modal presumably makes the matrix implicit agent available by existential closure. Yet the presupposition is false; temporal adjuncts (including *without*-adjuncts) perfectly support NOC readings with no matrix implicit argument ((88), (98e)). Examples like (92a–b), with matrix unaccusative verbs, are not hard to construct.

(92) a. The meeting ended without deciding on a course of action.
      b. Another day has passed without hearing her voice.

In fact, unmodalized passive examples are also attested. Tellingly, the controller can be either the matrix agent (93a) or some extrasentential entity (93b).

(93) a. The meeting was canceled without providing any reasons.
      b. The meeting was canceled without knowing the reasons.

Thus, the question to ask is not how a modal enables an OC dependency (Poole's question), but why it sometimes seems to facilitate NOC. My hunch is that the modal highlights the logophoric center in virtue of its "subjective" nature. That is, because the interpretation of the modal involves constructing a modal base, it necessarily involves the perspective of whoever does it. This may be true even for circumstantial modals ((91b) allows that reading), such as when A says, *Corn can grow here* and B replies, *No, it can't.*[3]

As a novel piece of evidence for the OC/NOC duality of temporal adjuncts, consider cases of remote control, analogous to those with RatC adjuncts in (77)–(79). Here, the subject of the copular clause is the pleonastic *it* ordinarily associated with time predicates (e.g., *It was Monday*). Such examples can be found on the internet, most naturally when the temporal clause is modified by *right*.[4]

(94) a. Poor Sam$_i$ has had to play that three times in four seasons now and each time it was [right before PRO$_i$ seeing a very important person in his life].
      b. I$_j$'ve only thrown up once (thank god) and it was [right after PRO$_j$ eating some raisins and drinking cherry juice].
      c. I remember when I$_i$ realized that samurai was the job for me. It was [right before PRO$_i$ getting to the Aht Urghan camps], and I played with some Japanese players.

No OC derivation is available to postcopular temporal clauses, so NOC is the only option. The NOC antecedent in all these cases is human. In contrast, remote control fails with inanimate antecedents, as these are excluded from NOC.

(95) a. *The bomb$_i$ was placed under the seats. It was [right before PRO$_i$ exploding and killing 7 passengers].
        (cf. *The bomb was placed under the seats right before exploding and killing 7 passengers.*)
      b. *The novel$_i$ became an international sensation. It was [right after PRO$_i$ being translated into English].
        (cf. *The novel became an international sensation right after being translated into English.*)
      c. *The wine bottles$_i$ were carefully packaged. It was [right before PRO$_i$ being shipped to Canada].
        (cf. *The wine bottles were carefully packaged right before being shipped to Canada.*)

Consider the following minimal pair from Green 2018:277 (repeated from (89)).

(96) The hamburgers$_i$ became much more popular at the school carnival . . .
      a. . . . [after PRO$_i$ cooking just a little bit longer].
      b. . . . [after PRO$_{arb}$ cooking them$_i$ just a little bit longer].

The current proposal predicts that only (96b) will have a remote control paraphrase. This is correct.

(97) The hamburgers$_i$ became much more popular at the school carnival.
      a. *It was [after PRO$_i$ cooking just a little bit longer].
      b. It was [after PRO$_{arb}$ cooking them$_i$ just a little bit longer].

Thus, the test of remote control converges with the other tests for OC vs. NOC and confirms the ambiguous nature of temporal adjuncts.

Propositional variants of controlled gerunds occur with either accusative or genitive subjects, a distinction of no significance for present purposes (98a–b). For some idiosyncratic reason, *while/when*-gerunds exclude lexical subjects.[5]

(98) a. John retired [before/after Bob's announcing his replacement].
      b. He managed to climb to the top [without anyone helping him at any stage].
      c. She was very dreamy [while/when PRO/*Bob/*Bob's talking to us].
      d. She was very dreamy [while/when Bob was talking to us].
      e. The night sky can be an unforgettable spectacle [while/when PRO camping in the desert].

It is legitimate, I think, to consider the finite adjunct in (98d) as a propositional variant of the gerund in (98c), for their meaning is indistinguishable *qua temporal modifiers* (as already noted for (22)); see Reuland 1983:129 for remarks in that spirit. If so, the occurrence of NOC in (98e) is expected under the PVC. Indeed, the OC/NOC alternation of all temporal adjuncts is precisely what (19b) predicts.[6]

5.4 Absolutive Clauses

Absolutive clauses in English are also constructed with gerunds; their semantic relation to the matrix event is rather loose, ranging from temporal precedence to circumstantial, manner, causal, or conditional modification. Inanimate controllers and weather predicates are acceptable, indicating that OC is available (examples are from the internet[7]).

(99) a. [PRO_i having run smoothly until then], the economic engine$_i$ began
          to sputter already at the beginning of the year.
      b. It$_i$ was pitch dark and very cold, [PRO_i having snowed and thawed
          recently].

Although absolutive clauses have occasionally been classified as OC constructions (Mohanan 1983, Pires 2007), research has repeatedly shown NOC to be available as well, with indisputable evidence going back at least to Jespersen 1954, and many examples documented in Kortmann 1991. First, a nonc-commanding controller is possible (examples from Kortmann 1991:60 and Green 2019:12, respectively).

(100) a. [Being PRO_i not yet fully grown], his$_i$ trousers were too long.
       b. [PRO_i sitting in class the day after the party], my$_i$ eyes refused to
           stay open.

Extrasentential control is possible too, as (101a–d) illustrate (Jespersen 1954:409, Kortmann 1991:58, Williams 1992:300, Hartman 2008:206, respectively).[8]

(101) a. Looking out of the window, there were the flower beds in the front
           garden.
       b. Motoring down the road to New York, numerous signs read "Visit
           Our Snake Farm."
       c. [PRO having travelled all day], the hotel was a vision indeed.
       d. [PRO standing on the patio], the plants obscure/highlight the duck pond.

Absolutive clauses frequently occur with lexical subjects, confirming the existence of a propositional variant. A subordinating *with* is possible but not necessary.[9]

(102) a. [Fanaticism having cooled down], no moral principle remained in
men's souls.
b. [My family being financially secure], there was no reason to take on
another day job.
c. [With George watching every step of hers], Lyn could hardly
experience her new freedom.

Thus, the OC/NOC alternation and the availability of a propositional variant
are correlated.

5.5 Justification Clauses

In justification clauses, the adjunct provides justification for the action in the
main clause. The notion of justification subsumes the notion of reason, with an
additional implication of some moral judgment (positive or negative). Most frequently, justification clauses are used to convey acts of punishment or reward.[10]
The adjunct is introduced by the preposition *for*, which selects a gerund.

Green (2018:163) suggests that with a few main verbs (*blame, praise, thank*)
the clause may, in fact, be a selected argument. However, the fact that it can
be stranded under VP-ellipsis, as Green himself observes (p. 168), suggests
that it is an adjunct even in these cases.

(103) Peter thanked/praised Justin for eating all of his dinner, and Jill did so
for cleaning up after himself.

In section 7.3, I consider further constituency tests with justification clauses.

In general, either subject or object control is allowed with justification
clauses, depending on contextual information. Sometimes the interpretation is
ambiguous, as in Green's (2018:164) example (104) (on the subject control reading, the flowers are an apology; on the object control reading, they are a reward).

(104) Jack$_i$ brought Sharon$_j$ flowers [for PRO$_{i/j}$ working so late].

Because of their "ethical" flavor, justification clauses are rarely felicitous
with inanimate controllers. However, insofar as such controllers can be the
target of moral judgment, they are acceptable. First, consider object control
((105a–d) are from the internet and (105e) is from Green 2019:10).[11]

(105) a. Every photographer should hate Instagram$_i$ [for PRO$_i$ making our
job look easy].
b. I hated going out because of the cold and I resented winter$_i$ for
[PRO$_i$ making me dress like a potato].
c. Our food took about 30 minutes to get to us, and two of us sent the
steak$_i$ back [for PRO$_i$ being undercooked].

d. He criticized the project$_i$ [for PRO$_i$ being too expensive].

e. I included the book$_i$ in the book fair [for PRO$_i$ being so well-written].

Inanimate subject control is also possible.

(106) a. The Italian novel$_i$ won the prize [for PRO$_i$ being so well-written].

b. Coconuts$_i$ were the survivors' favorite choice of food [for PRO$_i$ being so nutritious].

For a second OC diagnostic, observe that local subject control passes the sloppy reading test.

(107) Mary$_i$ hated music school [for PRO$_i$ having to take violin classes], and her brother$_j$ did ~~hate school [for PRO$_{*i/j}$ having to take violin classes]~~ too.

As Green (2018:169) observes, implicit arguments can serve as controllers of justification clauses, as well as non-c-commanding controllers, indicating that NOC is also possible.

(108) a. They awarded it [for PRO winning the contest].

b. I put roses on the front porch of [her$_i$ house] [for PRO$_i$ being so kind to me].

As we would now expect, "implicit control" manifests the [+human] restriction, since it is, in fact, NOC. Example (109c) was found on the internet,[12] and (109a,b,d) were constructed from it.

(109) a. Hauptman$_i$ won the Nobel Prize [for PRO$_i$ using statistical methods to radically speed up the techniques by which X-ray crystallography can map the structure of molecules].

b. The experiment$_i$ won the prize [for PRO$_i$ being performed with groundbreaking X-ray techniques].

c. The Nobel Prize was won [for PRO$_i$ using statistical methods to radically speed up the techniques by which X-ray crystallography can map the structure of molecules].

d. *The prize was won [for PRO$_i$ being performed with groundbreaking X-ray techniques].

Finally, justification clauses can even occur with no sentence-internal controller, as in the following example (also found on the internet[13]). Notice that neither the scores nor the canceler are the ones cheating.

(110) Another five scores were canceled [for PRO cheating by other means].

Like other alternating OC/NC adjuncts, justification clauses have propositional variants (examples taken from the internet[14]).

(111) a. Robin Lasky started the piling on Bill Thompson by offering
           several bucks [for him helping Mary Martin find her lost and
           abandoned phone on a desert island].
       b. Our life was blessed [for her being so much a part of it].

These adjuncts, then, conform to the correlation stated by the PVC. They do,
however, raise an interesting question for the compositional analysis developed
below. While subject control, alternating between OC and NOC, can be explained
along the lines of the other adjuncts, object control presents a challenge. Insofar as
the object controller can be inanimate, it controls by predication, which requires
the adjunct to attach quite low in the VP—but subject control requires high
attachment. I return to this puzzle in section 7.3, where I use VP-targeting tests to
narrow the range of possible solutions.

5.6   Telic Clauses

In telic clauses, the adjunct specifies an unexpected outcome (or *telos*) of the
action in the main clause. It is interpreted as factive and is (nearly) always
introduced by *only*. The matrix predicate cannot be stative but is otherwise
unrestricted (example (112c) is from Huettner 1989:117). Constituency tests,
as well as prosodic phrasing, indicate that telic clauses are adjoined to TP.

(112) a.   Mary worked very hard, only to see that nobody appreciated that.
       b. #Mary worked very hard, only to finish the contract in time.
       c. *Mary resembled her mother, only to be left out of her father's will.

Uncontroversially, telic clauses manifest control by inanimate DPs, including
weather *it*, so they allow OC (examples are from Whelpton 2001:331, 319).

(113) a. The sun$_i$ radiated heat to the surrounding planets, [only PRO$_i$ to dim
           just as life began to develop].
       b. It$_i$ was sunny in the morning, [only PRO$_i$ to rain later].

The literature is unanimous in claiming that telic clauses *only* display OC, by
the matrix subject, and never NOC (Huettner 1989:120, Whelpton 2002:330,
Green 2018, 2019). This claim, I submit, is false.

Although Green (2018) claims that telic clauses resist "implicit agent control,"
such examples are not hard to find ((114)–(116) are all from the internet[15]).

(114) a. Names of different facilities were suggested and calls were made [only
           PRO to find out that those facilities don't have any meeting space].
       b. A welcome cup of tea was prepared [only PRO to find that the water
           was full of soot].

Long-distance, non-c-commanding, implicit, and deictic control of telic clauses are also possible, if rare. In the examples below, PRO is controlled by a logophoric antecedent, set up in the previous discourse: in (115a), it is whoever is responsible for launching the products, which is not even an implicit argument (*launch* being used as an unaccusative verb); in (115b), it is the possessor of the matrix subject; in (115c), it is the matrix implicit agent; and in (115d) and (115e), it is the speaker.

(115) a. Many well-researched products can launch with all the data in the world behind them [only PRO to find that no one wants to buy them].
   b. Our$_i$ road to the quarter final was fantastic [only PRO$_i$ to lose to a team like Saudi Arabia on penalties].
   c. 547 hours played, [only PRO to realize everything gets stuck]!
   d. There's a lot of tension building up throughout the film, [only PRO to be let down by the final twist].
   e. And then this one stupid emergency landing [only PRO to find you on the moon] huh?

Finally, telic clauses have propositional variants with lexical subjects.

(116) a. The major indexes will look like they're about to take off, with leading stocks flashing buy signals, [only for the market to pull back down].
   b. You can spend weeks waiting for a window of moonless sky to come around, [only for the weather to turn against you and rain].

This concludes the discussion of alternating OC/NOC adjuncts. All six adjuncts identified in this class pattern as predicted by the PVC: they all have a propositional variant. Therefore, they can all denote propositions, even when appearing with a PRO subject. As predicates with a PRO subject, they display OC; as propositions with a PRO subject, they display NOC.

6   A Compositional Analysis

With the empirical terrain of adjunct control mapped out, we can turn to the theoretical analysis. The gist of the analysis to be developed in this chapter is as follows. Strict OC adjuncts invariantly denote predicates and attach very low, as root modifiers. Alternating OC/NOC adjuncts denote relations (between predicates as OC or between propositions as NOC) and attach to Voice′, VoiceP, or TP. While predication is implicated in both forms of OC, only strict OC adjuncts achieve it by genuine structure sharing of the controller; OC in the alternating adjuncts is achieved by "plugging in" the controller twice. NOC, on the other hand, arises when the adjunct's head relates saturated propositions, with the adjunct's predicate applying to a free logophoric variable.

Section 6.1 lays out the basic inventory of VP representations that serve as structural inputs to clausal adjunction. These structures must be articulated enough to be able to reflect the differences among OC by the object, OC by the subject, and NOC. Section 6.2 presents compositional formats for the different adjuncts: strict OC, alternating OC, and alternating NOC. It also highlights the central role played by the P head of the adjunct in selecting for the right type of clause and in mediating the modificational relation. Section 6.3 then presents the explicit compositional analysis for strict OC adjuncts (section 6.3.1) and for OC/NOC adjuncts (section 6.3.2), going through all the possible adjunction sites.

6.1   VP Structure and Event Composition: Background Assumptions

In this section, I lay out a number of fundamental assumptions about the structure of VP that will play a role in the following sections. All are motivated independently of the material discussed in this work; however, none is self-evident.

First, the basic semantic types I will be using are <e> (individuals), <t> (truth values), and <s> (eventualities). Propositions are type <s,t> and properties are type <e,<s,t>>. Modifying adjuncts will be of higher types, constructed from those above. Throughout the discussion, I will abstract away from other elements in the linguistic ontology that are obviously relevant to a full semantic account of adjuncts (times, places, reasons, etc.). In Landau 2015, logophoric clauses are analyzed as sets of contexts, type <κ,t>, where a context includes the world, time, author, and addressee of the relevant speech/thought event. Logophoricity is eminently relevant to the analysis of NOC, as we will see. However, since I will be concerned only with how the meaning of an adjunct externally composes with the meaning of the main clause, not with how the adjunct's meaning is internally constructed, the traditional <s,t> type will be sufficient. I assume that a suitable translation to context-based semantics is always possible.

Consider next the structure of the VP. I follow the growing consensus in the last decade, drawing on a broad range of morphological and semantic evidence, that the functions originally attributed to little v are distributed across a number of functional heads that expand the root (see Harley 2009, 2012, 2013 and the papers collected in D'Alessandro, Franco, and Gallego 2017). The lowest light v verbalizes the root; the highest light v is a Voice head, which introduces the external argument, checks accusative case, and marks the phase boundary.

I further adopt a fully Davidsonian event decomposition, in which not only the external argument but also the internal argument are introduced by a dedicated head; $v_{undergo}$ in the latter case (see Ritter and Rosen 1998, Borer 2005, and Ramchand 2008 for analyses in this spirit; the implementation below is my own adaptation). As will become clear, this articulation is necessary to accommodate, both structurally and semantically, object-controlled adjuncts. Causative and inchoative verbs are constructed with a dedicated v_{caus} head (distinct from Voice) that contributes the causative semantics. Each may appear with or without a result phrase (ResP), yielding telic and atelic predicates, respectively (the lexical content of ResP below is marked as δ). Finally, unergative verbs are constructed with an activity head, v_{do}. Overall, the building blocks of verb meanings are roots and light v heads, the latter coming in four flavors.[1]

Skeletal structures for the basic verb classes are provided in (117), followed by standard denotations for the functional elements.

(117) *Basic VP structures*

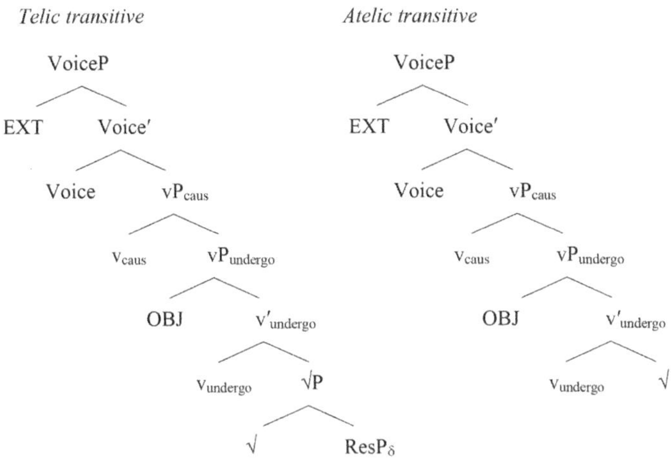

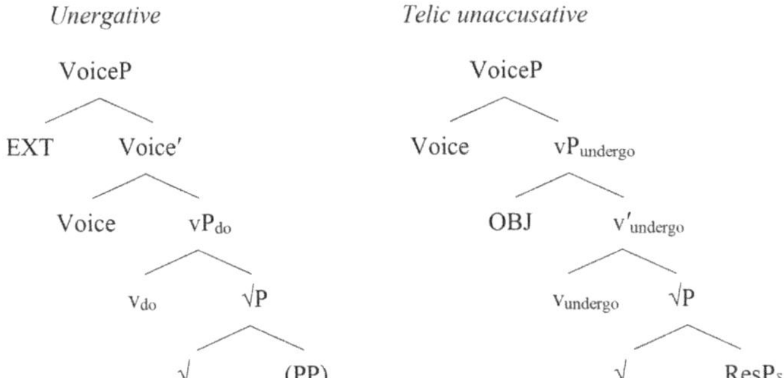

(118) *Basic denotations*

    a. $[\![\sqrt{}]\!] = \lambda e.\sqrt{}(e)$

    b. $[\![\text{ResP}_\delta]\!] = \lambda e.\exists e_2[\text{Result}(e,e_2) \wedge \delta(e_2)]$

    c. $[\![v_\text{undergo}]\!] = \lambda x.\lambda e.\text{Undergoer}(x,e)$

    d. $[\![v_\text{caus}]\!] = \lambda P_{<s,t>}.\lambda e.\exists e_3[P(e_3) \wedge e{\rightarrow}e_3]$

    e. $[\![v_\text{do}]\!] = \lambda e.\text{Do}(e)$

    f. $[\![\text{voice}]\!] = \lambda x.\lambda e.\theta(x,e)$ (θ = *Agent, Causer, Experiencer*, etc.)

These "atoms" combine with three compositional rules: Function Application (FA), Predicate Modification (PM), and Event Identification (EI). Specifically, $\sqrt{}$ combines with ResP by PM; v_undergo combines with $\sqrt{}$P by EI; v_do combines with $\sqrt{}$P by PM; v_caus combines with vP$_\text{undergo}$ by FA; and Voice combines with vP$_\text{caus}$ or vP$_\text{do}$ by EI.[2] Note that at each step, the choice of compositional rule is not stipulated, but fully predictable from the semantic types involved. Arguments (OBJ and EXT) saturate their sisters by FA.

Adjunction possibilities within the extended VP are constrained by the semantic types of the nodes in the VP and those of the adjuncts. Propositional adjuncts denote relations between propositions; therefore, they may only attach to VoiceP (or TP, to which I return below). Predicative adjuncts may, in principle, combine with predicative nodes (by PM) or with nodes denoting predicates of events (by EI). As we will shortly see, the former option is realized with OC variants of alternating adjuncts and the latter with strict OC adjuncts.

6.2 Modes of Adjunct Composition

What exactly is meant by the term "predicative control"? In (119a), the predication **angry'(j)** pretty much exhausts the contribution of the secondary predicate. The simultaneous interpretation (i.e., Jane turned to us while in a state of anger) is an automatic outcome of the event variables of the secondary and primary predicates being co-bound by the same temporal operator. However, the predication **angry'(j)** clearly does not exhaust the contribution of the adjunct in (119b). At least the temporal/concessive relation denoted by *after/despite* is not included in it.

(119)   a. Jane turned to us angry.

        b. Jane turned to us after/despite being angry.

This is typical of clausal predicative adjuncts. The head of the adjunct is a functor that specifies some semantic relation between the matrix and the embedded eventualities, a relation that is overlaid on top of the predication relation. How is this achieved?

In principle, a predicative adjunct may combine with the main clause in two different ways. One way is for the adjunct to modify the main predicate, thereby creating a complex predicate, which then applies uniquely to the subject. Another way is for the adjunct and the main predicate to be indirectly related: each first combines with the subject, yielding a proposition, and subsequently the two propositions are related by the semantic relation denoted by the adjunct's head. In the first case, the adjunct modifies an unstructured root; in the second case, it modifies a verbal projection. Correspondingly, the former type of modification underlies strict OC adjuncts and the latter type underlies OC/NOC adjuncts.

To get an initial "feel" for the semantic distinction, consider the following contrast.

(120) a. *Goal clause (Strict OC)*
 John works hard to stay out of jail.
 b. *Rationale clause (OC/NOC)*
 John works hard in order to stay out of jail.

In fact, (120a) might be interpreted as (120b), with a null *in order*. But its salient reading, the goal reading, is distinct. On that reading, John works hard *at* staying out of jail. Another paraphrase is 'John tries to stay out of jail with great effort'.[3] Tellingly, in this paraphrase the adjunct is replaced by a complement, highlighting their semantic similarity. The function of *works hard* in (120a) is rather like *with great effort*, a predicate modifier, only intensionalized. Notice that no such reading exists in (120b). The latter implies that John *literally* works hard—that is, the main predicate functions as an event description. While in (120a) John may be sitting at home all day, clenching his teeth and resisting the temptation to return to a life of crime, in (120b) John must be performing some actual, demanding work. The null head of the goal clause modifies the embedded action with the main predicate *work hard*; the overt head of the RatC (*in order*) sets up a relation between the embedded and main propositions.

Here is another illustration, using different types of adjuncts.

(121) a. *Result clause (Strict OC)*
 The roots spread to form a wide base.
 b. *Temporal clause (OC/NOC)*
 The roots spread before forming a wide base.

The modifier in (121a) is, intuitively, the adjunct clause. In particular, the atelic unaccusative verb *spread* encodes no inherent resultant state; the result clause adds and specifies such a state, similarly to a resultative predicate (e.g., *spread wide*). In (121b), however, the adjunct does not modify the spreading action at all. Rather, via the relational functor *before*, a temporal relation is established between the main event and the embedded event.

What we see, then, is that strict OC modification is a symmetric relation. One can think of the main predicate as modifying the embedded one, as in (120a), or conversely, of the embedded predicate as modifying the main one, as in (121a). This is an important clue that points to a symmetric semantic type. In contrast, OC/NOC adjuncts take part in an asymmetric relation; that relation, in turn, may involve properties (in the OC variant) or propositions (in the NOC variant), but it is ultimately the same—a relation between two events or propositions.

The first step in the analysis, therefore, is to distinguish among the semantic types of the three manifestations of controlled adjuncts.

(122) *Semantic types for controlled adjuncts*

	Strict OC	Alternating OC/NOC	
		OC variant	NOC variant
P head	$\langle\langle e,\langle s,t\rangle\rangle,\langle e,\langle s,t\rangle\rangle\rangle$	$\langle\langle e,\langle s,t\rangle\rangle,\langle\langle e,\langle s,t\rangle\rangle,\langle e,\langle s,t\rangle\rangle\rangle\rangle$	$\langle\langle s,t\rangle,\langle\langle s,t\rangle,\langle s,t\rangle\rangle\rangle$
PP adjunct	$\langle e,\langle s,t\rangle\rangle$	$\langle\langle e,\langle s,t\rangle\rangle,\langle e,\langle s,t\rangle\rangle\rangle$	$\langle\langle s,t\rangle,\langle s,t\rangle\rangle$

Syntactically, the P head merges with its clausal complement to yield the structure [$_{\text{PP}}$ P CP]. Semantically, the (denotation of the) P head applies to (the denotation of) the clause, yielding the denotation of the PP adjunct. The resulting adjunct denotes a property of individuals in the case of strict OC adjuncts, and a relation between such properties, or between propositions, in the case of alternating OC/NOC adjuncts.

In terms of s-selection, the system incorporates the claim that heads of nonfinite adjuncts, by default, s-select a property. In addition, a subset of these heads can also s-select a proposition.[4] In effect, we extend Chierchia's (1984) V-complement system of selection to the P-complement system.

(123) *S-selection in nonfinite adjuncts*

	Adjunct's head s-selects	Propositional variant
Strict OC adjuncts	property	–
OC/NOC adjuncts	property/proposition	+

These selectional requirements are ultimately the source of the surface contrast between adjuncts that allow NOC and those that do not. They are rooted in the intrinsic semantics of the modifying P head—whether it operates by modifying the main action or by establishing a specific relation between the main event and the embedded event. Importantly, s-selection is not exhausted by semantic types; otherwise, nothing would guarantee that strict OC adjuncts and alternating OC adjuncts attach at different sites. The P head of strict OC adjuncts specifically s-selects the root (or a restricted class of roots), while the P head of an alternating OC adjunct selects an event. Ultimately, this is the source of the structural difference in where they attach.

Notice that *some* lexical distinction between the two types of adjuncts is needed on *any* theory; even "binary configurational" theories of adjunct control (see chapter 10), which claim to fully derive the OC-NOC distinction from the attachment site, must resort to some lexical difference between the two types of adjuncts in order to explain in a noncircular way *why* they must attach where they actually do. They simply rarely spell out that difference.

In a sense, the current proposal shortcuts the configurational detour directly to the lexical distinction, although the latter does, as we will see, inevitably constrain the range of available attachment sites for any adjunct. In chapter 10, I will critically assess binary configurational accounts of adjunct control and indicate their shortcomings. Importantly, my explicit appeal to a lexical distinction between the heads of OC and OC/NOC adjuncts is safely noncircular, in virtue of the independent empirical correlation established between the control type and the existence of a propositional variant—that is, the second column in (123).

Using the semantic types in (122), we can proceed to state the general interpretive schemas for combining a matrix predicate with any one of the three categories of adjuncts: namely, strict OC adjuncts and the two variants of OC/NOC adjuncts. These schemas are completely abstract; they will be fleshed out with illustrative substantive content in sections 6.3.1–6.3.2.

We begin with strict OC adjuncts. A strict OC adjunct is a predicate. Its P head specifies some modificational relation, call it f, between the matrix predicate and the predicative adjunct clause. The output of this relation is a complex predicate that applies directly to the controller (subject for unergative verbs, object otherwise).

(124) *Format for predicative strict OC adjuncts*
Given the structure $[DP_i \ldots [[\ldots V \ldots]_\alpha \, [_{PP} \, P \, [PRO_i \ldots]]_\beta]]_\gamma$,
where PP $(= \beta)$ is a predicative adjunct to α, controlled by DP, and P
introduces the relation f: $[\![\gamma]\!] = f([\![\alpha]\!], [\![\beta]\!])([\![DP]\!])$
Values for f: $f_{\text{Result}}, f_{\text{Goal}}, f_{\text{Stimulus}}, f_{\text{SPC}}$

Alternating OC/NOC adjuncts are relational, expressing some relation g between the matrix and the embedded eventualities. The OC variant expresses this relation indirectly: it first constructs two propositions from the two predicates by separately applying them to the controller DP, and then relates the resulting propositions via g.

(125) *OC/NOC adjuncts: Predicative format*
Given the structure $[DP_i \ldots [[\ldots V \ldots]_\alpha [_{PP} P_{pred} [PRO_i \ldots]]_\beta]]_\gamma$, where PP $(= \beta)$ is a predicative adjunct to α, controlled by DP, and P_{pred} introduces the relation g: $[\![\gamma]\!] = g([\![\alpha]\!]([\![DP]\!]),[\![\beta]\!]) ([\![DP]\!])$
Values for g: $g_{Rationale}$, g_{OPC}, $g_{Temporal}$, $g_{Absolutive}$, $g_{Justification}$, g_{Telic}

Suppose that β' is the propositional variant of β (e.g., the gerund–finite adjunct pair in (22)). This means that the P head has a variant, P_{prop}, that s-selects a proposition and relates it to the main clause *via the same g.*

(126) *OC/NOC adjuncts: Propositional format*
Given the structure $[[DP_i \ldots]_\alpha [_{PP} P_{prop} [DP_j/PRO_{i/j} \ldots]]_{\beta'}]_\gamma$, where PP $(= \beta')$ is a propositional adjunct to α, and P_{prop} introduces the relation g: $[\![\gamma]\!] = g([\![\alpha]\!], [\![\beta']\!])$

The claim that an adjunct β has a propositional variant β', then, amounts to the claim that both adjuncts are semantically related to the main clause by the same conceptual functor g. Likewise, if β has no propositional variant in the language, then no propositional β' is related to the main clause by the same conceptual functor that relates β to the main clause. Because strict OC adjuncts introduce a modification relation between properties only, they have no propositional variants.

6.3   Putting the Pieces Together

In this section, I present the characteristic syntax of each adjunction structure in the VP domain, together with its semantic composition. Section 6.3.1 discusses strict OC adjuncts, distinguishing between those that are object-controlled and those that are subject-controlled. Section 6.3.2 discusses alternating OC/NOC adjuncts, providing an analysis for each variant.

6.3.1   Adjunction and Composition of Strict OC Adjuncts

In section 6.2, I proposed that strict OC adjuncts attach to the root projection, establishing selection under sisterhood. This accounts for their high selectivity for specific subsets of specific verb classes. Because √P is the lowest projection, and because OC involves predication, the controller of an adjunct attached to √P will be the first argument merged in the verbal projection. Thus, unaccusative and transitive predicates will manifest object control (result and justification/SPC clauses, respectively), and unergative predicates will manifest subject control (goal and stimulus clauses).

Let us begin by considering how the strict OC adjunct itself is composed. The P head takes a property complement (syntactically, FinP) and returns a property of the same type. Semantically, it introduces the embedded eventuality and relates it to the main event through some conceptual relation (result, goal, etc.). Schematic denotations for such P heads are provided below.

(127) a. $[\![P_{Result}]\!] = \lambda Q_{<e,<s,t>>}.\lambda x.\lambda e.\exists e_1[Q(x)(e_1)$ is the natural result of e]
  b. $[\![P_{Stimulus}]\!] = \lambda Q_{<e,<s,t>>}.\lambda x.\lambda e.\exists e_1[Q(x)(e_1)$ is the stimulus of e]
  c. $[\![P_{Goal}]\!] = \lambda Q_{<e,<s,t>>}.\lambda x.\lambda e.\exists e_1[Q(x)(e_1)$ is the goal of e]
  d. $[\![P_{SPC}]\!] = \lambda Q_{<e,<s,t>>}.\lambda x.\lambda e.\exists e_1[Q(x)(e_1)$ is the purpose/utility of x in e]

Clearly, these denotations do not begin to scratch the surface of what is meant by "result" or "goal," nor are they designed to do so. A fuller semantic analysis will have to include many more ingredients: specific presuppositions (e.g., the eventuality in stimulus clauses must be involuntary), intensional operators (the eventualities of goal and SPC adjuncts are restricted to worlds in some intention-relative modal base), and so on. These matters deserve explication but fall well beyond the scope of the present work. What matters at this stage is only the compositional aspects of the relevant denotations.

The strict OC PP adjunct and the predicate it modifies are of the same semantic type: <e,<s,t>>. In the resulting complex predicate, both the individual variable and the event variable of each constituent predicate are shared with those of the other; this is what accounts for the OC interpretation and for the temporal cohesion of the two eventualities. The effect is similar to what PM achieves, except that PM, as standardly defined, applies to sisters of type <e,t> or <s,t>. In fact, PM can be readily generalized to higher types, as has been suggested in a number of works (Heim 1994, Klecha 2014, Zobel 2018, Bondarenko 2019). The version in (128) (due to Heim 1994:40) is sufficient for our purposes.

(128) *Generalized Predicate Modification (GPM)*
  If α is a branching node with daughters $\{\beta,\gamma\}$, and $\{\beta,\gamma\}$ are both in
  $D_{<e,<s,t>>}$, then $[\![\alpha]\!] = \lambda x.\lambda e. [\![\beta]\!](x)(e) = [\![\gamma]\!](x)(e) = 1$

Although GPM subsumes PM, I will keep their labels distinct for perspicuity below.

Let us now turn to the derivation of the full sentence, using a result clause as an example. These clauses may modify either telic or atelic unaccusative predicates; that is, they may elaborate on an already entailed result or add one themselves. I illustrate the telic option below. Note that each "result"—the one contributed by the predicate and the one contributed by the adjunct—is predicated of its own eventuality. The two eventualities may sometimes coincide but need not. Thus, the sentence *The sofa folds out to make a bed* entails that the folding results in two eventualities: one is the state of being "out" (= to a complete degree), the other is the inchoative eventuality of becoming a bed.

(129) *Adjunction of strict OC adjuncts with unaccusative verbs*
The sofa$_i$ folds out [PRO$_i$ to make a bed].

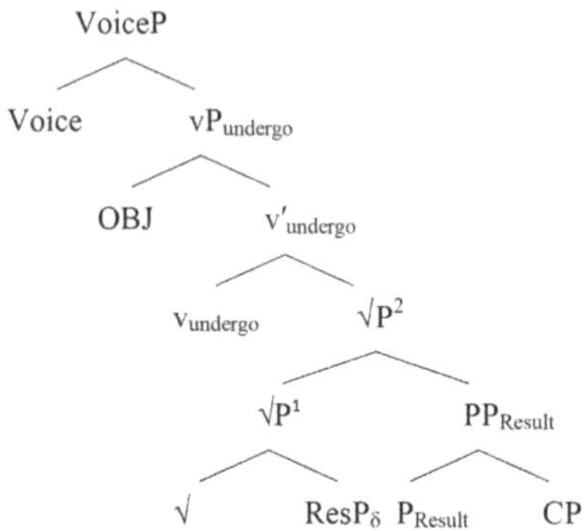

a. $[\![\sqrt{P^1}]\!] = \lambda e.\exists e_2[\sqrt(e) \wedge \text{Result}(e,e_2) \wedge \delta(e_2)]$
b. $[\![PP_{\text{Result}}]\!] = \lambda x.\lambda e.\exists e_1[CP(x)(e_1)$ is the natural result of e]
c. $[\![\sqrt{P^2}]\!] = \lambda x.\lambda e.\exists e_2[\sqrt(e) \wedge \text{Result}(e,e_2) \wedge \delta(e_2)] \wedge \exists e_1$ *by EI*
$[\![CP]\!](x)(e_1)$ is the natural result of e]
d. $[\![v'_{\text{undergo}}]\!] = \lambda x.\lambda e.\text{Undergoer}(x,e) \wedge \exists e_2[\sqrt(e) \wedge \text{Result}(e,e_2) \wedge \delta(e_2)]$
$\wedge \exists e_1[[\![CP]\!](x)(e_1)$ is the natural result of e] *by GPM*
e. $[\![VoiceP]\!] = [\![vP_{\text{undergo}}]\!] = \lambda e.\text{Undergoer}([\![OBJ]\!],e) \wedge \exists e_2[\sqrt(e) \wedge$ *by FA*
$\text{Result}(e,e_2) \wedge \delta(e_2)] \wedge \exists e_1[[\![CP]\!] ([\![OBJ]\!])(e_1)$ is the natural result of e]

Object control with strict OC adjuncts is manifested in transitive clauses as well—specifically, in SPCs. The structure is identical to (129) except for the presence of a causative layer and an external argument.

(130) *Adjunction of strict OC adjuncts with transitive verbs*
I ordered this floating shelf$_i$ [PRO$_i$ to hold all my art books].

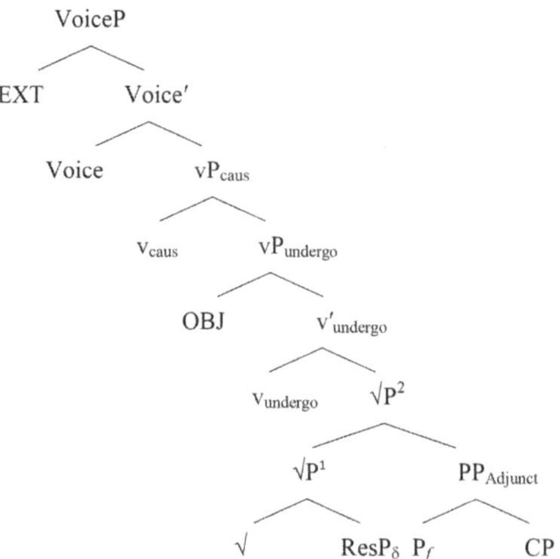

a. $[\![\sqrt{P^1}]\!] = \lambda e.\exists e_2[\sqrt{(e)} \wedge Result(e,e_2) \wedge \delta(e_2)]$

b. $[\![PP_{SPC}]\!] = \lambda x.\lambda e.\exists e_1[[\![CP]\!](x)(e_1)$ is the purpose/utility of x in e]

c. $[\![\sqrt{P^2}]\!] = \lambda x.\lambda e.\exists e_2[\sqrt{(e)} \wedge Result(e,e_2) \wedge \delta(e_2)]$ *by EI*
   $\wedge \exists e_1[[\![CP]\!]\ (x)(e_1)$ is the purpose/utility of x in e]

d. $[\![v'_{undergo}]\!] = \lambda x.\lambda e.Undergoer(x,e) \wedge \exists e_2[\sqrt{(e)} \wedge Result(e,e_2) \wedge \delta(e_2)]$
                                                                by GPM

   $\wedge \exists e_1[[\![CP]\!]\ (x)(e_1)$ is the purpose/utility of x in e]

e. $[\![vP_{undergo}]\!] = \lambda e.Undergoer([\![OBJ]\!],e) \wedge \exists e_2[\sqrt{(e)} \wedge Result(e,e_2)$
   $\wedge \delta(e_2)]$ *by FA*
   $\exists e_1[[\![CP]\!]\ ([\![OBJ]\!])\ (e_1)$ is the purpose/utility of $[\![OBJ]\!]$ in e]

f. $[\![vP_{caus}]\!] = \lambda e.\exists e_3[e{\rightarrow}e_3 \wedge Undergoer([\![OBJ]\!],e_3) \wedge \exists e_2[\sqrt{(e_3)}$ *by FA*
   $\wedge Result(e_3,e_2) \wedge \delta(e_2)]$
   $\wedge \exists e_1[[\![CP]\!]\ ([\![OBJ]\!])\ (e_1)$ is the purpose/utility of $[\![OBJ]\!]$ in e_3]

g. $[\![voiceP]\!] = \lambda e.Agent([\![EXT]\!],e) \wedge \exists e_3[e{\rightarrow}e_3 \wedge Undergoer([\![OBJ]\!],e_3)$
                                                      by EI+FA

   $\wedge \exists e_2[\sqrt{(e_3)} \wedge Result(e_3,e_2) \wedge \delta(e_2)]$
   $\wedge \exists e_1[[\![CP]\!]\ ([\![OBJ]\!])\ (e_1)$ is the purpose/utility of $[\![OBJ]\!]$ in e_3]

Let us turn now to strict subject OC adjuncts. In English, this category includes goal and stimulus clauses, both of which modify unergative verbs. Once again, the adjunct attaches to √P and modifies the matrix action *before* the controller is merged; that is, the modification is subpropositional. Because no object is present, the first argument to be merged and saturate the complex predicate is the subject. Note that the label "Agent" in the semantic composition in (131) is merely a cover term (i.e., the controller of a stimulus clause may be an experiencer).

(131) *Adjunction of strict OC adjuncts with unergative verbs*
   John_i worked hard [PRO_i to stay out of jail].

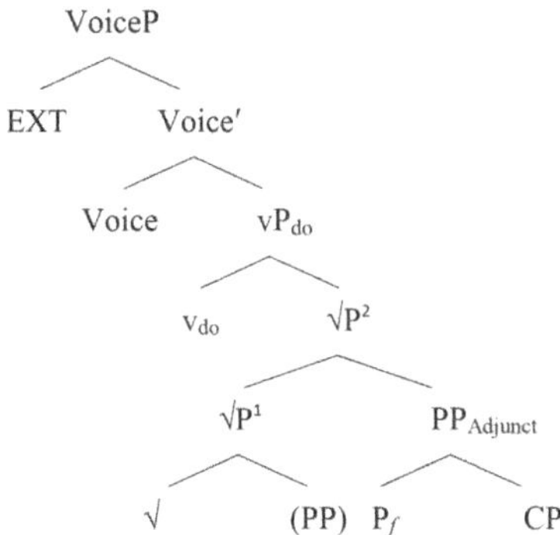

a. $[\![\sqrt{P^2}]\!] = \lambda x.\lambda e.\sqrt{(e)} \wedge \exists e_1[[\![CP]\!]\ (x)(e_1)$ is the goal of e]   *by EI*
b. $[\![vP_{do}]\!] = \lambda x.\lambda e.Do(e) \wedge \sqrt{(e)} \wedge \exists e_1[[\![CP]\!](x)(e_1)$ is the goal of e]   *by EI*
c. $[\![Voice']\!] = \lambda x.\lambda e.Agent(x,e) \wedge Do(e) \wedge \sqrt{(e)}$ *by GPM*
   $\wedge \exists e_1[[\![CP]\!]\ (x)(e_1)$ is the goal of e]
d. $[\![VoiceP]\!] = \lambda e.Agent([\![EXT]\!],e) \wedge Do(e) \wedge \sqrt{(e)}$ *by FA*
   $\wedge \exists e_1[[\![CP]\!]\ ([\![EXT]\!])(e_1)$ is the goal of e]

Like purpose clauses, goal clauses are modalized and so the embedded property will be relativized to goal-achieving worlds. Note that one can sensibly talk about "the goal of the event" without directly referring to its agent; the latter is only implicated by inference. For stimulus clauses, the embedded event is presupposed to have happened in the actual world.

6.3.2 Adjunction and Composition of OC/NOC Adjuncts

The following salient properties of OC/NOC adjuncts need to be captured: (i) they display either OC or NOC; (ii) they have a propositional variant; (iii) they can be stranded under VP-targeting operations.[5] On the present analysis, properties (i) and (ii) reduce to a common source: the said adjuncts map either as properties or as propositions, giving rise to OC or NOC, respectively (see (125)–(126)). Property (iii) reflects the high attachment site of these adjuncts, Voice' or VoiceP (see section 7.2 for discussion).

The simple case is the propositional variant. Semantically, the P head of that variant is a function from propositions to a function from propositions to propositions. The P head introduces a semantic relation, call it *g*, holding between the main and embedded propositions. For proper semantic composition, the PP must adjoin to some propositional node, VoiceP or TP. The result is an adjunct with a lexical subject or a NOC adjunct. The structures below focus on the higher layers of VP, leaving the root layer unspecified.

(132) *OC/NOC adjuncts: Propositional variant (at VoiceP)*
       The meeting ended [without PRO_{arb} deciding on a course of action].

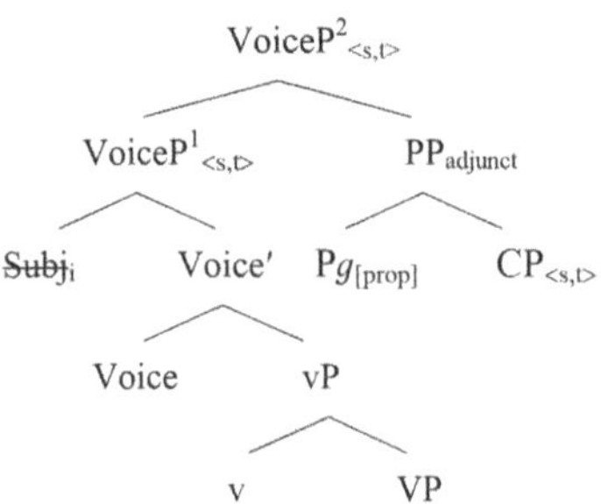

a. $[\![P_{g[\text{prop}]}]\!] = \lambda p_{<s,t>}.\lambda q_{<s,t>}.\lambda e.g(p,q)(e)$
b. $[\![PP]\!] = \lambda q_{<s,t>}.\lambda e.g([\![CP]\!],q)(e)$ *by FA*
c. $[\![\text{VoiceP}^2]\!] = \lambda e.g([\![CP]\!], [\![\text{VoiceP}^1]\!]) (e)$ *by FA*

For temporal clauses, "$g(p,q)(e)$" may mean 'The time interval of p precedes/ follows/includes the time interval of q in e'. For justification clauses, "$g(p,q)$ (e)" may mean 'p is the justification for q in e'. For telic clauses, it may mean 'p is an unexpected consequence of q in e'. And similarly for other adjuncts. Note that there is no requirement at all that p and q share any participant. Thus, the propositional variant does not deliver any control relation. If the subject of the clause denoting p happens to be PRO, NOC will apply.

With the predicative variant, OC is forced. The P head of the adjunct introduces the same semantic relation g (which is why it is indeed a *variant* of the propositional adjunct), but the arguments of that relation are put together differently. The head is a high-order function from properties to a function from properties to properties. Unlike strict OC adjuncts, the predicative clause does not directly compose with the main predicate. Instead, each of the two predicates is separately applied to the subject; the resulting propositions are then related by g. Specifically, after composing with vP and with Voice^0, the adjoined structure composes with the subject, which simultaneously saturates both predicates. The result is OC, but crucially not via "structure sharing" (as in strict OC adjuncts), because the subject is "fed" twice into the semantics.

The OC/NOC duality of this class of adjuncts is therefore not due to the content of g, the semantic relation itself, which is invariant per any given P head; rather, it is due to their mode of composition. I illustrate Voice'-adjunction before turning to TP-adjunction, which involves a slight complication.

(133) *OC/NOC adjuncts: Predicative variant (at vP)*
Around here, it$_i$ always snows [before PRO$_i$ raining].

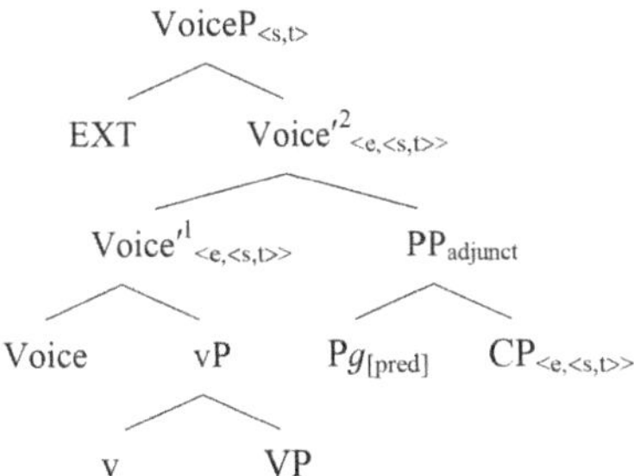

a. $\llbracket P_{g[pred]} \rrbracket = \lambda P_{<e,<s,t>>}.\lambda Q_{<e,<s,t>>}.\lambda x.\lambda e.g(P(x),Q(x))(e)$

b. $\llbracket PP \rrbracket = \lambda Q_{<e,<s,t>>}.\lambda x.\lambda e.g(\llbracket CP \rrbracket (x),Q(x))(e)$ *by FA*

c. $\llbracket Voice'^2 \rrbracket = \lambda x.\lambda e.g(\llbracket CP \rrbracket (x), \llbracket Voice'^1 \rrbracket (x))(e)$ *by FA*

d. $\llbracket VoiceP \rrbracket = \lambda e.g(\llbracket CP \rrbracket (\llbracket EXT \rrbracket), \llbracket Voice'^1 \rrbracket (\llbracket EXT \rrbracket))(e)$ *by FA*

For temporal clauses, "$g(P(x),Q(x))(e)$" may mean 'The time interval of x having the property Q precedes/follows/includes the time interval of x having the property P in e'. And similarly for other OC/NOC adjuncts, on their OC variant. As far as the *g* relation itself is concerned, whether its arguments are atomic propositions or not makes virtually no difference; the modification relation is the same. But from the standpoint of the selecting P head, the difference is crucial: only when the propositional arguments of *g* are decomposed into predicate-argument pairs can the OC relation be established (between the arguments of the two predicates).

It is instructive to compare how OC comes about in strict OC adjuncts, (131), with how it comes about in alternating OC/NOC adjuncts, (133). In (131), the predicative adjunct is *directly* linked to the main predicate and *indirectly* linked to the matrix subject via the complex predicate created by the adjunct's head. In (133), the situation is reversed: the predicative adjunct is *directly* linked to the matrix subject (by FA) and *indirectly* linked to the main predicate (via *g*). Although both processes fall under predication—and hence show all its characteristic properties—the compositional process is different.

Let us now turn to sentence-initial adjuncts, which also display either OC or NOC (Landau 2013, 2017; see (146)–(147) below). The NOC option is straightforward, closely paralleling (132).

(134) *OC/NOC adjuncts: Propositional variant (at TP)*
      [PRO standing on the patio], the plants obscure/highlight the duck pond.

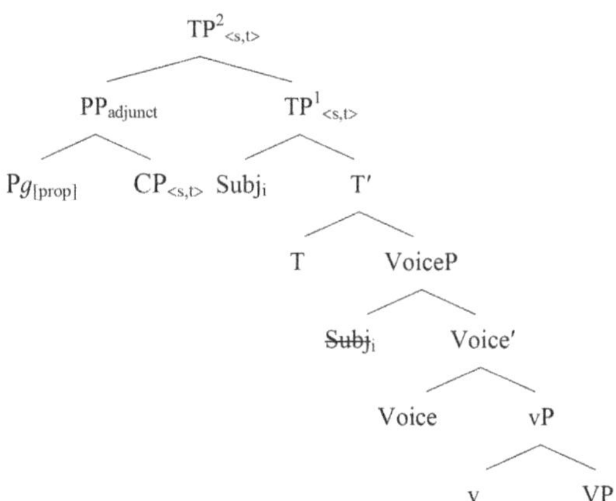

a. $[\![P_{g[\mathrm{prop}]}]\!] = \lambda p_{<s,t>}.\lambda q_{<s,t>}.\lambda e.g(p,q)(e)$

b. $[\![\mathrm{TP^2}]\!] = \lambda e.g([\![\mathrm{CP}]\!], [\![\mathrm{TP^1}]\!])(e)$ *by FA*

Note that VoiceP and TP denote the same proposition (abstracting away from the contribution of tense and modality). Movement of the subject from Spec,VoiceP to Spec,TP abstracts over that argument, creating a property, and then re-feeds the subject to the property, restoring the proposition. The sentence-initial adjunct combines with that proposition via g, the semantic relation delivered by P.

There is also indisputable evidence that sentence-initial adjuncts can display OC; hence, there must be a way for predicative variants to compose there too. Here, however, we face a problem. TP is a propositional node, so a predicative adjunct cannot compose with it. To mimic (133), the adjunct must find a property-denoting node to adjoin to. The only possibility is T′, but T′-adjunction would place the adjunct to the right of the subject. Such medial adjuncts are indeed possible, enclosed between pauses (e.g., *Harry, before talking to Ron, left the room*; Green 2018:17), but not necessary. Moreover, there is strong evidence (see (172)) that sentence-initial adjuncts do not (or need not) reconstruct; hence, their composition cannot be reduced to (133). Therefore, the puzzle is how an unambiguous OC adjunct composes with a property-denoting node in its surface position, above TP.

To solve this puzzle, I will recruit a device developed by Nissenbaum (1998) to account for the regular composition of main clauses with adjuncts containing parasitic gaps (PG). In PG constructions, two Ā-movements take place: the licensing movement in the main clause, and a null operator movement inside the adjunct. Both create derived predicates of type <e,<s,t>>. On Nissenbaum's analysis, these derived predicates compose by predicate modification at the vP level (our GPM), forming a complex predicate, which is saturated by the intermediate trace of the licensing movement, the outermost adjunct to vP. The structure is sketched below (irrelevant details omitted).

(135) *Nissenbaum's analysis of PG constructions*
Which document did you file without reading?

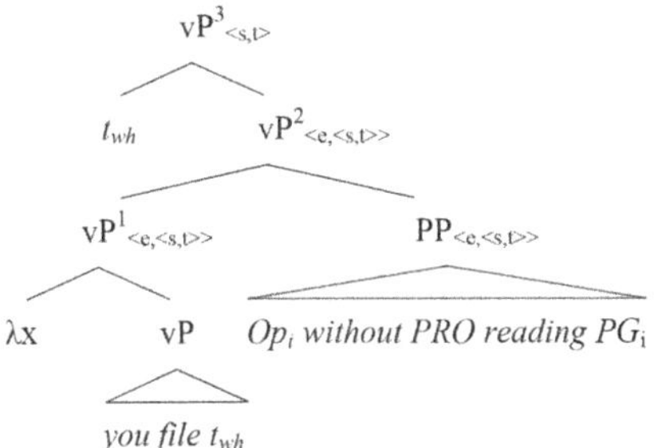

The theoretical innovation in this representation consists in the idea that predicates derived by movement (along the lines of Heim and Kratzer 1998) are visible to syntactic computation. In particular, the vP^1 node, created by λ-abstraction as a side effect of *wh*-movement, can serve as an attachment site for the PG-containing adjunct. It is only in virtue of providing this attachment site that the PG construction can be properly interpreted. Saturation of the derived predicate is suspended until after adjunction. Let us call this analysis *suspended saturation*. Nissenbaum further shows how it derives all the main properties of PG constructions as well as making surprising new predictions.

The idea of suspended saturation is particularly apt for the problem at hand: how can a predicative adjunct compose with a propositional node (TP)? The answer is simple: it actually composes not with the core propositional TP but with a derived, predicative TP. To produce this predicate, the subject moves at LF, and precisely as in (135), the predicative adjunct "tucks in" between the moved element and the derived predicate that it forms.

(136) *OC/NOC adjuncts: Predicative variant (at TP)*
   [After PRO$_i$ falling into this liquid], sugar$_i$ never dissolves.

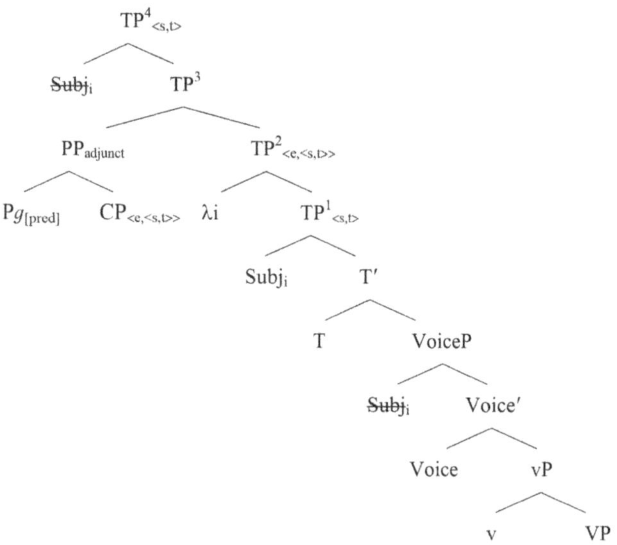

   a. $[\![P_{g[\text{pred}]}]\!] = \lambda P_{<e,<s,t>>}.\lambda Q_{<e,<s,t>>}.\lambda x.\lambda e.g(P(x),Q(x))(e)$
   b. $[\![TP^2]\!] = \lambda x.\lambda e.\, [\![TP^1]\!](x)(e)$ *by Predicate Abstraction*
   c. $[\![TP^3]\!] = \lambda x.\lambda e.g([\![CP]\!](x), [\![TP^2]\!](x))(e)$ *by FA*
   d. $[\![TP^4]\!] = \lambda e.g([\![CP]\!]([\![Subj]\!]),[\![TP^2]\!]([\![Subj]\!]))(e)$ *by FA*

A number of differences between (135) and (136) need to be addressed.

First, in the PG derivation the licensing movement is *triggered* by some feature (*wh*, topic, focus, relative, etc.), whereas in the OC derivation the movement of the subject is not triggered by any formal feature. Nonetheless, the latter is no less motivated, for it is required for interpretability. It is analogous to QR (Quantifier Raising) and other scope-shifting operations that apply covertly. Some of these operations are required to repair a type mismatch that would occur if they did not take place; others are justified by yielding novel interpretations (Fox 2000). The adjunction of the subject to TP in (136) belongs to the former category and calls for no special assumptions. Note also that being non-feature-driven, it is exempt from the antilocality imposed on movement within the same projection (Grohmann 2012).

Second, in (135) the adjunct composes with its sister by GPM; in (136), by FA: the adjunct's head first applies to its clausal sister and the result applies to the derived TP predicate. Again, these differences are innocuous insofar as the structure is interpretable in both cases. Actually, the fact that Nissenbaum's derivation is not inherently wedded to any specific compositional rule is all the more in its favor.

The third and most substantive difference is the fact that predicate-forming movement is overt in (135) but covert in (136). This is no small matter, for it is a classical trait of PG constructions that they are licensed only by *overt* movement (e.g., not by *wh*-in-situ). Indeed, Nissenbaum (2000) derives this restriction by assuming that tucking-in is forced whenever possible. The PG-containing adjunct, then, must merge below the *wh*-trace, producing (135). But if the *wh*-trace is only formed at LF, the adjunct—which must be merged overtly, being pronounced—will merge first, and the *wh*-trace will tuck in below it, yielding a type mismatch. If LF movement cannot license PG constructions, then it is not clear how it can license the isomorphic OC construction in (136).

However, more recent developments cast doubts on Nissenbaum's account. First, the single-output model has replaced the Y-model, so that overt and covert syntactic operations are no longer temporally sequenced. Given that, the inability of *wh*-in-situ to license PG constructions in English cannot be traced to any derivational logic that capitalizes on *when* overt or covert *wh*-traces appear on the stage. Second, the "classical trait" has been called into question with the discovery that *wh*-in-situ constructions do license PGs in a number of languages (see Bošković 2002 on Romanian, Manetta 2013 on Hindi-Urdu, and Branan and Sulemana 2019 on Bùlì). It is likely that English-type *wh*-in-situ constructions are not derived by movement anyway (Reinhart 1998), hence their failure to license PG constructions.

LF movement and suspended saturation of the subject are presumably exceptional devices that come with an extra cost. Furthermore, they involve surface opacity: a node that looks saturated is nonetheless interpreted as unsaturated at a more abstract level. This feature of the analysis is potentially advantageous, for it is well-known that sentence-initial adjuncts are more prone to NOC than sentence-final adjuncts (Kortmann 1991, Landau 2013, Green 2018). If OC and NOC derivations exist side by side, as I assume here, a preference for NOC is equivalent to a *dis*preference for OC. Although the OC derivation is the one preferred by default, this preference is weakened in sentence-initial position due to the extra machinery involved in (136). This might explain (among other reasons) why NOC is easier to obtain.

Furthermore, the derivational complexity of suspended saturation might be beyond the computational capacity of young children. We may then expect them to allow NOC even more robustly in sentence-initial adjuncts—and indeed, this is what we find (see section 12.2). Thus, the proposed analysis of OC in sentence-initial adjuncts receives independent support from other sources.[6]

Hierarchical Consequences for VP-Targeting Tests

Syntax and semantics go hand in hand in the selectional theory of adjunct control proposed here. While the previous chapter focused on how the different syntactic configurations of adjunction are interpreted to yield the observed categories of strict OC (by subject or object) and OC/NOC (at vP or TP), the present chapter examines the way these configurations interact with syntactic operations that apply at the VP level. We will see that these operations work in tandem with the compositional hierarchy. Thus, we will have converging evidence for the proposed structures. To wit, the fact that these structures yield testable predictions that are confirmed both semantically (the range of control options, the range of modification relations) and syntactically (permissible movement and ellipsis operations) furnishes a particularly compelling argument that these structures are indeed correct.

7.1 VP-Targeting Tests Meet Articulated VP Projections

The most common tests for the position of adjuncts involve VP-ellipsis, VP-fronting, and pseudoclefting. For adjuncts, all these tests yield identical results. That is, if an adjunct can be elided by VP-ellipsis, it can be fronted with VP and occur in the focus zone of a pseudocleft (following the copula). An adjunct that VP-ellipsis spares, in turn, can be stranded by VP-fronting and can occur in the *wh*-clause of a pseudocleft.

With the articulated VP structures standardly employed in current work, however, it is no longer clear which VP layer these classical tests target. Can they target any VP layer? Only layers from a certain point upward? Are there principled constraints at work? Current research does not offer definitive answers to these questions. Nevertheless, I would like to advance the following two concrete hypotheses.

(137) a. Neither √P nor what it dominates can be targeted by syntactic operations.

   b. VP projections below Voice cannot be targeted by syntactic operations.

The rationale behind (137a) is straightforward. The root is an uncategorized head without any formal features. Movement and ellipsis, however, are necessarily mediated by such features: for instance, [uWh] for *wh*-movement, the [E]-bearing feature for ellipsis. This implies that syntax will not be able to target projections of the root for these purposes. Specifically, formal features that underlie Agree/Move dependencies do not appear on roots and their projections, hence cannot mediate applying these processes to them.[1] Because strict OC adjuncts are adjoined to √P, they too will be syntactically inert. Both predictions are confirmed. The data below, repeated from chapter 4, indicate that VP-targeting operations cannot strand strict OC adjuncts (because they cannot target √P), nor can these adjuncts be moved (because movement cannot target anything within √P).

(138) *Goal clauses*

   a. *What Max did to stay out of jail was work hard.

   b. *To smoke, John went out.

   Result clauses

   c. The sofa folds out to make a bed, and so does the chair (*to form a pup tent).

   d. *To shatter on the floor, the glass fell.

   Stimulus clauses

   e. John said that Mary would tremble to hear of her father's wrath, and tremble she did (*to hear of her father's wrath).

   f. *To see what a fool Sam was making of himself, Susan blushed.

   Subject purpose clauses

   g. She bought a bobcat to play with her children although I wouldn't (*to play with mine).

   h. *To talk to them$_i$, they$_i$ brought John along.

Turning to (137b), I suggest a morphological rationale. Successive head movement within the extended VP creates various types of complex heads.

(139) *Complex heads formed in VP*

$$\begin{bmatrix} \text{Voice} - \begin{bmatrix} \text{v}_{\text{caus}} - \text{v}_{\text{undergo}} - \sqrt{} \\ \text{v}_{\text{do}} - \sqrt{} \\ \text{v}_{\text{undergo}} - \sqrt{} \end{bmatrix} \\ {}_{\alpha} \qquad\quad {}_{\beta} \end{bmatrix}$$

The idea is that morphology can spell out either the maximal complex head α or the submaximal β, without the Voice head, *but nothing smaller*. That is, uncategorized roots are not pronounceable by themselves; likewise, v_{caus}, being an affix, cannot be pronounced in isolation from $[v_{undergo}\text{-}\sqrt{}]$ in a synthetic causative VP. Voice is different, presumably because it is not a locus of Vocabulary Insertion (VI). Rather, it *regulates* VI on the head below it via Agree (Merchant 2013b). Thus, by the time VI takes place, the necessary voice value (active/passive) will be present on whatever light v Voice selects.

If β is the minimal pronounceable verbal complex, then any derivation that breaks up this complex will crash at PF. This would precisely be the outcome of any operation that renders a substring of β silent. In fact, movement and ellipsis can do just that. If, in a causative VP, $vP_{undergo}$ is fronted, v_{caus} would be stranded, producing a PF crash. Likewise if $vP_{undergo}$ is deleted under ellipsis.

Because the minimal VP projection that can be targeted for ellipsis or fronting is the complement of Voice, adjuncts at the VoiceP level will display systematic optionality with respect to these operations. Specifically, a Voice′ adjunct will be included by a VoiceP operation and excluded by a vP operation (where vP is the complement of Voice). In addition, a VoiceP adjunct can be either included or excluded by a VoiceP operation, depending on whether it targets the higher or lower VoiceP segment, respectively. Note that a Voice′ adjunct corresponds to the OC variant and a VoiceP adjunct to the NOC variant of an alternating OC/NOC adjunct.

To sum up, VP-targeting tests will be unable to target the host of strict OC adjuncts, namely, $\sqrt{}$P. This prediction is fully confirmed in (138a,c,e,g). Furthermore, these tests will either include or exclude alternating OC/NOC adjuncts *of both variants* (as long as they are inside VoiceP). Finally and obviously, these tests will not be applicable to TP adjuncts of either variant. We thus derive a surprising but—as we will presently see—robust result: The standard configurational tests cannot distinguish OC from NOC variants—a serious problem for all the "binary configurational" accounts (see chapter 10), but not for the present proposal.

7.2 OC/NOC Adjuncts under VP-Targeting Tests

Let us turn to the evidence. Alternating OC/NOC adjuncts are, in fact, hierarchically heterogeneous. Four out of the six types adjoin at the VoiceP level, one adjoins to $\sqrt{}$P, and one to TP. In table (140), *VP-included/excluded* indicates whether the adjunct is included or excluded in the standard VP-targeting tests.

(140) *Adjunction sites for OC/NOC adjuncts*

	√P-adjunction	Voice′-adjunction	VoiceP-adjunction	TP-adjunction
OPC	❶ OC/NOC VP-included	–	–	–
Rationale Temporal Absolutive Justification	–	❷ OC VP-included **or** VP-excluded	❸ NOC VP-included **or** VP-excluded	❹ OC/NOC VP-excluded
Telic	–	–	–	❺ OC/NOC VP-excluded

To track all the predictions, I will use the numbers in the filled boxes in the table.

Let us start with prediction (1). OPCs are exceptional in being the only OC/NOC adjuncts that must adjoin to √P (see (81)). Why is that? Recall that OPCs are exceptional in another sense: their "propositional variant" is not truly propositional, as they are predicative adjuncts, formed by abstraction over the object gap. This makes them *necessarily* predicative regardless of control; even with a lexical subject or as NOC adjuncts, they remain predicative. It is this property, I propose, that accounts for their low attachment. Just like strict OC adjuncts, OPCs, being inherently predicative, combine with √P by Event Identification. For the OC variant, the outcome is still a predicate (on the subject position), which undergoes the compositional process of (133) to yield OC by the matrix goal/benefactive/agent. For the NOC variant, after the matrix theme is merged, the clause turns into a propositional adjunct, which is integrated along the lines of (132).[2]

That OPCs display either OC or NOC was shown in (82) and (85). Observe that both the OC variant (141a) and the NOC variant (141b) are VP-internal (i.e., must be included in any VP-targeting test). Recall that "implicit agent control" is an instance of NOC; even so, the subject of the OPC in (141b) need not refer to the matrix implicit agent.

(141) a. They first provided my device with a connector cable to be charged with, (*and then they did ___ to be scanned with).

b. The sterile bandages have been placed in the small backpack to use in case of serious injury, (*but the plasters have been ___ to use for bruises only).

Both OC and NOC variants of OPCs, then, are VP-internal, confirming prediction (1).

Prediction (2) states that OC variants of rationale, temporal, absolutive, and justification clauses are either included or excluded in VP-targeting tests. For the first two types of adjuncts, these facts are familiar, although cited examples usually involve human controllers, which cannot single out OC. The following examples demonstrate that unambiguous OC variants of each of the four adjunct types can be included in VP-targeting tests.[3]

(142) a. *RatC*

His first book was written in order to be read, but his second book wasn't ___.

b. *Temporal clause*

Up north it always snows before raining, but down here, it rarely does ___.

c. *Absolutive clause*

I washed these clothes yesterday. The trousers dried hanging in the sun a few hours after the T-shirt did ___.

d. *Justification clause*

The Italian novel won first prize for being emotionally captivating, just like the Spanish novel did ___ last year.

However, the very same OC adjuncts can also be excluded from these tests.

(143) a. *RatC*

His first book was written in order to be read, and his second book was ___ in order to be sold in the millions.

b. *Temporal clause*

Up north it always snows before raining, but down here, it often does ___ *after* raining.

c. *Absolutive clause*

I washed these clothes yesterday. The trousers dried hanging in the sun, but the T-shirt did ___ merely lying on the armrest.

d. *Justification clause*

This year, the Italian novel won first prize for being emotionally captivating, while last year the Spanish novel did ___ for being politically poignant.

Prediction (3) states that the same structural duality with respect to VP-targeting tests will be observed with NOC variants of these adjuncts. Indeed, this is what we find. On the one hand, these variants can all be VP-included.

(144) a. *RatC*

The lights in the backyard were on all night to see any burglars approaching, and the lights on the front porch were ___ too.

b. *Temporal clause*

In the summer, the night sky is frequently an unforgettable spectacle when camping in the desert, but in the winter it rarely is ___.

   c. *Absolutive clause*
     A: My head exploded reading this crap.
     B: Yeah, mine did ___ too.
   d. *Justification clause*
     There were five scores that were canceled for cheating by imperson-
     ation, but there were four scores that weren't ___.

On the other hand, the same NOC adjuncts can be external to the VP projection targeted by these tests.

(145) a. *RatC*
     The lights in the backyard were on all night to see any burglars
     approaching, but the lights on the front porch were ___ to spot the
     thieving raccoon.
   b. *Temporal clause*
     In the summer, the night sky is an unforgettable spectacle when
     camping in the desert. In the winter, it is ___ when hiking up the
     mountain ridge.
   c. *Absolutive clause*
     A: My head exploded reading this crap.
     B: Well, mine did ___ writing it!
   d. *Justification clause*
     There were five scores that were canceled for cheating by imperson-
     ation, and there were four that were ___ for cheating with fake
     documents.

We now come to predictions (4) and (5), concerning TP adjuncts. These
sentence-initial adjuncts are trivially VP-external, so the VP-targeting tests
are unnecessary. All we need to establish is that any adjunct that can occur
sentence-initially can alternate between OC and NOC. This is indeed the
case. OC is possible in sentence-initial position (*pace* Fischer and Flaate
Høyem 2017).

(146) a. *RatC*
     In order to catch fire from a glowing coal, tinder must be dry.
   b. *Temporal clause*
     After falling into this liquid, sugar never dissolves.
   c. *Absolutive clause*
     Having run smoothly until then, the economic engine began to
     sputter already at the beginning of the year.

    d. *Justification clause*
      For being designed with impeccable elegance, the Ferrari 488 won
      the California luxury car contest this year.

At the same time, sentence-initial adjuncts allow NOC; indeed, they most easily allow it in that position. Note that the subject of the RatC in (147a) (adapted from Green 2018:86, originally from Williams 2015) is plausibly not the young girl. ((147b) is from Kawasaki 1993:173, (147c) is from Williams 1992:300, and (147d) is adapted from Green 2018:69.)

(147) a. *RatC*
      In order to acquire the support of female voters, the ribbon was cut
      by a young girl.
     b. *Temporal clause*
      After pitching the tents, darkness fell quickly.
     c. *Absolutive clause*
      Having just arrived in town, the hotel was a vision indeed.
     d. *Justification clause*
      For being so kind to me, I put roses on the front porch of her house.

Telic clauses belong in this class of TP-adjoined OC/NOC adjuncts, but they are subject to a peculiar linearization restriction: the adjunct must follow the main clause, whether displaying OC or NOC.

(148) a. The storm subsided on Wednesday, only to return with a ven-
       geance on the weekend.
     b. *Only to return with a vengeance on the weekend, the storm
       subsided on Wednesday.
     c. You always warned us that you'd be gone one day, and then you
       were gone, only to find you in Berlin.
     d. *You always warned us that you'd be gone one day, and then only to
       find you in Berlin, you were gone.

I suspect that this restriction is not syntactic but reflects discourse constraints on information sequencing. Because the telic clause expresses an unexpected outcome, it can only appear after the information that generates the expectations that it (the telic clause) defeats. Intuitively, something cannot be unexpected in the absence of expectations. Importantly, this restriction concerns linear order, not hierarchy, for the sentence-final position is clearly VP-external, with both OC and NOC variants. Showing it with VP-fronting or pseudocleft tests is tricky because they too reverse the order of the main clause and the adjunct. Consider, however, the scope interaction with negation.

(149) a.   It's not the case that the storm subsided on Wednesday, only to
             return with a vengeance on the weekend.
       b.   It's not the case that you were gone, only to find you in Berlin.
       c. #The storm didn't subside on Wednesday, only to return with a
          vengeance on the weekend.
       d. #You weren't gone, only to find you in Berlin.

(149a–b) show that sentences with telic clauses—either OC or NOC—can occur
under the scope of negation. The resulting reading is what we expect, given that
the telic clause is conjoined with the main assertion (Whelpton 2001): either the
main event didn't take place, or the embedded one didn't take place, or neither
did. However, normal sentential negation does not generate these readings in
(149c–d). Instead, only the main event is negated, with the telic clause modifying it just as it modified the affirmative version. The result clashes with the
required "unexpectedness" implication, hence the anomaly. Thus, if the storm
didn't subside on Wednesday, its return on the weekend is anything but surprising. The fact that telic clauses scope above negation tells us that they are not
adjoined to VP; hence, TP-adjunction is indirectly supported.

Thus, factoring out the linearization restriction, which is specific to telic
clauses, predictions (4)–(5) in table (140) are fully confirmed: all the adjuncts
that can attach to TP alternate between OC and NOC, and the alternation is
attested in the very same TP-adjoined position.

This almost concludes the discussion of the hierarchical correlations predicted by the present proposal. Before I conclude this section, let me highlight
one striking feature of table (140): both OC and NOC are found at the lowest
and highest adjunction sites. Voice′ and VoiceP do align with the OC-NOC
distinction, but given that they are virtually indistinguishable for VP-targeting
tests, the implication is this: *OC and NOC are not definable by adjunction
site*. This is a *fact* about adjunct control, not a theoretical point. This fact is
crucial, for it demonstrates the fundamental inadequacy of what I have called
"binary configurational" accounts of adjunct control—namely, accounts that
posit simple implicational relations between adjunction site and control type.
I will look closely into such accounts in chapter 10, yet table (140) already
indicates that syntactic structure and control type interact in a more intricate
(though no less systematic) way than those theories envision.

7.3   Object-Controlled Justification Adjuncts: A Constituency Paradox?

I have classified justification clauses as OC/NOC adjuncts (table (14)) and
accordingly placed them in adjunction to Voice′ or VoiceP (table (140)). Voice′
adjunction works well for OC by the subject, as the complex predicate formed

with the adjunct applies to the external argument in Spec,VoiceP; see structure (133). Object control poses a problem, however: the object in Spec,vP$_{undergo}$ is merged too low to saturate this complex predicate. In fact, the system so far allows predicative *object* control only in strict OC adjuncts, as in (130). How, then, can object control arise in justification clauses?

One possibility, which can be immediately dismissed, is that object control in justification clauses is an instance of NOC. In fact, this is precisely what I will propose for "unusual" object control into temporal clauses (see section 11.3). For justification clauses, however, this is a nonstarter, given clear cases of control by inanimate objects in (105) (repeated here), which demand no special pragmatic context.

(150) a. Every photographer should hate Instagram$_i$ [for PRO$_i$ making our job look easy].
 b. I hated going out because of the cold and I resented winter$_i$ for [PRO$_i$ making me dress like a potato].
 c. Our food took about 30 minutes to get to us, and two of us sent the steak$_i$ back [for PRO$_i$ being undercooked].
 d. He criticized the project$_i$ [for PRO$_i$ being too expensive].
 e. I included the book$_i$ in the book fair [for PRO$_i$ being so well-written].

Another possibility is that justification clauses are multiply ambiguous: they surface not only as alternating OC/NOC adjuncts at the VoiceP level, but also as strict OC adjuncts at the √P level. In their latter guise, they attach below the object, as in (130), deriving the interpretations in (150).

This possibility raises a number of nontrivial difficulties. First, it implies that OC by the object and OC by the subject come about by very different compositional processes. Second, more fundamentally, it implies that for some unknown reason, the concept of justification, and *only* that concept, is grammaticalized in two very different ways. One (propositional) involves a relation between fully saturated events; the other (predicative) involves augmentation of the root's meaning. It would then be somewhat mysterious how the two modificational processes end up with no perceptible semantic difference between them.

The strongest argument against a strict OC version of justification adjuncts, however, comes from constituency considerations. Recall from (138) that adjunction to √P renders the adjunct inseparable from the VP for all VP-targeting tests. A √P-adjoined justification clause, then, should not be strandable under these tests. However, Green (2019:14) observes that object-controlled justification clauses can be VP-external.

(151) Last month Billy's mom washed the car for him$_i$ [for PRO$_i$ working so hard in school], and yesterday his dad did so [for PRO$_i$ passing his exams].

Because the controller in (151) is human, one might suppose that this is a propositional NOC adjunct, attached to VoiceP. To exclude this possibility, we may adduce parallel examples with inanimate object controllers.

(152) a. He criticized the project for being too expensive, but I did for being just plain stupid.
     b. Criticize the project though he did for being too expensive, in the final meeting he voted for it.
     c. Include the book in the book fair though I did for being so well-written, no publisher seemed to be interested in purchasing the copyright.

These examples must involve OC by the matrix object. Hence, we face a paradox—specifically, a constituency paradox. VP-targeting tests point to high attachment of object-controlled justification clauses (at least as high as Voice′); at the same time, the predicative relation with the matrix object requires them to attach no higher than $v'_{undergo}$. What is the right syntactic analysis for these constructions?

To solve the problem, I will employ suspended saturation once more—the combination of covert LF movement and adjunction to a λ-abstract, already invoked to explain predicative control (by the subject) at the TP level in (136). That is, I take the VP-targeting tests at face value and assume that the object-controlled justification clause attaches at VoiceP; specifically, it adjoins to the node created by covert movement of the object. The structure thus formed is a one-place predicate, which applies to the raised object, yielding OC (low vP and √P projections are suppressed in structure (153)).

(153) *Predicative OC by the object in justification clauses*

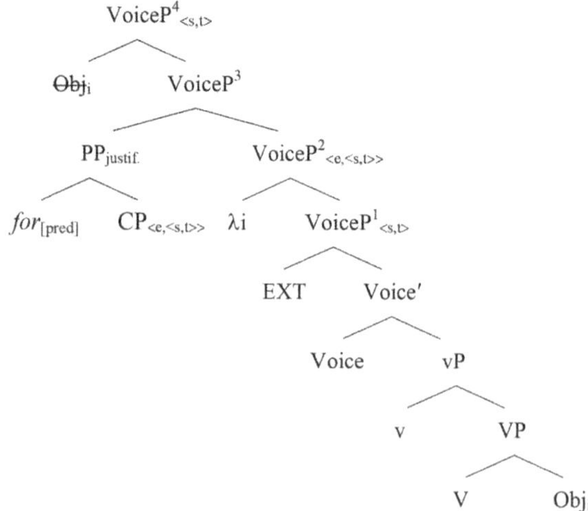

The compositional process is entirely parallel to (136), except that the abstracted position is the object's. Importantly, the modificational relation introduced by the P head *for* is the same relation that mediates propositional modification with justification clauses. In this way, we preserve the underlying semantic unity of the OC-NOC variants, seen in pairs like the following.

(154) Orban forced the Central European University out of Hungary . . .
    a. . . . for PRO being used by students as an intellectual hub for freedom activists.
    b. . . . for students using it as an intellectual hub for freedom activists.

An obvious question is, what is it about justification clauses that allows them to enter such derivations? Note that the mechanism of suspended saturation, if made completely free, would generate OC by objects with all adjuncts. This would clearly be *over*generation, as object control into adjuncts is severely restricted; other than SPCs and justification clauses, it shows the hallmarks of NOC, not OC (sections 11.2–11.3).

At this point, I can only offer speculative remarks. It seems that covert raising to VoiceP is not a free operation like covert raising to TP. Some lexical trigger is needed. Perhaps the head of the justification adjunct, *for*, introduces an "edge feature" at the VoiceP level, specifically [uD], and this feature triggers the necessary object shift, albeit covertly. While this is still far from a genuine explanation, it at least locates the property that needs to be explained in order to make sense of the exceptional susceptibility of justification clauses to object OC, subject OC, and NOC. After all, any solution would have to posit, at one point or another, some special lexical property of these adjuncts to account for their exceptional control profile.

There is some independent evidence that a solution of this nature must be available in the grammar. The evidence comes from the interaction of control into temporal adjuncts and object cliticization in Spanish. Normally, as Van-Dyne (2020) observes, direct objects may not control these adjuncts. ((155a–b) are from Katie VanDyne, pers. comm.)

(155) a. *Tiré   la   carta$_i$ [después de PRO$_i$ estar   en   la   mesa
          por   dos   semanas].
          threw.away.1SG the letter after   of   be.INF on the table
          for   two   weeks
          (Intended: 'I threw the letter away after it was on the table for two weeks.')
     b. *Cosechó   el   maíz$_i$ [antes de PRO$_i$ florecer].
          harvested.3SG the corn   before of   flower.INF
          (Intended: 'He/She harvested the corn before it flowered.')

Interestingly, object control becomes possible once the object is cliticized onto the finite verb (examples from VanDyne 2020:10).

(156) a. La_i tiré   [después de PRO_i estar   en la mesa por dos semanas].
it   threw.away.1SG after   of   be.INF   on the table for two weeks
'I threw it away after it was on the table for two weeks.'

b. Lo_i cosechó   [antes de PRO_i florecer].
it   harvested.3SG before of   flower.INF
'He/She harvested it before it flowered.'

VanDyne interprets the contrast between (155) and (156) as evidence that OC into adjuncts is structurally determined: the higher position of the clitic allows it to c-command the adjunct, while the low, base position of the object does not. The insight is no doubt correct, though what clitic position is targeted in OC is less obvious. On VanDyne's analysis, the clitic stops at Spec,vP on its way to its surface position, Spec,TP, from which it controls the adjunct. However, if predication is the grammatical mechanism of OC in adjuncts, the relation between Spec,TP and a vP adjunct is not local enough. Instead, I would like to suggest that it is the intermediate copy of the clitic in Spec,VoiceP that controls the adjunct—exactly as it is normally the external argument in Spec,VoiceP (rather than the derived position in Spec,TP) that establishes subject control. Specifically, the predicative adjunct tucks in below the intermediate clitic copy but above the λ-binder it introduces.

(157) $[_{TP}$ *pro* $[la_i$ $[_{T'}$ T $[_{VoiceP}$ ~~*la*~~$_i$ $[\lambda_i$ $[_{VoiceP}$ *pro* $[_{Voice'}$ v $[_{VP}$ V ~~*ta*~~$_i$]]]] $[_{Adjunct}$ · · · PRO_i · · ·]]]]]

Note that adjunction to Voice′ will yield subject control—as desired, since "clitic control" is an option that does not exclude subject control, according to VanDyne.

As with justification clauses in English, clitic control in Spanish seems fundamentally different from the highly variable, context-dependent, sporadic occurrence of NOC by matrix objects (section 11.3). First, it is easily available with inanimate objects, as seen above. More importantly, *unmoved* clitics do not license it. This demonstrates that the enhanced control capacity of moved object clitics is solely due to their superior syntactic position and not to any pragmatic advantage they harbor, such as being topic-oriented. Unmoved clitics occur on infinitival verbs; (158) patterns with (155) and not with (156) (Katie VanDyne, pers. comm.).

(158) a. *Quiero   [tirar-la$_i$ [después de PRO$_i$ estar   en la   mesa
           por   dos   semanas]].
           want.1SG throw.away.INF-it after   of   be.INF on the table
           for   two weeks
           'I want to throw it away after it was on the table for two weeks.'
      b. *Quiero   [cosechar-lo$_i$ [antes de PRO$_i$ florecer]].
           want.1SG harvest.INF-it before of   flower.INF
           'I want to harvest it before it flowers.'

Structure (157) is formally isomorphic to structure (153). In both, VoiceP is turned into a predicative node by the λ-binder associated with a shifted object/ clitic. This node hosts a predicative OC adjunct. The adjunct, normally predicated of the external argument, is thus predicated of the object/clitic, specifically its shifted, unpronounced copy, merged outermost in VoiceP. Seen that way, the difference between the two scenarios is rather superficial. In (153), the silent copy of the controller is the head of its chain, whereas in (157), it is an intermediate link. Yet for all practical purposes, OC is established the same way.

Whether shifted objects always enjoy greater control capacity is an unexplored question. Object control in Turkish temporal clauses (see (219)) may be another such case if analyzed with covert object shift/scrambling. Another case in point is Brazilian Portuguese, in which Ā-movement of the object makes it a possible controller of the adjunct (Modesto 2000, Rodrigues 2004). Nunes (2014) argues that this is bona fide OC, but Modesto (2008, 2011) has shown that these facts fall under a more general pattern of topic chains (observed with complements as well). However these matters are resolved, the apparatus developed for exceptional object control in justification clauses in English may have broader applicability for these and related patterns crosslinguistically.

8 A Strict NOC Adjunct?

If some adjuncts only display OC and others alternate between OC and NOC, it is natural to ask whether there are any adjuncts that only display NOC.

Green (2018) proposes that speaker-oriented adjuncts (see Quirk et al. 1985:1068–1073, Meinunger 2006, Lyngfelt 2009b) fit the bill.

(159) a. [PRO to be honest], John would be better off without Mary.
     b. [PRO judging from experience], John would be better off without Mary.

For the MTC, which Green advocates, the absence of OC is somewhat problematic, since sideward movement should be able to target any clause before it is adjoined.

There is no general agreement on whether there is a productive class of speaker-oriented (clausal) adjuncts, as opposed to a small set of conventionalized idioms. Quirk et al. point out that this group can be listed comprehensively, and Kortmann (1991:51) attributes this to their "idiomatic, quasi-formulaic character."[1] On the other hand, Duffley (2014:99–102) cites many diverse instances of these adjuncts, all attested in corpora, which seem to defy any idiomatic characterization.

Nevertheless, these adjuncts display certain curiosities that set them apart from genuine NOC adjuncts. The following discussion will be mostly descriptive; the ultimate analysis of these adjuncts still needs to be worked out.

First, the term "speaker-oriented adjuncts" is a misnomer. In an interrogative context, these adjuncts shift to addressee orientation.

(160) a. [PRO judging from my/*your experience], John would be better off without Mary.
     b. [PRO judging from your/*my experience], would John be better off without Mary?
     c. [PRO putting myself/*yourself in his shoes], John should consult a doctor.
     d. [PRO putting yourself/*myself in his shoes], should John consult a doctor?

This phenomenon is known as "origo shift": a discourse-dependent item that is oriented to the speaker in declarative clauses shifts to the addressee in interrogative clauses. The term was coined by Garrett (2001) to describe how evidential markers in declarative-interrogative pairs shift their interpretation, but was subsequently found to be relevant to other phenomena like agreement morphology (Zu 2018) and the interpretation of high adverbs in general, including *as*-phrases (Woods 2014, Spadine 2018). A better term for these adjuncts, then, is *speech-act-oriented (SA-oriented) adjuncts*, where "SA orientation" is understood as linking to the AUTHOR or ADDRESSEE role.

SA-oriented adjuncts are superficially similar to NOC adjuncts in accepting long-distance controllers when they are embedded. The controllers correspond to the shifted speaker or addressee in the speech act embedding the adjunct.

(161) a. *NOC* (PRO = embedded AUTHOR/ADDRESSEE)
Mary$_i$ told John$_j$ that [PRO$_{i/j}$ having such experience], this job would be a piece of cake.

     b. *SA-oriented adjunct under declarative* (PRO = embedded AUTHOR)
Mary$_i$ told John$_j$ that [PRO$_{i/*j}$ judging from experience], such offers were very rare.

     c. *SA-oriented adjunct under interrogative* (PRO = embedded ADDRESSEE)
Mary$_i$ asked John$_j$ whether, [PRO$_{*i/j}$ judging from experience], such offers were very rare.

Could we then simply classify SA-oriented adjuncts under NOC, with the special proviso that the interpretation of their PRO subject is somewhat more restricted than usual?

A number of considerations militate against this move. First, SA-oriented adjuncts are fundamentally different from other NOC adjuncts in another way: they reject lexical subjects, even the obvious first/second person pronoun. This already casts doubt on the idea that these adjuncts are propositional. Indeed, by the PVC, they should be predicative.

(162) a. *[For me to be absolutely frank], John would be better off without Mary.

     b. *[For you to be absolutely frank], would John be better off without Mary?

     c. [PRO/*me taking into account all the difficulties], it's feasible.

     d. [PRO/*you taking into account all the difficulties], is it feasible?

Second, embeddability of these adjuncts is highly sensitive to the embedding verb. While speech act verbs and some cognitive verbs can shift the orientation of these adjuncts, most attitude verbs cannot.

(163) Mary$_i$ thought that [PRO$_i$ judging from experience], such offers were
    very rare.
    . . . ?knew/??realized/*imagined/*denied/*forgot/*feared . . .

True NOC, as in absolute adjuncts, does not show this sensitivity to the
embedding verb.

(164) Mary$_i$ thought/knew/realized/imagined/denied/forgot/feared that
    [PRO$_i$ having no experience in photojournalism], such offers were very
    rare.

The high selectivity of embedded SA-oriented adjuncts is a signature of
indexical shift, whose distribution obeys the same implicational hierarchy
found among attitude verbs (Deal 2017, Sundaresan 2018a). As Sundaresan
makes clear, logophoric pronouns are much less "choosy" than shifted indexicals in the range of attitude verbs they require. The same asymmetry holds of
NOC adjuncts vs. SA-oriented adjuncts. It therefore seems plausible to associate SA-oriented adjuncts with some shifted indexical element (as yet to be
identified) rather than with standard NOC.

A third outstanding difference between the two classes concerns the *depth*
of embedding. While NOC adjuncts can be indefinitely remote from their
antecedents (up to processing and memory limitations) (165c), SA-oriented
adjuncts can be separated from their controller by at most one clause boundary (165a–b).

(165) a. John$_i$ said/claimed that [PRO$_i$ speaking from his$_i$ experience], such
        matters require the intervention of the police.
    b. John$_i$ said that Mary$_j$ claimed that [PRO$_{*i/j}$ speaking from her$_j$/*his$_i$
        experience], such matters require the intervention of the police.
    c. John$_i$ said that Mary claimed that [PRO$_i$ having shared his$_i$
        experience with them], the task was much more manageable.

Taken together, these special properties indicate that SA-oriented adjuncts
are not a species of NOC, contrary to previous claims. Instead, I propose that
they are a special kind of *OC* adjunct. Following Cinque 1999, Ernst 2014, and
much related literature, assume that SA-oriented adjuncts attach very high in
the left periphery; specifically, they adjoin to the Speech Act projection that
hosts the AUTHOR (in declaratives) or the ADDRESSEE (in interrogatives) participant of the local context of evaluation. This context may be shifted from
the utterance context under very restricted circumstances (parallel to indexical shift elsewhere), but even when shifted, it consistently registers the immediately embedding attitude eventuality, along with its speaker and addressee
arguments.

Like all strict OC adjuncts, SA-oriented adjuncts are predicative. This immediately captures the lack of a propositional variant. They must be predicated of a local nominal, which in their case happens to be universally null— the AUTHOR/ADDRESSEE nominal occupying the specifier of a Speech Act projection. We may grammaticalize this restriction by letting the head of the SA-oriented adjunct s-select a property restricted to one of these roles.

The proposal that SA-oriented adjuncts fall under OC may seem counterintuitive if one construes OC as demanding a sentence-level overt controller. Yet there is no reason to adhere to this "literal" sense within a theory that interprets OC as a syntactic dependency with particular testable properties. To the extent that these properties are attested with SA-oriented adjuncts, the classification is supported. We have already seen a number of ways in which SA-oriented adjuncts differ from NOC adjuncts. More positively, we can look at ways in which they pattern with OC adjuncts. Consider the strict/sloppy ambiguity.

(166) a. A: [PRO_A to be honest], there is little to be done.

      B: [$PRO_B/_{*A}$ to be honest], it doesn't matter.

    b. John$_i$ *might* claim that [PRO_i speaking from his$_i$ experience], this can work, and Mary$_j$ certainly *will* Δ.

      Δ = *claim that [$PRO_{j/*i}$ speaking from her$_j$/*his$_i$ experience], this can work*

In matrix contexts, the reference of PRO inside an SA-oriented adjunct sloppily shifts with the speaker, (166a). This may look trivial, given that these adjuncts are often defined as "speaker-oriented," yet definitions cannot substitute for causal explanations; one still needs to explain what rules out the strict reading (which is pragmatically reasonable: for example, *If you were totally honest, it wouldn't matter*). Similarly, in embedded contexts, PRO must pick out the local matrix speaker, and not the speaker of the antecedent sentence, (166b). These sloppy readings are obligatory, confirming the OC status of SA-oriented adjuncts.

All of this still leaves many questions open, in particular with respect to the relation between this class of adjuncts and shifted indexicals, regarding their embeddability restrictions and so on, but I will set these aside for now. The important conclusion is that there does not seem to be a class of strict NOC adjuncts. This lacuna raises an intriguing puzzle for typology and Universal Grammar: *why* are strict NOC adjuncts absent from natural languages (if indeed they are)? Deriving this lacuna will be the task of chapter 13.

Let us take stock of the empirical picture drawn so far. The starting point, in chapter 2, was a fundamental semantic distinction between heads that introduce strict OC adjuncts and heads that introduce alternating OC/NOC adjuncts. Each type of head is responsible for a cluster of syntactic and semantic properties.

Heads of strict OC adjuncts denote functions from properties to properties, and the adjuncts they introduce modify the most minimal projection of the verbal root by Event Identification. At this level, they "augment" the root's meaning, either by elaborating on one of its intrinsic entailments (goal, result, or purpose) or by adding one such natural extension. For this reason, their contribution is sometimes very close to that of a clausal complement and occasionally can be paraphrased with one. Similarly, at this level they can restrict the range of light v heads that the root is to combine with (unaccusative or unergative). Because they attach below the minimal verbal projection that is visible to syntactic operations, they can neither be stranded nor be targeted in isolation from the VP. Finally, because the head of the adjunct rigidly selects a property, these adjuncts have no propositional variant; this is what accounts for the absence of a NOC version with them.

Heads of alternating OC/NOC adjuncts come in two types. The predicative type denotes a function from properties to a function from properties to properties. This type is utilized in OC environments. The propositional type denotes a function from propositions to a function from propositions to propositions. It is utilized in uncontrolled environments—adjuncts with lexical subjects or NOC adjuncts. Importantly, at the denotational level both types introduce the same relation between the main clause proposition and the embedded one. They only differ in whether these propositions are read directly off of the syntactic structure or put together in the semantics. The former option corresponds to adjunction to some propositional node (VoiceP or TP). The latter option corresponds to adjunction to a predicative node (Voice′ or the "derived predicative TP"). These adjunction sites cannot interact with the root's semantics directly, nor with specific selection for some light v. On the other hand, they afford OC/NOC adjuncts syntactic flexibility and relative independence from the VP.

The table in (167) pulls together the important findings and correlations from the earlier chapters.

(167) *Empirical profile of adjunct control in English*

Adjunct type	Control	Propositional variant	Attachment site
Goal	OC	–	√P-adjunction
Result	OC	–	
Stimulus	OC	–	
SPC	OC	–	
OPC	OC/NOC	+	
Rationale	OC/NOC	+	OC: Voice′/TP-adjunction
Temporal	OC/NOC	+	
Absolutive	OC/NOC	+	NOC: VoiceP/TP-adjunction
Justification	OC/NOC	+	
Telic	OC/NOC	+	TP-adjunction

The table clearly shows there to be a *perfect correlation* between control type and the existence of a propositional variant. Over ten different types of adjuncts, such a perfect correlation cannot be an accident. Therefore, it sets a novel, exacting empirical challenge for any theory of control to meet. As demonstrated in chapter 2, the theory derived from the combination of the TTC and very minimal assumptions about s-selection can successfully meet this challenge.

Another correlation, this one nearly perfect, holds between the adjunct type (OC vs. OC/NOC) and its attachment site(s). Strict OC adjuncts are always adjoined to the lowest projection, √P. Most OC/NOC adjuncts are found adjoined to Voice′/VoiceP and TP. Two notable exceptions are OPCs, which are restricted to √P-adjunction, and telic clauses, which are restricted to TP-adjunction.

The following entailments, then, can be extracted from the data, and should define part of the empirical desiderata of any theory of adjunct control.

(168) *Correlations between adjunct control and attachment sites*
    a. Strict OC → Only √P-adjunction (= VP-internal)
    b. Voice′/TP-adjunction possible → OC possible
    c. VoiceP/TP-adjunction possible → NOC possible

These entailments are rather different in nature from the ones often seen in the literature. Two types of entailments that are glaringly absent are of the form XP-adjunction $\rightarrow$ OC, YP-adjunction $\rightarrow$ NOC. There are simply no such valid entailments, although current accounts of adjunct control assume that they exist (see the next chapter). An important goal of this work, then, is to recalibrate the empirical desiderata of studies of adjunct control, in line with (167)–(168). As the preceding chapters have demonstrated, the present analysis successfully accounts for these empirical correlations.

I now turn to alternative views of the underlying factors that determine the control behavior of adjuncts and ask whether they can provide an equally satisfactory account. These alternatives are dubbed "binary configurational" accounts, a term that highlights the claimed implication from attachment site (VP, vP, etc.) to control type (OC or NOC). Although the present proposal clearly engages with configurational claims (derived from assumptions of compositionality), it differs sharply from these accounts in avoiding such one-to-one implications.

10 Against Binary Configurational Alternatives

One of the leading ideas in control theory, which goes back to Williams 1980, is that NOC is the "elsewhere" case of OC; that is, NOC applies only when OC fails (Lebeaux 1984, Jones 1992, Kawasaki 1993, Hornstein 1999, 2003, Landau 2000, 2013:254, Manzini and Roussou 2000, Boeckx and Hornstein 2007, Boeckx, Hornstein, and Nunes 2010). Call this the "classical view." The classical view is binary in the sense that it only envisions two relevant configurations: one in which OC is possible and hence necessary, and a different one in which OC is not possible and hence NOC is. The empirical content of this view lies in identifying independent correlates of these two configurations.

Recently, the classical view has been defended by Fischer (2018), by McFadden and Sundaresan (M&S) (2018), and most explicitly by Fischer and Flaate Høyem (F&FH) (2017). Abstracting away from what OC reduces to on various theories—predication, movement, or Agree—failure of OC, on the classical view, is due to failure of PRO to be c-commanded by any DP in its local domain; under these circumstances, and *only* under these, NOC emerges.

In this chapter, I present two sets of arguments against current versions of the classical view. In section 10.1, I closely examine the configurational predictions made by these accounts—in particular, the correlations they predict between the type of control (OC or NOC) and various structural dependencies (variable binding, scope, NPI licensing, and extraction). In each case, I show that the predictions are not fulfilled because the syntax of OC and NOC is, in fact, more subtle than these accounts assume. In section 10.2, I discuss the difficulties these accounts face in explaining the fundamental correlation established in chapters 4–5—that is, the PVC.

10.1 Structural Arguments against OC-NOC Complementarity

Appealing as the classical view may be, it is false beyond redemption. The growing body of evidence accumulated in Williams 1992, Reed 2014, Landau 2017, Green 2018, and the present study, clearly demonstrates that OC and

NOC are not in complementary distribution in adjuncts.[1] At least six types of adjuncts in English display either OC or NOC in the same structural position (i.e., the same according to the approaches cited above). Under the right circumstances, in fact, OC and NOC readings may coexist in a single sentence (examples from Green 2018:40, 277).

(169) a. The pool$_i$ was the perfect temperature [after PRO$_{i/arb}$ being in the hot sun all day].
    b. The hamburgers$_i$ became much more popular at the school carnival . . .
        . . . [after PRO$_i$ cooking just a little bit longer].
        . . . [after PRO$_{arb}$ cooking them$_i$ just a little bit longer].

The classical view is empirically wrong in two crucial ways. First, it predicts that OC adjuncts must be c-commanded by their controller. Yet such adjuncts may occur sentence-initially, which indicates that they are at least TP-adjoined (Landau 2013:226, 2017). This was shown in (146a–d), repeated here.

(170) a. *RatC*
        In order to catch fire from a glowing coal, tinder must be dry.
    b. *Temporal clause*
        After falling into this liquid, sugar never dissolves.
    c. *Absolutive clause*
        Having run smoothly until then, the economic engine began to sputter already at the beginning of the year.
    d. *Justification clause*
        For being designed with impeccable elegance, the Ferrari 488 won the California luxury car contest this year.

In fact, plain secondary predicates can attach there too, whether introduced by a subordinator or not. ((171a–b) are from Kortmann 1991:8 and Williams 1994:39, respectively.)

(171) a. If in doubt, you can phone me at any time.
    b. Sad, John left.

The locality required between the predicative adjunct and the subject can be satisfied at the TP level, but crucially without the latter strictly c-commanding the former.[2] Even if c-command in the sense required for Agree/Move holds between the subject and the adjunct in these cases, it cannot be the only option, for the same attachment site readily supports NOC. However, for the same attachment site to support either OC or NOC is a contradiction in terms for F&FH (2017), Fischer (2018), and M&S (2018).

Nor can reconstruction be invoked, for the initial adjunct often shows no signs of having originated below the subject.[3] (172a) only supports the unreconstructed scope relation $\forall \gg \neg$. (172b) shows that an epistemic modal cannot scope above the initial adjunct; the only accessible reading is the anomalous, unreconstructed one, with the adjunct scoping over the modal. This reading is sensible only with a deontic modal (172c), confirming that the problem is not with these structures per se.[4]

(172) a. [After falling into every liquid], this crystal does not dissolve.
        (cf. *This crystal does not dissolve after falling into every liquid.*)
    b. #[In order to be expensive], this dress must have been designed this way.
        (cf. *This dress must have been designed this way in order to be expensive.*)
    c. [In order to be a head-turner], this dress must be designed this way.

Second, the classical view predicts that NOC adjuncts cannot be c-commanded by any local DP. This is disconfirmed by many examples already given above ((73), (85b), (88), (98e), (110), (115)). Lest one suspect that these sentence-final adjuncts are somehow adjoined even higher than the subject (hence, lack any local c-commanding DP), it is easy to construct examples that require the NOC adjunct to be c-commanded by the local subject—although it is *not* controlled by it. In (173), I use NPI licensing, variable binding, and association with focus to establish this hierarchical relation.[5]

(173) a. The door is not open in order to greet anyone, I just needed some fresh air.
    b. Every road$_i$ in this area is dangerous when driving on it$_i$ during the rainy season.
    c. Bill admitted that his fridge was only full before hosting a party.
        [→ *his fridge isn't full at other times*]

Likewise, VP-targeting tests can "capture" NOC adjuncts, demonstrating their ability to attach below the subject. This was demonstrated in (144), repeated in (174). Note that the VP gaps in (174) are naturally interpreted as including the antecedent adjunct.

(174) a. *RatC*
        The lights in the backyard were on all night to see any burglars approaching, and the lights on the front porch were ___ too.
    b. *Temporal clause*
        In the summer, the night sky is frequently an unforgettable spectacle when camping in the desert, but in the winter it rarely is ___ .

    c. *Absolutive clause*
      A: My head exploded reading this crap.
      B: Yeah, mine did ___ too.
    d. *Justification clause*
      There were five scores that were canceled for cheating by imperson-
      ation, but there were four scores that weren't ___ .

Green's (2019) theory fares better, as it allows for OC/NOC noncomple-
mentarity. However, it is still committed to certain problematic configurational
assumptions. Building and expanding on Boeckx and Hornstein's (2007)
account of NOC in subject clauses, Green assumes that OC into high adjuncts
results from sideward movement, and NOC only arises if movement is impossible or—and this is where Green's innovation lies—is "costly."[6] Specifically,
adjuncts that adjoin inside the VP and do not project a CP layer (hence, are not
phases) will be transparent for movement. Moreover, this movement will be
upward (to Spec,vP, the base position of the subject controller), just as it is with
complements, resulting in OC.

In contrast, OC into vP adjuncts must involve sideward movement (between
trees), since the landing site—Spec,vP—does not c-command the adjunct.
Green hypothesizes that sideward movement is more costly than upward
movement (within a tree), giving rise to an alternative NOC derivation. Likewise, OPCs, despite being VP-internal (see (81a)), employ OC by sideward
movement; the reason is the presence of a CP projection (needed to host the
operator in Spec,CP), which forces the adjunct to be linearized before it is
adjoined, making it an island upon adjunction. Given the cost of sideward
movement, NOC is allowed with OPCs too.

Green's analysis of strict OC (VP-internal) adjuncts effectively obliterates
any configurational difference between them and complements: extraction
from either proceeds by upward movement. Yet OC adjuncts still retain a
salient distinctive property: they are weak islands. While extraction of arguments from them is acceptable to varying degrees (see (183)–(188)), extraction of adjuncts ranges from marginal to impossible.

(175) a. *Adjunct extraction from goal clause*
      A: When did John fight to renovate the building?
      B: Last Tuesday. / #Next Tuesday.
      A: How did John fight to teach ecology to the students?
      B: Very hard. / #Scientifically.
    b. *Adjunct extraction from stimulus clause*
      A: Why did Mary laugh to see John getting red?
      B: Because she's tactless. / #Because he was deeply embarrassed.

Being smaller than CPs on Green's account, these adjuncts are not linearized prior to merging with the matrix clause. This allows OC (= A-movement) to target their subject, but it also allows Ā-movement to target any other constituent in them, overgenerating island violations of the sort seen in (175). One may also question the assumption that SPCs are constructed differently from OPCs. If the former also project a null operator in Spec,CP, they too should be linearized prior to extraction. OC would proceed by sideward movement, so NOC should be attested as well. Yet this is false: SPCs exclude NOC. Green's account may reject the parallelism between the two purpose clauses and take SPCs to be smaller than CPs. This would correctly rule out NOC, but—just as in (175)—would incorrectly allow Ā-extraction from them. As Jones (1991:77) observes, SPCs are weak islands.

(176)　How did John bring Bill in to fix the car? (#With metric tools.)

I conclude that Green's (2019) account of strict OC adjuncts rests on untenable syntactic assumptions.

　Is there *any* sure configurational predictor of the type of control an adjunct displays? The table in (140) has already undermined this idea, but we can bolster the conclusions with further combinations of control type and VP-targeting tests. Consider the following candidates.[7]

(177)　*Potential configurational predictors of adjunct control*
　　　a. TP-adjunction → NOC
　　　　(F&FH 2017, Fischer 2018, M&S 2018)
　　　b. vP-adjunction ↛ NOC
　　　c. vP-adjunction ↛ OC
　　　　(F&FH 2017, Fischer 2018)
　　　d. VP-internal → OC
　　　　(F&FH 2017, Fischer 2018, M&S 2018)

(177a) has already been proven false by (170). (177b) is falsified by the sentence-final adjuncts in (178). OC is detected by the inanimate controllers. The adjuncts survive VP-ellipsis, so they must be adjoined at least as high as vP. Yet they scope under negation (178a) and under a vP-adjoined adverb (178b), ruling out TP-adjunction. These examples thus demonstrate unambiguous OC into vP adjuncts.

(178)　a. A: When did your book become famous?
　　　　　　B: It didn't before being adapted to film.
　　　b. Psychedelic country music rarely annoys me when played loud, but industrial jazz often does ___ when played very low.

(177c) has already been refuted in (173)–(174), to which we can add (179), where a NOC adjunct scopes under the matrix negation (to license the NPI), ruling out TP-adjunction.

(179) The way to Cincinnati wouldn't become shorter by using any of these maps.

Finally, (177d) fails to accommodate NOC readings of OPCs (cf. (85)). One can demonstrate that even on a NOC reading, the OPC stays VP-internal. Notice that in (180a–b) PRO need not refer to the matrix implicit agent. VP-ellipsis must include the OPC, proving it is VP-internal.

(180) a.   The sterile bandages have been placed in the small backpack [PRO$_{arb}$ to use in case of serious injury], and the plasters have been ___ too.
       b. *The sterile bandages have been placed in the small backpack [PRO$_{arb}$ to use in case of serious injury], but the plasters have been ___ [PRO$_{arb}$ to use for bruises only].

In sum, there is no one-to-one configurational predictor of the OC-NOC distinction in adjuncts, at least not among the ones that have been entertained in the literature. In fact, *any* attachment site supports OC or NOC with some adjunct. By contrast, the (un)availability of a propositional variant, as seen in table (167), is a faultless predictor.

Once again, this does not imply that hierarchical distinctions are not relevant to adjunct control. Empirically, the generalizations stated in (168) (repeated here) hold.

(181) *Correlations between adjunct control and attachment sites*
       a. Strict OC → Only √P-adjunction (= VP-internal)
       b. Voice′/TP-adjunction possible → OC possible
       c. VoiceP/TP-adjunction possible → NOC possible

Theoretically, hierarchical distinctions reflect adjunction to different nodes, and different nodes may map to denotations of different semantic types. The point is that the internal structure of the system prevents simplistic inferences of the sort proposed in (177), and indeed, the facts to do not bear them out.

At the same time, subtle interactions between control and islandhood align with the correlations in (181), as already hinted in note 5 of this chapter. It is well-known that in English, nonfinite adjuncts are weak islands at best. Green (2019:30), defending the MTC against the objection that adjuncts are islands for movement (and so the OC-creating movement should not be possible), cites the following examples, which indicate that violations caused by *wh*-extraction are "often weak or nonexistent."

(182) a. What did you go to the store in order to buy?
     b. What did you give flowers to Jake for doing?

Importantly, in Green's theory alternating OC/NOC adjuncts have a uniform internal syntax and a uniform attachment site (adjunction to vP)—regardless of whether they display OC or NOC. The control alternation is due not to any structural factor but to the tie between two constraints—one against sideward movement (producing OC), the other against pronominalization (producing NOC). The prediction is that extraction would be equally possible out of NOC adjuncts. However, this is false.[8] ((185b) is from Jones 1991:77.)

(183) *RatC*
     a.   Alice is well-dressed to greet passing neighbors.
     b.   Who is Alice well-dressed to greet?
     c.   The door is open to greet passing neighbors.
     d.   *Who is the door open to greet?

(184) *Justification clause*
     a.   The Italian novel won the prize for captivating young readers.
     b.   Which readers did the Italian novel win the prize for captivating?
     c.   The prize was won for captivating young readers.
     d.   *Which readers was the prize won for captivating?

(185) *OPC*
     a.   John brought these tires over to put on the blue car.
     b. ?Which car did John bring these tires over to put on?
     c.   Those tires are over there to put on the blue car.
     d.   *Which car are those tires over there to put on?

Truswell (2011:133–134) observes facts similar to (183a–d).[9]

(186) *RatC*
     a.   I tapped my nose to signal the presence of an intruder to Mary.
     b.   What did you tap your nose to signal to Mary?
     c.   This story will appear on the back page in order not to embarrass the president.
     d.   *Who will this story appear in the paper to please?

Truswell (2011:140) also observes that *wh*-extraction out of temporal OC adjuncts is marginally possible if the answer is coherently related to the matrix eventuality (187b). Although he does not compare the NOC counterpart, it is distinctly worse (187d), in line with the pattern of RatCs and justification clauses.

(187) *Temporal clause*
   a.   John rewrote his paper after meeting the professor who graded it.
   b. %Which professor did John rewrite his paper after meeting?
   c.   The fate of the paper was unclear after meeting the professor who graded it.
   d. *Which professor was the fate of the paper unclear after meeting?

Williams (1992:307) observes a parallel contrast: when the controller does not c-command PRO, extraction is worse than when it does.

(188) a.   John loses control of his fears when listening to Larouche.
   b.   Larouche, who John loses control of his fears when listening to, . . .
   c.   John's fears always go out of control when listening to Larouche.
   d. *Larouche, who John's fears go out of control when listening to, . . .

Lack of c-command precludes OC; hence, (188c–d) must involve NOC. Williams proposes that the control distinction corresponds to a structural one: OC adjuncts are adjoined to VP, NOC adjuncts are external to it. The latter claim cannot be correct in view of (173), (174), and (179). Yet I concur with Williams that the extraction contrast is syntactically rooted.

By contrast, Truswell's account of extraction from adjuncts is wholly semantic, invoking the Single Event Grouping Condition ("The minimal constituent containing the head and the foot of the chain can be construed as describing a single event grouping"; 2011:157). Notably, Truswell's criteria for "event grouping" require neither OC nor any kind of argument sharing; hence, they are met in the (d) examples in (183)–(188). Truswell writes:

I must confess that I have little idea what's going on here. I must leave this unresolved here, taking some comfort in the fact that things are at least as mysterious on a syntactocentric approach: there is a semantic difference here which has some chance of being pertinent, but no obvious syntactic difference of any relevance between good and bad cases of extraction from rationale clauses. (2011:134)

On the present analysis, there *is* a highly relevant syntactic difference between the (b) and the (d) examples in (183)–(188). In fact, there are two such differences. The OC variants project a smaller clausal structure, up to FinP, and adjoin below the phase level (to Voice′). The NOC variants project a larger clausal structure, up to CP, and adjoin above the phase level (to VoiceP). Each of these distinctions, or both taken together, may be responsible for the greater transparency of OC adjuncts to extraction. There are natural ways to proceed in exploring these matters, but they involve spelling out locality constraints at a level that goes beyond my present concerns. Suffice it to say that both domain size and structural position are the two key determinants in theories of locality;

hence, the present analysis is in a better position to explain these facts than alternatives that posit a single structure, such as Green's or Truswell's.

At the same time, the empirical landscape is rich enough to rule out other alternatives that do posit two structures. Discussing the interaction of control with extraction out of adjuncts, M&S (2018:494–495) propose that the OC variants are attached below the matrix subject and the NOC examples are attached above it. Because M&S take OC to be Agree and Agree depends on c-command, OC cannot apply in the (c) and (d) examples in (183)–(188), and NOC is licensed (a version of what I have called the "classical view"). Island-hood is tied to the higher-than-TP adjunction site, hence the ungrammaticality of the (d) examples.

However, we have already seen conclusive evidence in (173), (174), and (179) that NOC variants can attach below the surface subject and occur inside its c-command domain. While the present analysis concurs with the idea that OC variants are attached lower than NOC variants (Voice′ adjunction vs. VoiceP adjunction), it does not require the latter to be as high as outside VoiceP. NOC adjuncts do not have to adjoin to TP, although they can; see table (167). Conversely, OC adjuncts do not have to adjoin below the subject.

To conclude this section: Binary configurational accounts fail to map the OC-NOC distinction to empirically validated syntactic configurations. Some accounts are too weak; they offer no structural distinctions between the adjunction sites of OC and NOC variants to explain their different behavior under certain tests (e.g., extraction). Other accounts are too strong; they impose structural conditions on the two variants that, in fact, are not confirmed (e.g., by c-command tests). These problems do not afflict the present analysis, whose structures are now doubly motivated—both by the underlying compositional semantics and by the full battery of syntactic diagnostics surveyed here.

10.2   An Explanatory Lacuna: The Propositional Variant Criterion

The deeper problem with binary configurational accounts is their inability to connect the OC-NOC distinction to the (un)availability of a propositional variant. In other words, these accounts have no natural substitute for the PVC, repeated here.

(189) *The Propositional Variant Criterion (PVC)*
  For a clausal adjunct $[P [PRO \ldots]]_W$:
  a. W has no propositional variant $\Leftrightarrow$ W is predicative $\Leftrightarrow$ W displays strict OC
  b. W has a propositional variant $\Leftrightarrow$ W is either predicative or propositional $\Leftrightarrow$ W displays OC or NOC

On the MTC account, all adjuncts are expected to allow OC, given side-ward movement. If no lexical DP is merged in the subject position of the adjunct, no OC chain will be formed, and a last-resort *pro* will be inserted instead. Thus, the path to a NOC derivation is open to *any* adjunct on this theory, clearly an overgeneration problem. A major goal of Green 2019 is to curb this unwanted overgeneration by limiting NOC adjuncts to VP-external positions and stipulating that upward movement is forced when possible.

However, even within Green's adaptation, the fundamental question remains: why are the OC adjuncts the ones that resist lexical subjects and the NOC adjuncts the ones that permit them? This correlation is completely accidental. On the MTC, lexical subjects may surface only if case-licensed. So one would have to stipulate that VP-internal adjuncts are headed by a defective, caseless T. A parallel stipulation is needed to guarantee that vP-adjoined adjuncts are headed by a nondefective T. Notice that even this would not cover all the relevant facts. With RatCs, the lexical subject is case-licensed not by T but by the complementizer *for*. Even worse, sometimes the propositional variant is finite, so one would have to link the adjunction site of the *nonfinite* adjunct (the source of NOC on Green's account) to the existence of a *finite* variant. Obviously, the resulting array of disconnected facts misses the simple generalization concerning the semantic types of all the adjuncts involved.[10]

Consider next how M&S's (2018) configurational theory would deal with the correlations documented in table (167). M&S are mainly concerned with DP/PRO alternations in nonfinite adjuncts, as in the following Tamil example. In particular, their analysis of PRO and *pro* as manifestations of the same underlying (unspecified) element is designed to explain the absence of a *pro* interpretation in such adjuncts ((180) is taken from M&S 2018:470–471).

(190) Raman$_i$ [Vasu/PRO$_{i/*j}$ puuri-jæ   porikk-æ] maavǔ
      vaaŋg-in-aan.
      Raman.NOM Vasu.NOM   puuri-ACC fry-INF   flour.ACC
      buy-PST-M.3SG
      'Raman bought flour [(for Vasu) to fry puuris].'

Prima facie, (190) looks like a counterexample to the PVC. The availability of a propositional variant should make NOC possible, contrary to the indexation options provided. Yet on a closer look, the Tamil example is no more of a counterexample to the PVC than its English translation is, although the latter is also restricted to the OC reading. Plainly, a RatC (if this is what the Tamil clause really is) allows either OC or NOC, but with an agentive matrix subject, both procedures will pick out that subject as antecedent; see the discussion surrounding (38). Unambiguous NOC can only raise its head when leading to a distinct interpretation—most typically (but not always; see below), with an inanimate main subject, as shown extensively in chapter 5. M&S do not construct the relevant type of examples in Tamil to tell whether DP/PRO alternating adjuncts in this language (of which they sample only one kind, RatCs) can support NOC. The same is true of the Spanish absolutive clauses they mention. Indeed, there is reason to be skeptical about claims about allegedly strict OC adjuncts that have been made for many other languages. In section 11.1, I survey representative cases that do not withstand closer inspection.

As to propositional variants and NOC, no mutual relation is expected on the Agree-based theories. In fact, M&S (2018) skirt the source of the alternation between DP and PRO subjects, for they explicitly reject the case-licensing approach. This leaves them with no clear stand on *necessarily* predicative adjuncts, namely, adjuncts that *only* tolerate a PRO subject (see their footnote 21). Elsewhere (Sundaresan and McFadden 2009) they do suggest, following Chierchia (1984), that the alternation between DP and PRO subjects in *complements* (*try* vs. *want*) is ultimately rooted in s-selection: verbs selecting properties disallow embedded DP subjects and verbs selecting propositions allow them. However, they make it clear that this (correct) story does not apply to adjuncts: "Adjunct clauses and clauses which contain enough structure to place a locality boundary between their subject and the matrix verb thus cannot have a selectional effect on the type of the embedded subject" (2009:26).

Notice that this description ignores a crucial player: the (prepositional) head of the adjunct. That head *can* and does s-select the semantic type of the adjunct clause, a fundamental observation that underlies the present analysis. At any rate, with no principled distinction between strict OC adjuncts and OC/NOC adjuncts, the theory cannot correlate their distribution with anything, let alone with the existence of a propositional variant, as needed.

Finally, recall the central fact that "implicit argument control" into adjuncts is always a species of NOC, not OC (see the argumentation in chapter 3 and examples (35), (36), (41), (84), (109)). This fact falls out of the predicational analysis of adjunct OC (implicit arguments being invisible to predication) but not out of the MTC or the Agree-based theories. On the latter approaches, implicit controllers are just null *pro* elements (Boeckx and Hornstein 2004) or φ-bundles (Landau 2010a); their θ-role and referential properties are identical to those of overt OC controllers, a conclusion required for *complement* implicit control. Therefore, the robust effect of the "emergence of the [+human] restriction" under "implicit adjunct control" is a total mystery. Nor can these theories predict the strict correlation—an adjunct allows "implicit control" if and only if it displays NOC—given that for these theories, the two types of control are distinct.[11]

To sum up, we see that the explanatory scope of binary configurational theories is rather limited. First, the inferences they draw from attachment site to control type are not borne out (setting aside the issue of *motivating* the different attachment sites independently of control). Second, they do not examine the full gamut of adjunct clauses in detail and so rest on an incomplete database. Third, they underestimate the range of NOC possibilities by testing examples in which OC converges with the NOC reading. Fourth, they fail to note the striking correlation between control type and the (non)existence of propositional variants. Fifth and last, they are intrinsically incapable of assimilating implicit control to NOC.

11 Ever-Growing NOC

In the preceding chapter, I discussed two empirical areas in which current accounts of adjunct control face problems: the distribution of OC adjuncts and the distribution of NOC adjuncts. I showed that because these accounts fail to appreciate that inanimate controllers only operate by OC, they underestimate the true range of OC configurations. In fact, OC adjuncts can be found at *every* adjunction site. In a parallel fashion, the true range of NOC configurations has been underestimated. Here, however, the problem is different. Many control configurations that in principle allow NOC have been misclassified as OC configurations. I have demonstrated this above for the entire class of alternating OC/NOC adjuncts in English; my goal in this chapter is to make the case much more general.

First, I will show that NOC has been systematically underestimated in many languages. Sample data from nine languages reveal a consistent pattern: constructions described as OC adjuncts in fact allow NOC (section 11.1). As in English, these adjuncts are systematically ambiguous, but the NOC variant is rarely recognized or even properly tested.

I then look at "unusual" or "exceptional" object control into adjuncts normally described as requiring strict subject control—typically, temporal adjuncts. In section 11.2, I revisit the classical finding that object experiencers can control adjuncts, now reinterpreted as NOC by a logophoric center (which happens to be the local matrix object); in section 11.3, I examine even rarer cases of object control into adjuncts, which can only be attributed to the high topicality of the object's referent. In section 11.4, I try to tease apart the two often-conflated properties of NOC antecedents: being logophoric centers and being discourse-salient (topics). I show that either property is sufficient in itself for NOC and that the [+human] feature nearly (but not quite) always prevails by default.

11.1 NOC Is Underestimated Crosslinguistically

The alternation between OC and NOC presents a serious challenge to nearly all current accounts of adjunct control. Yet the problem is rarely acknowledged, because the reported judgments (outside English) do not reflect an alternation. Often, authors are content in presenting an environment that behaviorally patterns with OC, and do not seriously probe the possibility of NOC.

As we have seen, this methodology is ill-advised, because NOC cannot be distinguished from OC in the most common type of example, involving a matrix human subject. Moreover, even when the matrix subject is inanimate, a nonlocal antecedent may fail to control because it is not a possible logophoric center. Finally, even when the local subject is inanimate and a nonlocal antecedent is a logophoric center, the latter may fail to control because it is less prominent than other logophoric centers with respect to the adjunct.

All these pitfalls must be carefully avoided when testing for OC and claiming that NOC is not available. This has been done for English only recently, in Landau 2017, Green 2018, 2019, and the present work. Studies of adjunct control in other languages, even the most recent ones, seldom apply this rigorous methodology; consequently, their conclusions about the OC-NOC divide are not compelling.

While it is beyond my goals here to delve in any depth into adjunct control in languages outside English, I would simply like to point out where further empirical work is needed. In particular, in this section I will review claims for OC in adjuncts in Italian, Spanish, Umdurk, Greek, German, Norwegian, Polish, French, and Turkish. In each case, we will see that slight modifications in the examples or in the contextual setting all of a sudden make the "impossible" NOC possible again.[1]

Italian. Sundaresan (2014:78) presents sentence (191a) as a case of OC. Clearly, though, NOC would also choose the local agentive subject (which is the most prominent logophoric center). Indeed, once the matrix subject is inanimate, the same type of adjunct, in the same position, supports extrasentential control (191b–c) (Carlo Cecchetto, pers. comm.).

(191) *Italian*

    a. Detestando il   pesce, Gianni compró solo carne.
       detest.GER   the   fish   Gianni bought only meat
       '[PRO$_{i/*j}$ detesting fish], Gianni$_i$ bought only meat.'

    b. Detestando gli   altri, la   vita   diventa difficile.
       hate.GER   the   others the life   gets   difficult
       'Life gets difficult when one hates others.'

    c. Andando   a   Roma, la   strada   diventa   molto   stretta.
       go.GER   to   Rome the   street   gets   very   narrow
      'If one takes the direction to Rome, the street gets very narrow.'

Spanish. Similarly, Sundaresan (2014:75) presents the absolute adjunct in
(192a) as a case of OC, which is resistant to pragmatic manipulation; the
extrasentential *María* is not a possible controller. Once again, due to the conflu-
ence of OC and NOC, it is impossible to determine that OC is attested here.
Notice, in particular, that the sentence strongly suggests a causal relation
between the adjunct and the main clause: because Carlos realized he showed the
first symptoms of the flu, he got vaccinated. This paraphrase illustrates how
natural it is to select *Carlos* as the prominent logophoric antecedent. In fact,
María is a possible controller for some speakers, contra Sundaresan's description (Victoria Mateu, pers. comm.).

Once again, extrasentential control *of the same adjunct in the same posi-*
tion is facilitated by a local inanimate subject (192b) (Karlos Arregi, pers.
comm.). In fact, even a local human subject controller can yield to an extrasentential one if the latter is made salient enough in the context (192c) (Catalan;
Rigau 1998:105). Quite generally, not only absolutive but also temporal
adjuncts in Spanish allow arbitrary control in the right circumstances (192d)
(Paz 2019:11). See Herbeck 2020 for further evidence and discussion of NOC
into adjuncts in Spanish.

(192) *Spanish*

    a. Según   María$_j$, [al   mostrar PRO$_{i/*j/*k}$ los primeros síntomas
      de la   gripe], Carlos$_i$ se   vacun-ó.
      according.to Maria, at.the show.INF   the first   symptoms
      of the flu   Carlos REFL vaccinate-PST
      'According to Maria, (with Carlos) showing the first symptoms of
      the flu, Carlos got vaccinated.'
    b. María$_j$ admitió a regañadientes que, [al   mostrar PRO$_j$ los primeros
      síntomas de la gripe], las vacaciones se   hecharon a perder.
      Maria admitted reluctantly   that at.the show.INF   the first
      symptoms of the flu   the vacation   REFL throw.pst to lose.inf
      'Maria$_j$ reluctantly admitted that [PRO$_j$ showing the first symptoms
      of the flu], the vacation went to hell.'
    c. [En/Al PRO no   telefonar-nos], ens   vam   intranquil-litzar.
      in/at.the   not to.phone-us   REFL got   worried-1PL
      'Because she/he didn't phone us, we got worried.'

   d. Concierto   de   Ozuna$_i$ fracasa   rotudamente   en   México
      concert   of   Ozuna   fails   outright   in   Mexico
      tras PRO$_{arb}$ haber-lo$_i$ cancelado   dos   veces antes.
      after   have.INF-CL.ACC.3M.SG   canceled   two   times before
      'Ozuna's concert fails hugely in Mexico after having canceled it
      twice before.

Umdurk. Georgieva (2018) describes a number of adjunct clauses in Umdurk (Uralic; Permic), among them absolutive-like adjuncts that are headed by the converb *-sa*. At one point, they are described as OC adjuncts, resisting non-c-commanding control, but at another point they are described as NOC, permitting it (examples from pp. 173, 183).

(193) *Umdurk*
   a. [Rinok-iś   berti-sa]   Liza-len   anaj-ez   śijon peźi-i-z.
     market-ELA come.home-CVB Liza-GEN mother-3SG food cook-PST-3SG
     '[PRO$_{i/*j}$ having come home from the market], Liza's$_j$ mom$_i$ prepared
     a meal.'
   b. [Vaškala kirʒan-jos-iz kilzi-sa] [Maša-len   tod-a-z] likt-i-z Pet'a.
     old song-PL-ACC listen-CVB Masha-GEN mind-INE/ILL-3SG come-PST-3SG Petya
     '[PRO$_i$ listening to the old songs], Masha$_i$ thought of Petya.'
     (Lit. '. . . to Masha's mind came Petya')

   Clearly, a human DP cannot control out of another human DP, but can control out of a nonhuman DP—an old observation and a familiar feature of NOC (Chomsky 1986b:128, Giorgi and Longobardi 1991:179, Landau 2013:248). In (193a) the possessor's perspective is not invoked but in (193b) it is. (193a), then, provides no evidence for OC in *-sa* adjuncts (although inanimate control does, as Georgieva (2018:177) demonstrates).

Greek. Consider (194a), from Kotzoglou 2016:177. Kotzoglou's point is that gerund adjuncts in Greek must be controlled by a matrix argument, explicit or implicit. A long-distance antecedent cannot directly control the subject of the gerund if the dependency is not mediated by any matrix argument. Accordingly, Kotzoglou claims that (194a) only affords the nonsensical, OC reading (where the television wakes up). I should note that not all Greek speakers agree with this judgment, and some do allow long-distance control by 'the parents'. The important methodological point, however, is that the context does not highlight the parents' subjective perspective; rather, the implicit experiencer object of the verb 'respect' is the prominent logophoric center. It is therefore not surprising that speakers have some difficulty in retrieving 'the parents' as a controller for the gerund. Once the parents' perspective is made explicit, as in (194b), long-distance control becomes completely natural (examples from Ioanna Siratidou, pers. comm.).[2]

(194) *Greek*

    a. Sto spiti mas o mesimerianos ipnos ton γonion$_i$ mu itan praγma iero . . .
       'In our house, my parents' siesta was a thing to respect . . .'
       #[PRO$_{*i/j}$ ala ksipnondas] i   tileorasi$_j$ aniγe   sti ðiapason.
       but wake.up.GER the.NOM television.NOM open.IMP.PST.3SG at.the loudest
       (Intended: '. . . but once they woke up, the volume of the television used to be turned up.')

    b. I γonis$_i$ mu θimonan pandote mazi mas ean kaname θorivo otan kimodusan . . .
       'My parents were always getting angry at us if we made noise while they were sleeping . . .'
       [PRO$_i$ ala ksipnondas] i   tileorasi   aniγe   sti ðiapason.
       but wake.up.GER the.NOM television.NOM open.IMP.PST.3SG at.the loudest
       '. . . but once they woke up, the volume of the television used to be turned up.'

German. Consider next infinitival adjuncts headed by *ohne* 'without' in German. Fischer and Flaate Høyem (2017:7) describe them as forcing OC, presenting (195a) as evidence. Once again, if we set up a context favorable to NOC, the facts are different (195b), in fact identical to the English (88a) (Florian Schäfer, pers. comm.). Fischer and Flaate Høyem also classify RatC *um*-adjuncts under OC, but NOC is possible there too (195c) (example from Stefanie Bode, pers. comm.).

(195) *German*

    a. Sie$_i$ gingen vorbei, [ohne PRO$_{i/*j}$ etwas   zu bemerken].
       they   passed by   without   anything to comment.on
       'They passed by without commenting on anything.'

    b. Fortschritt wird hier nie   passieren,
       progress   will   here never   happen
       [ohne PRO$_{arb}$ eigene Fehler   zuzugeben].
       without   own   mistakes to.admit
       'Progress will never happen here without admitting one's own mistakes.'

    c. [Um   sich PRO$_{arb}$ zu entspannen], wäre   eine Pause gut.
       in.order SELF   to relax   would.be a   break good
       'In order to relax, a break would be good.'

Norwegian. Likewise, Fischer and Flaate Høyem (2017:12) claim that the adjunct in (196a), translated as a RatC, is restricted to OC. The same adjunct, however, in the same position, reveals the possibility of NOC, when the matrix subject is inanimate (196b) (example from Peter Svenonius and Kristine Bentzen, pers. comm.). Note that on its natural interpretation, PRO in (196b) is understood to be *disjoint* from the matrix implicit agent.

(196) *Norwegian*

    a. Vi$_i$ trenger mer informasjon [for PRO$_i$ å kunne gi råd].
       we need   more information for   to can   give advice
       'We need more information in order to give advice.'

    b. Skjemaet må være ferdig utfyllt [for PRO å kunne gi råd].
       the.form must be finished filled.out for to could give advice
       'The form must be filled out completely in order to give advice.'

Polish. Gerunds headed by *bez* 'without' have been claimed to force OC by the local subject (197a) (Witkoś and Żychliński 2014:ex. (4a)). This is evidently false, as long-distance control is possible in examples like (197b) (example from Anna Bondaruk, pers. comm.).

(197) *Polish*

    a. Szef$_i$ zwolnił swego najlepszego pracownika [bez PRO$_{i/*j}$zawahania].
       boss fired   his   best   worker   without hesitating
       'The boss fired his best worker without hesitation.'

    b. Jan$_i$ był   rozczarowany, że   trzecia randka minęła
       Jan   was   disappointed that third   date   passed
       [bez   PRO$_i$ całowania].
       without   kissing
       'Jan was disappointed that a third date passed without kissing.'

French. Haug et al. (2012) argue that gerundive adjunct clauses in English and French display what they term "loose control." "Loose control" is situated somewhere between OC and NOC: essentially, it is control by some matrix participant, overt or implicit. True arbitrary or long-distance control, however, lies outside of it. But in fact, alongside standard OC, French gerundive adjuncts allow this type of control just like their English counterparts (198a–b) (examples from Fabienne Martin, pers. comm.). See Duffley and Dion-Girardeau 2015 for some quantitative data on nonsubject control with free adjuncts in French.

(198) *French*

    a. Jean était très nerveux. Arrivant au lieu de rendez-vous,
       Jean be.IMP quite nervous arrive.GER at.the place of meeting
       personne n'était encore arrivé.
       nobody NEG-be.IMP already arrived
       'Jean was very nervous. Arriving at the meeting place, nobody had
       arrived yet.'

    b. Marie était dans tous ses états. S'étant préparée depuis
       Marie be.IMP in all her states REFL-being prepared since
       si longtemps, la cérémonie s'est déroulée à merveille.
       so long the ceremony REFL-is unrolled marvelously
       'Marie was very excited. Having prepared herself for so long, the
       ceremony went perfectly well.'

No doubt, the sentences in which the adjuncts of (198a–b) are embedded display the perspectives of Jean and Marie, respectively. However, these perspectives are not grammatically encoded in these sentences; one would be hard pressed to locate implicit arguments with the unaccusative verbs 'arrive' and 'unroll', corresponding to *Jean* and *Marie*. Logophoric perspective is a global notion, which subsumes implicit arguments but cannot be reduced to them. More generally, there is no compelling evidence for the intermediate category of "loose control": any type of adjunct that allows implicit control also allows (in the right circumstances) long-distance, arbitrary, or deictic control. This is exactly what we expect if the only grammatically relevant categories in this domain are OC and NOC.

Turkish. Nominalized temporal clauses are described by Oded (2011:53) as OC constructions, disallowing non-c-commanding controllers (199a). As with the Umdurk examples in (193), however, a possessor can control out of a containing DP only if the sentence can be understood to report the possessor's perspective. Out of context, John's perspective is not clearly established in (199a). Indeed, the minimal change in (199b) does establish it without altering anything in the syntactic structure of (199a)—and possessor control becomes possible (example from Ümit Atlamaz, pers. comm.). This indicates that nonsubject control is possible and, as expected, displays the NOC signature. Furthermore, extrasentential control is also possible with these adjuncts (see (199c), from Ömer Eren, pers. comm.).

(199) *Turkish*

    a. *John'ın$_i$ resm-i [PRO$_i$ kendi-ne ayna-da   bak-tık-tan
       sonra] düş-tü.
       John-GEN   picture.POSS   self-DAT   mirror-LOC   look-NMLZ-ABL
       after   fall-PST.3SG
       (Intended: 'John's$_i$ picture fell [after PRO$_i$ having looked at himself
       in the mirror].')

    b. John'un$_i$ kaygı-sı   daha   da   artt-ı   [PRO$_i$ ayna-da
       John-GEN anxiety-POSS more also increase-PST.3SG mirror-LOC
       kendine   bak-tık-tan   sonra].
       self.3SG.DAT look-NMLZ-ABL   after
       'John's$_i$ anxiety rose even more [after PRO$_i$ having looked at
       himself in the mirror].'

    c. Biz$_i$ çok   üzgün-dü-k. [PRO$_i$ Tim-in   ortadan-yok ol-uş-u-nu
       we very upset-PST-1PL Tim-GEN disappear AUX-NOM-3POSS-ACC
       öğren-tık-tan   sonra] üç   uzun gün geç-miş-ti   ama
       learn-NMLZ-ABL after three long day pass-EVID-PST but
       o-ndan   hala hiçbir iz   yok-tu.
       she/he-ABL still any   sign   EXIST.NEG-PST
       'We were really upset. Three long days had passed after learning of
       Tim's disappearance but there was still no sign of him.'

Although classifying these adjuncts under OC is incorrect, Oded points out an interesting contrast with English: Turkish temporal clauses readily allow object control. This may be yet another instance of NOC (see section 11.3), although further evidence suggests the picture is more complicated; I briefly return to the Turkish data in section 14.4.

11.2 "Experiencer Control" Is NOC

During the 1980s, scholars of Relational Grammar (RG) accumulated data suggesting that experiencer objects have an enhanced potential to control nonfinite adjuncts. The evidence (drawn from Italian, French, Russian, and Japanese) showed that control options for various adjuncts display a curious disjunction: either the controller is a surface subject, or it is an experiencer object. Control by other objects (theme or goal) is not permitted, and often, neither is control by the demoted subject (the *by*-phrase); see Perlmutter 1984, Legendre 1989, 1993, Cresti 1990, and Legendre and Akimova 1993. Here is a representative paradigm in French from Legendre 1989:773, 774.

(200) a. [PRO$_{i/*j}$ ayant critiqué la politique étrangère du gouvernement],
              having criticized the policy foreign of.the government
       [les membres de l'opposition]$_i$ ont   attaqué   leur   chef$_j$.
       the members of the-opposition have attacked their leader
       'Having criticized the government's foreign policy, the members of
       the opposition attacked their leader.'
    b. [PRO$_i$ ayant   trimé   toute sa   vie], l'oisiveté   lui$_i$ répugne.
              having slaved all his life the-idleness him.DAT disgusts
       'Having slaved away all his life, he is disgusted by idleness.'
    c. [PRO$_{i/*j}$ s'étant   remis*(e)   à sortir], Marie$_i$ a   envoyé
       une   invitation   à   Pierre$_j$.
              SELF-being returned*(3SG.F) to go.out   Marie   has   sent
       an   invitation   to   Pierre
       'Having started to go out again, Marie sent an invitation to Pierre.'

(200a) allows subject control but not object (patient) control; (200b) allows
nonsubject (dative) experiencer control; and (200c) allows subject control but
not dative goal control.

    In fact, control by object experiencers is witnessed in English too (Kort-
mann 1991:8, 68).

(201) a. [PRO$_i$ sitting quietly here], the memory stirred him$_i$.
    b. [PRO$_i$ driving to Chicago that night, a sudden thought struck me$_i$.
    c. [PRO$_i$ having undergone the German academic education], the
       English university system impressed him$_i$ a great deal.

To account for this pattern, RG scholars developed the notion of a "working
1," defined as a term (= nonoblique) that is a subject at some grammatical
level. An experiencer is mapped as an "initial 1" (= deep subject), but may
undergo "inversion" to become a final 3 (= indirect object) or "antipassive" to
become a final 2 (= direct object). Yet in virtue of their "deep subjecthood,"
experiencers qualify as working 1s. Control of adjuncts, then, is restricted to
such working 1 nominals, a category subsuming both surface subjects and
object experiencers.

    In Landau 2010b:91–101, I reviewed the RG literature and suggested a way
to preserve its insights without adopting the idea of structural demotion—a
theoretical impossibility within modern grammatical theories. In particular, I
advanced the hypothesis that experiencers are "LF subjects," adapting an earlier proposal of Hermon (1985). Because object experiencers raise at LF to (a
second) Spec,TP position, their control potential is parallel to that of any other
surface subject.

The RG literature and Landau 2010b share the assumption that adjunct control by object experiencers falls under OC. They differ only in the level at which they take the OC dependency to be established (underlying structure for RG, LF in Landau 2010b). However, in light of the preceding section, that assumption must be rejected. As far as I know, all the adjuncts involved—chiefly temporal and absolutive adjuncts—alternate between OC and NOC, and *as NOC adjuncts* they may admit experiencer object control. The reason experiencers make such good controllers is not that they are structurally privileged, but that they introduce logophoric perspective holders; and NOC antecedents must be such logophoric perspective holders.[3] Indeed, this may also explain why the examples in the RG literature nearly always involve an experiencer controller that is either a clitic or a fronted topic—two strategies for highlighting a participant that increase its prominence for NOC antecedence (see section 11.4 on the role of topicality in NOC). From this perspective, then, the fact that patient/theme objects fail to control adjuncts via the NOC route is unsurprising.

Indeed, many of the examples cited in the RG literature do not probe for the possibility of NOC at all; logophoricity is not even recognized as a variable that should be manipulated. Competition is also not considered; the goal in (200c) competes with a more prominent potential controller, the subject, while the experiencer in (200b) is the only potential controller (subject control being semantically deviant). Examples like (198), where the sentence-internal controller is semantically inappropriate, are not considered.

Anticipating this alternative, in Landau 2010b:146n8 I offered two observations against the NOC analysis and in favor of the LF-subjecthood analysis. First, the adjuncts in question admit inanimate controllers, hence cannot be subsumed under NOC (example from Legendre 1989:780).

(202) *French*

Cette	chambre	conviendra	à	mes	parents	tout
this	room	suit.FUT	to	my	parents	completely
en	n'étant	pas	tout à fait	à	leur	goût.
in	NEG-being	NEG	completely	to	their	taste

'This room will be OK for my parents while not being quite to their taste.'

The observation, however, is fully consistent with the current view of these adjuncts as alternating between OC and NOC. The fact that subject control in (202) utilizes the OC path does not undermine the claim that nonsubject control in (200b) utilizes the NOC path—which must be available anyway, given examples like (198).

The second observation in Landau 2010b is that goal arguments (as opposed to, say, subject matter arguments) make for good logophoric antecedents in NOC (203a), but do not make for good controllers of adjuncts like the one in (200c).

(203) a.   John said to Mary$_i$ that it was possible that [PRO$_1$ praising herself] had been a mistake.

     b.   *John said about Mary$_i$ that it was possible that [PRO$_i$ praising herself] had been a mistake.

Again, note that the comparison is not minimal. The minimal clause containing the gerund in (200c) provides a more prominent controller (the subject *Marie*) while the one containing the gerund in (203a) provides no controller at all; furthermore, *Mary* is the closest potential controller (although control by *John* is not excluded in principle). Nevertheless, consideration of other data suggests that, compared with experiencers, *local* goals are constrained in their control capacity (as also observed in the RG literature). This raises the question of why *nonlocal* goals are not similarly constrained for long-distance control, if both environments involve NOC.

I believe that the answer lies in closer consideration of logophoric perspectives. *Mary* in (203a) is a natural logophoric antecedent because, in virtue of Mary's having received John's message, the proposition containing PRO (*that praising herself... mistake*) is part of her mental content. In contrast, the proposition *Pierre having started to go out again* is not necessarily part of Pierre's mental content in (200c). Although Pierre is probably aware of this fact about himself, the asserted event of Marie's sending him an invitation in no way invokes that proposition in his mind. This makes *Pierre* unsuitable for logophoric antecedence in this sentence. More generally, the notion of perspective holder cannot be simplistically reduced to a list of θ-roles (agent, experiencer, goal, etc.); instead, it must be determined globally, with the entire grammatical and extragrammatical context in sight.

In fact, local goal arguments *can* become NOC controllers when these considerations are carefully attended to.

(204) [PRO$_i$ having offered herself for the job], the committee's deliberations were not disclosed to Mary$_i$.

When we hear this sentence, our world knowledge leads us to attribute to Mary the understanding that her candidacy precludes her from having access to the deliberations. The entire sentence may well express her mental content, and thus NOC is perfectly possible, with the local goal argument, *Mary*, as controller.

In conclusion, the reasons I gave in Landau 2010b for keeping NOC and local, nonsubject experiencer control apart dissolve in light of the improved understanding we now have of NOC and its nuanced interplay with OC in nonfinite adjuncts. This finding is welcome from the standpoint of control theory, as it reaffirms that the fundamental OC-NOC dichotomy is powerful enough to handle all the relevant data, with no recourse to special assumptions. It also reaffirms the general point that the actual range of NOC has been seriously underestimated in the history of generative grammar. Finally, these conclusions have implications for the ultimate analysis of psychological predicates and how they map their arguments in the syntax—a topic obviously outside the scope of the present work.

11.3 Object Control in Alternating Adjuncts Is Also NOC

By now it will come as no surprise that under the right circumstances, NOC can extend to object control even with *non*experiencer objects. Indeed, this is the next logical step, and available evidence appears to support it.

Although the "official line" on absolute and temporal adjuncts holds that they only permit subject control, stubborn outlaws displaying object control have occasionally been noticed in the literature—noticed and swept aside, as they pose a serious threat to the conventional configurational account. On this textbook account, adjuncts are c-commanded by the subject and not by the object; hence, they only allow subject control.

Consider a few of these outlaws found in Green 2018:73, Paz 2019:7 (an internet example), and Lyngfelt 2009a:39, respectively.

(205) a. The security guard stopped the woman$_i$ [before PRO$_i$ boarding the plane].
   b. Woman's$_i$ family beats abusive husband$_j$ with sticks [after PRO$_j$ leaving her$_i$ with black eye].
   c. [After PRO$_i$ finishing the dissertation], they couldn't blame her$_i$ for taking a vacation.

A headline in *The Guardian* (2 May 2020) reads as follows (Vikki Janke, pers. comm.).

(206) Sir Michael Palin tells how elderly neighbor rescued him$_i$ [after PRO$_i$ setting house ablaze].

In the story, it is Palin who set his house ablaze.

In an experimental study with 70 native speakers of English, it was found that object control into final temporal adjuncts is a robust option (Janke and Bailey 2017). The study measured the effect of discourse priming—that is, salient topicality—on the likelihood that speakers will accept object control in temporal adjuncts. The effect was dramatic. While sentences of type (207a)/(208a) elicited on average only 4% object control judgments, the rate increased to 11% in weakly primed examples like (207b)/(208b) and to 51% in strongly primed examples like (207c)/(208c).

(207) a. Ron tapped Hermione while feeding the owl.
      b. I'm going to tell you something about Hermione. Ron tapped Hermione while feeding the owl.
      c. Hermione is looking after the birds. Hermione takes out the food. Ron tapped Hermione while feeding the owl.

(208) a. Luna lifted Ron while waving the wand.
      b. I'm going to tell you something about Ron. Luna lifted Ron while waving the wand.
      c. Ron is learning about magic charms. Ron tries out the new spell. Luna lifted Ron while waving the wand.

I should say that none of the speakers I consulted found object control in (207c)/(208c) natural, and most rejected it. This is probably due to interference from the default controller, the subject, which is not semantically excluded in these examples. I return below to these and related data. In general, one should keep in mind that object control into temporal adjuncts is a fairly marked phenomenon and subject to considerable variation. The judgments reported here are probably not universally shared, and this point too will need to be addressed.

Paz (2019:7) provides several examples of object-controlled temporal adjuncts in English, as in (205b), and also in Spanish.

(209) ICE arresta a madre$_i$ [tras PRO$_i$ dejar a su hija en la escuela].
      ICE arrests ACC mother after leave.INF ACC her daughter in the school
      'ICE arrests mother after she dropped off her daughter at school.'

Paz claims that Spanish is more tolerant than English to NOC interpretations of temporal adjuncts, but Janke and Bailey's (2017) findings suggest that the extent of object control in English temporal clauses has been systematically underestimated. Assuming these cases do fall under NOC, and in the absence of a comparable experimental study of Spanish, it is premature to draw any conclusions about potential crosslinguistic variation in this area.

Goncharov (2016:61n10) presents the following naturally occurring example of object control into an absolute adjunct in Russian, citing previous observations that "the subjects of the gerundives refer to the center of

empathy, which sometimes can be shifted to the object." This is exactly the
signature of NOC.

(210) V Germanii, [PRO$_i$ daže dostignuv 18-letnego vozrasta], invalidov$_i$ ne
       otlučaujt   ot   takix centrov.
       in Germany   even having. reached 18-years age handicaps.ACC   not
       exclude.3PL from such   programs
       '[Even after PRO$_i$ having reached the age of 18], they do not exclude
       people with handicaps$_i$ from such programs in Germany.'

Finally, there is evidence from Turkish temporal adjuncts, which, according to Oded (2011:56), allow either subject or object control. Oded analyzes
both options as OC. However, as noted above, the very same adjuncts allow
NOC as well (see (199)); hence, object control may also be included under
NOC. I return to the Turkish data in the next section, as they bear on the
proper pragmatic characterization of NOC antecedents.

Clearly, the empirical landscape of object control into temporal adjuncts
needs to be described more fully. However, let us suppose that the phenomenon
is real and is, in fact, NOC "in disguise." Then, in principle, it should be distinguishable from genuine OC by the object; that is, there should be a way of
removing the disguise. On the face of it, the [±human] distinction (see (42c)) is
just such a way: we would not expect object controllers, qua NOC antecedents,
to be inanimate. However, our assumptions about the pragmatic aspects of
NOC antecedents may have been oversimplified; I will put this issue aside until
the next section and seek other ways to tackle this analytic question.

Is object control into temporal adjuncts, if possible at all, an instance of OC
or NOC? To my knowledge, this question has only been seriously addressed
by Janke and Bailey (2017) and Janke (2018b). These authors advocate the OC
analysis. To allow OC between an object and an adjunct, however, they must
invoke a nonstandard VP-shell structure, where the "adjunct" is, in fact, the
lowest complement (as in Larson 1988, 1990, 2004), within the c-command
domain of the object.

(211) *OC structure for object-controlled temporal adjuncts in Janke and
       Bailey 2017*
       [$_{TP}$ Harry [$_{vP}$ tapped$_i$ [$_{VP}$ Hermione$_j$ [$_{V'}$ t$_i$ [$_{CP}$ while PRO$_j$ feeding the
       owl]]]]].

While the VP-shell structure produces object control, the standard VP-
adjunction structure produces subject control. The former is marked, Janke
and Bailey argue, because it involves the extra operation of V-movement
inside the VP shell. Hence, it is only selected under strong pragmatic pressure,

accounting for the increase in object control responses from (207a)/(208a) through (207b)/(208b) and up to (207c)/(208c).

This account is problematic for several reasons. First, on the widely accepted view of VP structure, V-movement applies in *all* VPs, from V to v, regardless of transitivity or the presence of adjuncts. Hence, derivation (211) should be no more costly than the adjunction derivation. Second, the causal chain between "pragmatic pressure" and the VP-shell structure is not clear. Presumably, economy comparisons restrict the availability of alternative derivations that lead to the *same* interpretation. Here, however, a *subject* control reading blocks an *object* control reading (under neutral pragmatic conditions) just because the latter is more "costly." But surely this extension of the economy logic is much too powerful, for it would block too many legitimate structures and interpretations. Closely parallel to adjunct control are depictive predicates, which display a subject-object ambiguity; see (212). Standard VP tests reveal that the object-oriented predicate is merged inside the VP, likely in a VP shell, whereas the subject-oriented predicate is adjoined to VP. Yet the two options coexist even though the former is less "costly" (on Janke and Bailey's assumptions).

(212) John met Mary very tired/in jeans.

In fact, on this extended notion of economy, it is not clear why matrix declarative sentences do not block matrix yes-no questions, as the latter involve an extra operation of (T-to-C) head movement compared with the former; or how topicalization is ever possible, being more costly than a sentence without it. In general, economy should not be able to look outside the reference set defined by equivalent interpretations; indeed, just this narrow notion of economy is invoked in chapter 13 to explain the preference for OC derivations over NOC derivations *that lead to the same interpretation.*

To corroborate the hypothesized correlation between low attachment and object control, Janke and Bailey (2017) presented those speakers who accepted the object control reading in (207c)/(208c) with the following examples. The point of VP-fronting in (213a) was to rule out the VP-shell structure. Similarly, the point of the matrix PP object in (213b) was to block c-command between the prepositional object, or its possessor, and the adjunct. Both configurations, then, leave VP-adjunction as the only possible parse.

(213) a. Harry is looking after the birds. Harry takes out the food. Harry
           expected Hermione to tap him and tap Harry Hermione did while
           feeding the owl.
       b. Peter talked to Jane's friend while pouring the drinks.

Janke and Bailey report that out of 26 participants who permitted object control in (207c)/(208c), 21 chose a subject control reading in (213a). For (213b), only subject control readings were allowed (no participant chose either *Jane* or *Jane's friend* as controller, although multiple options were allowed in the design).

Note, first, that the experimental setup of (213a) does not directly probe the most relevant question: do speakers *allow* object control in such situations? Instead, it probes which reading they *prefer*, when given a choice. Not surprisingly, they opt for subject control, which—on the present account—satisfies both the OC and the NOC derivations. The setup in (213b) did permit multiple responses, but given the dominance of the subject control reading, subjects may well have ignored other options, or simply "stopped" before making any special effort to retrieve them. As Janke and Bailey's own findings indicate, even strong contextual cueing of the object cannot cancel the natural prominence of subjects as NOC antecedents. Setups based on multiple choices can, at most, inform us about speakers' preferences or defaults, not about the scope of their underlying grammar.

Task-specific confounds make these judgments even less reliable. VP-fronting in the target sentence in (213a) (*and tap Harry Hermione did while feeding the owl*) removes the cued object from its base position, making the subject (*Hermione*) the linearly closest antecedent to PRO in the adjunct. Given the known role of linear proximity in antecedent retrieval, this change alone could account for the decline in object control choices. Furthermore, the fact that *Jane* was never chosen as controller in (213b) is completely predictable: it is neither cued as a salient topic nor construed as a logophoric center (see the related discussion of (193a) and (199a–b)).

Once the above confounds are carefully removed, object control reemerges. To see this, all we have to do is exclude the matrix subject from the "competition." (214a–b) are examples of object-controlled temporal adjuncts found on the internet.[4] (214c–d) were constructed from them; they illustrate that the object control reading is maintained even under VP-ellipsis that strands the adjunct, contrary to (213a).[5]

(214) a. The pilot reported a light which irritated him while flying.
       b. A road accident delayed us while driving to Oban for the first ferry.
       c. A red light irritated the pilot while flying, and later a yellow light did while landing.
       d. A road accident delayed us while driving to Oban for the first ferry, and then a nasty traffic jam did while driving back.

Similarly, prepositional objects may perfectly control temporal adjuncts, contrary to (213b), as the following examples, also culled from the internet,[6] illustrate.

(215) a. Sometimes it snowed on us while camping at Trout Camp.

    b. The welcome drinks were sent to us while waiting for the check-in.

There is no possible derivation for the VP-ellipsis examples in (214c–d) and for (215a–b) on Janke and Bailey's analysis. If object control of temporal adjuncts is a species of OC, it demands strict c-command between the object and the adjunct—absent in the above examples.

If, on the other hand, object control of temporal adjuncts is a species of NOC, then no structural relation between the object and the adjunct is needed. The adjunct attaches to vP as a saturated proposition (see (132)), and the antecedent of its null subject is determined outside syntax. Indeed, the fact that many of these examples feature an indexical pronoun as the object controller is exactly what we expect if logophoric (rather than syntactic) prominence conditions the control relation. Likewise, the strong dependence of object controllers on contextual salience is entirely natural on the NOC analysis, no different than the parallel dependence of any extrasentential controller; only local subject controllers have recourse to the OC route, which is free of pragmatic restrictions. Note that this patterning together of object control and extrasentential control is an accident on the view that takes the former to be a species of OC. Even if we accept that derivations like (211) come with a cost, nothing predicts that the grammatical factors required to offset the cost will be exactly those that facilitate NOC.

11.4   Logophoricity, Topicality, Either, or Both?

Certain data reported in the literature "stretch" the boundaries of NOC to the point that it blends with standard referential dependencies with *pro*. The paucity of these data makes it difficult to tell whether they truly challenge the conventional view of NOC or simply fall under a different rubric of pronominal dependencies. I will first present the problematic data and then propose a natural extension of the notion "NOC antecedent" to explain them.

Paz (2019) cites the English data in (216); the antecedent of the null subject (here marked as *ec*) is boldfaced. Indeed, given that it is an inanimate antecedent, Paz concludes that these cases should be analyzed with *pro* rather than with NOC PRO.

(216) a. [After ec_i displaying an error message], the ? signifies that **LaTeX**$_i$ is waiting for a response from you.

    b. This tells you everything about **this track**$_i$. The scene sets the tone of who Connor is and what his journey can be. [ec_i being one of the first tracks I wrote], I aimed to introduce and capture as many thematic ideas as possible.

My impression is that (216a) is not a real counterexample. By now it is customary to apply anthropomorphic language to complex machines, computers, or software. If LaTeX can be "waiting for a response," it is surely perspectival enough to qualify as a logophoric antecedent for PRO. Therefore, such examples are no more problematic than sentences like *My car hates me*, *The computer tried to connect to the network but failed*, and so on (see also note 1 in chapter 4). Example (216b) is more challenging, however, and so is the following one, found on the internet.[7]

(217) They tore [the old mansion house]$_i$ down in 1975. For a time the doors were closed, [only PRO$_i$ to see a re-emergence, and a new mission, as the Wood's Homes in the 1980s].

Similarly, the following corpus Spanish examples (from Paz 2019 and Herbeck 2020:5, respectively) exhibit long-distance control by an inanimate DP.

(218) a. **Este delito**$_i$ puede tener una pene de 1 a 6 meses de prisón. Sin
           embargo . . . ('This crime can carry a sentence of 1 to 6 months in
           prison. However . . .')
           [al   *ec*$_i$ no ser   considerado grave por la justicia mexicana],
           to.the   NEG be.INF considered   serious by   the court Mexican
           el   artista podría salir   bajo   fianza . . .
           the artist   could   leave.INF under bail
           '. . . since it is not considered serious by the Mexican court, the
           artist could
           get out on bail . . .'
       b. En Madrid$_i$ la   policía yo creo   que sí   que trabaja   bien
           in Madrid the police   I   think that yes that work.3SG well
           para *ec*$_i$ ser   una ciudad grande donde tienen   más
           for   be.INF a   city   big   where have.3PL   more
           problemas que   aquí.
           problems   than here
           'In Madrid$_i$ I think that the police do work quite well, [PRO$_i$ being a
           big city where they have more problems than here].'

The next data point comes from Turkish. As noted in section 11.1, Oded (2011:56) reports that temporal adjuncts in this language accept either subject or object control. Her examples, unfortunately, all involve *human* controllers, consistent with the NOC analysis. It turns out that inanimate objects can also control these adjuncts (Ümit Atlamaz, pers. comm.).

(219) John **yazıcı-yı**ᵢ [ecᵢ bozul-duk-tan sonra] çöp-e at-tı.

John printer-ACC break-NMLZ-ABL after trash-DAT throw-PST

'John dumped the printerᵢ in the trash after itᵢ broke.'

Returning to English, recall Janke and Bailey's (2017) finding, illustrated in (207)–(208), that object control in English temporal adjuncts can be facilitated up to a 51% acceptance rate when the referent of the object controller is a strongly established topic. ((220a–b) repeat Janke and Bailey's examples, (207c) and (208c) above.)

(220) a. Hermione is looking after the birds. Hermione takes out the food. Ron tapped Hermione while feeding the owl.

b. Ron is learning about magic charms. Ron tries out the new spell. Luna lifted Ron while waving the wand.

As already noted, these examples are not optimally designed, invoking competition between the subject and the object qua controllers. Being a logophoric center, the subject qualifies not only as an OC controller but also as a NOC one, masking the true extent to which object control is available for these adjuncts. Finally, Janke and Bailey did not test inanimate controllers at all.

To test the possibility of inanimate object control under comparable conditions of strong topicality, (221a–c) should be considered. Note that unlike in Janke and Bailey's examples, here subject control is not only disfavored in terms of topicality, it does not qualify as a logophoric center; and it is also semantically ruled out by the choice of predicate in the adjunct.

(221) a. The pool was uncovered. It was now clean. Chlorine water filled the poolᵢ [after PROᵢ staying empty the entire winter].

b. The stream was very strong. It glistened in the sun. Due to the landslide, heavy rocks fell from above and hit the streamᵢ [while PROᵢ flowing around big boulders].

c. Coffee prices have always been very susceptible to macro changes. Recently they have seen major fluctuations. The new regulation destabilized coffee pricesᵢ [before PROᵢ returning to their normal level].

I asked speakers to compare Janke and Bailey's examples (220a–b) with (221a–c). As it turns out, object control in the latter was no less accessible than it was in the former. If anything, it was more accessible, and the reason was even obvious to the speakers themselves (who pointed it out): the subject control reading is possible in (220a–b) but not in (221a–c), which makes the object control reading the only option. Once again, most speakers found all object control readings unacceptable; but the crucial point is that (220a–b) had no discernible advantage for speakers that in principle allowed object control. The implication is that even inanimate antecedents may control into temporal adjuncts when they are strongly established topics.

Some examples of absolutive adjuncts with inanimate controllers were mentioned in note 4 of chapter 3.

(222) a. [PRO$_i$ being stolen], the Bank of England refused to honor the note$_i$.
    b. [PRO$_i$ having swelled because of the rains], the workman was unable to remove the timber$_i$.
    c. [PRO$_i$ having run smoothly for years], it was finally time for my car$_i$ to be serviced.

These cases could be analyzed as fronted OC adjuncts, calling for no revision in the characterization of NOC, or as base-generated NOC adjuncts, licensed solely by the topicality of the matrix object controller (as suggested in Adler 2006:98).

The PRO subjects of the adjuncts in (216)–(219) and (221)–(222) pose a dilemma from the perspective of the present analysis. Being inanimate, they must be instances of OC.[8] However, temporal adjuncts attach too high for objects to c-command them, as OC requires, and we have already seen evidence in (214c–d) that indeed they attach higher than the objects. Furthermore, extrasentential antecedents obviously cannot participate in OC. How are such data to be analyzed, then?

As far as I can see, there are three possible solutions at this point.

Option 1: To allow OC by the object into temporal adjuncts, we may grant them the special derivation of "suspended λ-saturation" employed for object control into justification clauses in section 7.3. This, however, is far from an optimal solution. First, it does not carry over to long-distance control. Second, it is not clear how this derivation can be made selectively available to some speakers (in some contexts) but not to others.

Option 2: It is possible to treat all these *ec* subjects as *pro*. The pragmatic conditions on *pro* and NOC PRO are similar in that both pick out salient referents from the context; that is, both are topic-oriented in some sense. NOC PRO is still different in being restricted to human referents, in virtue of being logophoric (but see option 3 below). If the null subjects in examples like (216)–(219) and (221)–(222) represent a general exemption from the [+human] restriction, at least in some restricted domains, they may well instantiate *pro*. Indeed, both Paz (2019) and Herbeck (2020) advocate ideas in this spirit, according to which NOC PRO and *pro* are not two disjoint, encapsulated categories, but two points along a continuum of referential possibilities available to null subjects under complex discourse conditions.[9] Of course, the hard questions do not go away: Why does it still so often seem that the null subjects of nonfinite and finite clauses, even outside the OC domain, are not referentially equivalent? Why do null subjects in NOC overwhelmingly favor the [+human] reading?

Option 3: Regardless of how the ontology of *pro* vs. PRO is resolved, one can try to disentangle the notions of topicality and logophoricity, so often lumped together in discussions of NOC. This is the direction I will pursue, building on insights gathered from work on logophoric pronouns and long-distance reflexives.

It is a curious feature of the history of the field that some studies link NOC PRO to the discourse topic (Bresnan 1982, Kawasaki 1993, Adler 2006, Janke and Bailey 2017) while others link it to the logophoric center (Kuno 1975, Williams 1992, Landau 2001). Lyngfelt (2000:31) introduces the constraint Log, which is openly dualistic: "the pragmatically most salient referent in the present context—which corresponds to concepts like topic, empathy, point-of-view." Recognizing this confound at the heart of NOC, in Landau 2013:254–256 I pointed out potential empirical tests that might tease apart topicality, humanness, and logophoricity.

For example, an explicitly marked topic cannot control into a subject clause (a typical NOC environment) if it is [–human] (223a). This might seem like a side effect of logophoricity, but in fact, highly topical human DPs, which are not logophoric centers, can still function as NOC controllers ((223b), from Richardson 1986:257). In Landau 2013:255, I concluded from these (albeit isolated) data that "logophoricity is not a necessary condition on NOC, although the [+human] restriction is, which means that the latter is irreducible to the former, and constitutes a primitive feature of NOC PRO."

(223) a. ??As for the tomatoes$_i$, it is difficult to tell whether [PRO$_i$ being sold at retail price] would be required so soon.

     b. All I can say about Mary$_i$ is that most people I have spoken with agree that while [PRO$_i$ removing herself from the race so quickly] may have pleased the party hacks, it will surely distress the people whose interests she represents.

Whether the [+human] restriction is, in fact, "a primitive feature of NOC PRO" is now called into question by data like (216)–(219) and (221)–(222). To complicate the picture, topicality, just like logophoricity, is not a necessary condition (see Landau 2013:256). If a topic distinct from PRO's antecedent is explicitly set up, it does not diminish the latter's ability to control.

(224) Concerning Times Square, [PRO$_i$ to find himself alone there] became
        one of John's$_i$ most abiding fears.

While the examples in (223)–(224) involve subject clauses, it is possible to
construct parallel examples with adjunct control. The pair in (225) demonstrates that although topicality and logophoricity often converge, they need
not go hand in hand. NOC is licensed either way.

(225) a. *NOC by [–top,+log] antecedent*
           A: What about the certificates of appreciation? What happened to them?
           B: They were handed out before announcing the winners.
        b. *NOC by [+top,–log] antecedent*
           A: What about Mary? Is she available?
           B: Well, after sneaking outside last night, her father grounded her
           for a week.

In these cases, the (A) utterance establishes the topic for the (B) utterance.
The logophoric center is the implicit agent in (225a) and *her father* in (225b)
(the speaker and hearer are always available as topics and logophoric centers).
Recall that implicit arguments control adjuncts only via the NOC route, a
result established in chapters 3 and 5. An implicit agent of a passive is also
very low on the topicality scale, certainly compared with the surface subject,
and especially compared with a surface subject that is previously established
as a topic. (225a), then, displays NOC by a logophoric center that is neither a
topic from discourse nor a topic from the utterance situation (it need not be
the speaker). In (225b), *Mary* is the established topic, but not a logophoric
center (the patient argument of *ground* bears no mental perspective to the
event). Thus, it is a case of NOC by a topic that is not a logophoric center.

What such examples vividly show is that topicality and logophoricity are
each sufficient for NOC in themselves, but neither is necessary.[10] Importantly,
PRO is [+human] in all these examples, but we can no longer maintain that
this property derives from the concept of logophoric center, since being a
logophoric center is not necessary for NOC antecedents.

Two questions now arise: (i) What is the source of the [+human] restriction
for the vast majority of cases where it does seem to hold? (ii) Can topicality
successfully account for all instances of NOC by inanimate controllers? In
fact, I would like to suggest that a linguistically informed notion of topicality
holds the key to both these questions.

That topicality and humanness are tightly correlated is a robust typological
finding (Givón 1976). The very same animacy hierarchy that governs agreement in many of the world's languages (1 > 2 > Human > Animate > Inanimate)
governs topicality; that is, participants lower in the hierarchy are less likely to

be selected as topics than participants higher in the hierarchy (Comrie 1981, DuBois 1987, Song 2001, Swierskia 2004). The reasons are plausibly external to the grammar and rooted in human cognition. One possibility is to relate topicality and humanness via the notion of empathy—the degree to which the speaker identifies with a participant in the event. Kuno (2006:316) provides a list of grammatical properties that increase or decrease the level of empathy with a given participant. Two such properties are topicality and humanness:

Topic Empathy Hierarchy: Given an event or state that involves A and B such that A is coreferential with the topic of the present discourse and B is not, it is easier for the speaker to empathize with A than with B. . . . Humanness Empathy Hierarchy: It is more difficult for the speaker to empathize with a non-human animate object than with a human, and more difficult to empathize with an inanimate object than with an animate object.

Thus, topic-bound referents tend to be human because they attract the speaker's empathy, and the speaker's empathy is impeded by inanimate or nonhuman referents.

Turning to question (ii)—whether topicality can successfully account for all instances of NOC by inanimate controllers—the answer seems to be yes. At least, the scattered examples that I have collected from published sources are consistent with this view. A particularly interesting case, which we can now revisit, was mentioned in note 4 of chapter 3: absolute clauses with weather or temporal predicates. ((226a–c) are from Quirk et al. 1985:1122, Kortmann 1991:50, and Duffley 2014:181, respectively.)

(226) a. Being Christmas, the government offices were closed.
       b. Being Sunday, all banks were closed.
       c. Having rained all day long, the hill has become a virtual mud slide.

Herbeck (2020) cites a parallel example in Spanish.

(227) [Al   PRO   llover],   entra   agua.
      at.the   rain.INF   enters   water
      'When it rains, water enters.'

Erteschik-Shir (1997) suggests that the subject of these predicates is the spatiotemporal location of the event, a special kind of topic she terms "stage topic." When overt, this subject of predication surfaces as an "expletive," but this term is misleading in that the argument is not semantically vacuous.[11] On this view, (226a–c) are yet another instance of control by the topic, specifically by the stage topic, not unlike control by other parameters of the utterance situation, like speaker and addressee.

This view offers a natural account of the so-called ban on expletive PRO. It has long been observed that unlike the subject of weather/temporal predicates, a genuine expletive subject cannot occur in the position of NOC PRO. ((228a) is adapted from Chomsky 1981:327), and (228b–c) are taken from Safir 1985:34, 36.)[12]

(228) a. *[PRO to be clear that we're out of fuel] would be a nuisance.
  (cf. *For it to be clear that we're out of fuel would be a nuisance.*)
  b. *[PRO being obvious that John was late], we decided to go to the movies.
  (cf. *It being obvious that John was late, we decided to go to the movies.*)
  c. *French*

*[PRO avant	de	sembler	que	Jean	était	coupable],
before	of	seem.INF	that	Jean	was	guilty
il	était	évident qu'il	serait			condamné.
it	was	obvious	that-he would.be			condemned

  'Before seeming that Jean was guilty, it was obvious that he would be condemned.'

Pure expletives do not pick out any discourse entity that can possibly meet either the logophoricity or the topicality condition (including the special case of stage topics) on NOC PRO; hence, they are banned in such contexts.

Slightly modifying the descriptive characterization in Landau 2013:256, then, we may take logophoricity and topicality to each be sufficient for NOC antecedence. The [+human] restriction is entailed on the logophoric construal and is a strong (though not absolute) default on the topic construal.

(229) *Pragmatics of NOC*
  In a NOC configuration [. . . DP . . . [PRO . . .] . . .] (order irrelevant), DP may control PRO iff
  a. DP is [+top] *or* a logophoric center.
  b. Default: [+top] → [+human].

Clearly, (229) is not a theory. Rather, it is what a proper theory should explain. (229) is nonetheless useful as a prism through which to examine the bewildering set of data discussed above. In particular, it allows us to maintain option 3 while avoiding the drawbacks of options 1 and 2. For the problematic data with "inanimate NOC controllers," we need not invoke either a different derivation or a different element (*pro*). Instead, we should explore the possibility that the different ingredients of "NOC antecedence"—humanness, logophoricity, and topicality—may be calibrated differently for different speakers, and possibly even for the same speaker under different discourse circumstances. If, as seems likely, the concept of "NOC antecedence" is a cluster concept—more like *vegetable/fruit* and less like *odd/even*—then it is not surprising to find variation and high susceptibility to contextual information in how it is deployed.

Having said that, let me reiterate the empirical situation: NOC does fail with inanimate antecedents for most speakers in nearly all circumstances. This follows because logophoric antecedents *must* be human and topical ones strongly prefer to be so (229b). Therefore, using the [±human] criterion to distinguish OC from NOC, as I have done throughout this work, is a valid method, as long as one bears in mind potential outliers and takes care not to let them confound the empirical tests.

Continuing with the assumption that the worthiness of NOC antecedents is a multifactorial rather than binary matter, we can now understand what makes a local human subject such a favorite controller for alternating OC/NOC adjuncts. Human DP subjects most often bear an agent or experiencer role, which makes them natural logophoric centers, setting up the mental perspective from which the embedded (adjunct) eventuality is reported. Being subjects, they are also topical by default. Thus, they are ranked highest as NOC controllers. In parallel, they are also selected as OC controllers by virtue of their structural relation to the adjunct. This convergence places them at the top of the "controller-worthiness" scale. Below them are ordered DPs with less qualifying properties, as illustrated in (230) (where "controller-worthiness" decreases from left to right).

(230) *Controller-worthiness scale (a processing model)*

	Local [+human] subject	Local [–human] subject	Nonlocal [+human] DP	Nonlocal [–human] DP
OC-worthy	+	+	–	–
NOC-worthy: [+log]	+	–	+	–
NOC-worthy: [+top]	+	+ (weak)	+ (weak)	+ (weak)

The first column—local [+human] controllers—is a winner on all fronts. Examples of this type are traditionally described as OC, but strictly speaking, they reflect the joint power of the OC and NOC derivations converging on the same controller. In order to break up this convergence, a competing nonlocal controller must be very salient both as a logophoric center and as a topic; such cases are indeed very rare (see (2) in section 1.1).

As discussed above, [+human] DPs make better topics than [–human] ones. Similarly, local DPs make better topics than distant ones, simply because of the gradual decay of online discourse entries. Therefore, [–human] or nonlocal

DPs can be, at best, weak topics. Thus, the second and third columns in table (230) are (roughly) equally controller-worthy, each consisting of one positive rank, one negative rank, and one weak positive rank. This tie is reflected in the data on alternating adjuncts, where control by a local [–human] subject easily alternates with control by a nonlocal [+human] DP (see (231a–b))—sometimes in the very same sentence (see (231c)).

(231)   a. The chef thinks the potatoes$_i$ will sell better [after PRO$_i$ being salted].

       b. The chef$_i$ thinks the potatoes will sell better [after PRO$_i$ adding more salt].

       c. The pool$_i$ was the perfect temperature [after PRO$_{i/arb}$ being in the hot sun all day].

At the bottom of the scale we find [–human] nonlocal DPs, whose only claim to controller-worthiness rests on the possibility of being very weakly topical. This accounts for the marginal data reported in (216)–(219) and (221)–(222). Note that local object controllers are not represented as a separate class, being subsumed under general NOC, as argued in sections 11.2–11.3. Table (230) might be refined by including them. This would require distinguishing experiencer from nonexperiencer objects, and within the latter class, human from inanimate objects. Object controllers might also be ranked higher than nonlocal controllers in their [+top] degree insofar as they are more vividly present when the adjunct is encountered. To illustrate the joint effect of [+top] and [+log] in object control, consider this contrast from Adler 2006:100.

(232)   a. #The horror movie frightened Mary$_i$ [before PRO$_i$ going to bed].

       b.   As for Mary, she didn't sleep at all last night.

           ?The horror movie frightened her$_i$ [before PRO$_i$ going to bed].

Adler points out that once the object is made topical, as in (232b), object control is improved (though still marked for many speakers). However, she does not take into account the role of the psychological verb *frighten*. If indeed it is the joint workings of the logophoric perspective and the topicality of *Mary* that account for the improvement in (232b), we expect a worse outcome with nonpsychological verbs. This is confirmed.

(233)   a. #Heavy traffic delayed Mary$_i$ [before PRO$_i$ joining the rehearsal].

       b.   As for Mary, she was very late.

           #Heavy traffic delayed her$_i$ [before PRO$_i$ joining the rehearsal].

These are rather subtle contrasts, but they seem to go in the expected direction. It is probably not an accident that the RG literature on adjunct control (see section 11.2) focuses on *experiencers*. In any event, what the overall marginality of object control in adjuncts indicates is that in actual discourse, neither (229a) nor (229b) is guaranteed to be sufficient; sometimes it is only their additive, joint contribution that can elevate a NOC interpretation to the level of reasonable acceptability.

Accordingly, table (230) should be viewed as a rather abstract, half-formalized model, which cannot replace a real theory of performance. Many subtle variations and fluctuations in the actual rankings associated with [+top] and [+log] resist full formalization and are evidently left out. The weighted contributions of [+log] and [+top] will vary from one utterance to the next, giving rise to complex interactions, occasionally resulting in "unexpected" NOC readings. Nevertheless, the table and the scale it represents offer a reasonable rough pass at what an ultimate theory of performance should explain in addressing the complexities of adjunct control. In section 14.2, I will present additional evidence, from ellipsis resolution and from processing, for the claim that local human subject control does simultaneously utilize the OC and the NOC paths. Moreover, I will show that this model provides important clues about the acquisition and developmental course of adjunct control, the topic of the next chapter.

Table (230) is reminiscent of Lyngfelt's (1999, 2000) Optimality Theory tableaux, but the similarity is merely superficial. First and foremost, Lyngfelt's tableaux are intended to represent *competence* (i.e., grammatical knowledge of control), whereas table (230) describes some aspects of *performance*. That is, the controller-worthiness scale does not deliver a single "winner." The OC grammar and the NOC grammar operate in parallel, and as I have stressed repeatedly, each produces its own output. As long as selectional restrictions are observed, the grammar delivers one OC controller and one or more NOC controllers to the performance systems. It is only then that the different candidates are compared, and the choice among them will always be a matter of degree. Second, Lyngfelt's tableaux introduce a list of constraints that are already incorporated, in the present system, in the OC grammar (like the necessity of a controller and the c-command condition). These constraints do not apply to NOC candidates. Finally, Lyngfelt's system conflates topicality and logophoricity under a single constraint, whereas table (230) is precisely designed to tease apart their distinctive contributions.

Returning to the main thread of this section, we may ask what makes logophoricity and topicality a natural class with respect to NOC. The ultimate answer may well lie in general properties of the human cognitive system and how discourse participants are perceived and stored in working memory. What is quite clear is that NOC is no exception here. The coupling of logophoricity and topicality crops up in a number of long-distance referential dependencies. Following is a brief reminder.

Logophoric pronouns in West African languages are famous for being anchored to some logophoric center, thereby reflecting the mental perspective of some attitude holder. For example, the logophoric pronoun *òun* in Yoruba must be coindexed with the matrix attitude holder (see (234a), from Adesola 2005:163) (and the nonlogophoric, weak pronoun *ó* cannot be). Less famously, these logophoric pronouns are also licensed in nonattitude contexts, but only if referring to the discourse topic (see (234b), from Adesola 2005:169).

(234) a. Olú$_i$ ti   kéde   pé   **òun**$_{i/*j}$ máa   wá   ní   òla.
        Olu   ASP   announced   that   he   will   come   a   tomorrow
        'Olu has announced that he will come tomorrow.'

    b. A: Ta   ni   ó   kù   tí   è   ń
           who   be   he   remain   that   you   PROG
           wá   nínú   àwon   omo   Àjàó?
           seek   among   they   child   Ajao
           'Which of Ajao's kids are you still looking for?'
       B: Adémólá$_i$.
         'Ademola.'
       A: Mo   ti   rí   **òun**$_i$ lánàá.
         I   ASP   see   him   yesterday
         'I have seen him yesterday.'

To make sense of this duality, Adesola proposes that *òun* must be locally Ā-bound; the binder may be either the logophoric null operator or the topic null operator, both occupying an Ā-position in the left periphery of the clause. I return to this idea below.

The distribution of long-distance reflexives in East Asian languages displays the same duality. Nishigauchi (2014:181–182) points out that when the antecedent of *zibun* in Japanese is explicitly logophoric (like an experiencer argument), it need not be marked as a topic (235a). Yet when the antecedent is not logophoric (as when someone is asleep), it *must* be marked as a topic (235b). This shows quite clearly the functional equivalence of these two strategies (see Han and Storoshenko 2012 and Huang 1994 for parallel observations on the distribution of Korean and Chinese reflexives *caki* and *ziji*, respectively).[13]

(235) a. Iinkai-ga   zibun$_i$-o   erabi   soo ni   nat-ta   toki,
       committee-NOM   self-ACC   elect   likely   become-PST   when
       Takasi$_i$-**wa/ga**   huan-ni   nat-ta.
       Takashi-TOP/NOM   worried   become-PST
       'When it came to be likely that the committee might elect self$_i$,
       Takashi$_i$ became anxious.'

     b. Iinkai-ga   zibun$_i$-o   eran-de   kuire-ta   toki,
       committee-NOM   self-ACC   elect-do   favor-PST   when
       Takasi$_i$-**wa/*ga**   gussuri   nemut-te   i-ta.
       Takashi-TOP/NOM   fast   asleep   be-PST
       'When the committee did the favor of electing self$_i$, Takashi$_i$ was
       fast asleep.'

Nishigauchi proposes that *zibun* is always locally bound by a *pro* hosted in a POV (point of view) projection, and it is this *pro* that is subject to NOC (see Sundaresan 2018b and Charnavel 2020 for analyses in this spirit). Although he only considers distributional parallels between *zibun* and NOC PRO (non-locality, strict readings, etc.), the parallels extend, as we have seen, to the pragmatic felicity conditions as well.

The idea that discourse topics are represented as null elements—pronouns or operators—at the periphery of the clausal spine has been a cornerstone of much research ever since the seminal work by Huang (1984), inspiring many analyses of null arguments and subject *pro*-drop in particular (Cardinaletti 1990, Haegeman 1990, Sigurðsson 2011). Frascarelli (2007) analyzes *pro* in null-subject languages as a variable bound by an "aboutness topic" (specifically, aboutness-shift topic) occupying the highest projection (ShiftP) in the left periphery. When overt, it surfaces as a clitic-left-dislocation construction; when null, it refers to the continuous topic. In an attempt to integrate this analysis of referential *pro*-drop with the analysis of NOC, McFadden and Sundaresan (2018) propose that just as referential *pro* is valued by Agree with the topic in ShiftP, NOC PRO is valued by Agree with a logophoric center in Pers(pective)P. This is pretty much equivalent to Adesola's (2005) proposal mentioned above.

Let us assume that this line of research is basically correct. The question is how to integrate its results into the present framework. At the descriptive level, (229) already recognizes that NOC may arise through either one of two pragmatic routes—logophoricity or topicality. This duality needs to be incorporated into the constitution of NOC adjuncts. Recall that these are generated by projecting a *pro* variable in a CP layer above the predicative FinP, thereby saturating the latter. This *pro* should introduce *either* the logophoric center *or* the current aboutness topic. I thus minimally expand (20) as follows.[14]

(236) a. *Predicative adjunct:* $[_{PP}$ P $[_{FinP}$ PRO$_i$ Fin $[_{TP}$ ~~PRO~~$_t$ . . .]]]
   b. *Propositional adjunct:*
   (i) $[_{PP}$ P $[_{CP}$ *pro* C$_{[+log]}$ $[_{FinP}$ PRO$_i$ Fin $[_{TP}$ ~~PRO~~$_t$ . . .]]]]
   (ii) $[_{PP}$ P $[_{CP}$ *pro* C$_{[+top]}$ $[_{FinP}$ PRO$_i$ Fin $[_{TP}$ ~~PRO~~$_t$ . . .]]]]

I take *pro* to be a minimal pronoun with no inherent features. Its denotation is determined by the head of its projection (C$_{[+log]/[+top]}$), which encodes the relevant contextual information. Note that P itself only selects the semantic type of its clausal complement (<s,t>) and its category (CP); it doesn't select anything more specific. Thus, the [+log]/[+top] distinction is not encoded on P. This captures the empirical observation that there is no NOC adjunct that only permits a topic-bound PRO or one that only permits a logophoric PRO; the choice between these two possibilities is purely pragmatic and available in principle to all NOC adjuncts. At the same time, the mechanism of NOC in the current analysis is not purely pragmatic, relying as it does on the "discourse variable" *pro* as a "syntactic relay." Is this assumption necessary?

On a purely pragmatic theory of NOC (such as Kortmann's (1991) or Duffley's (2014)), there is only one null category in the adjunct: PRO. Principles of anaphora resolution, operating at the discourse level, operate to determine the reference of PRO in particular utterances: logophoric or deictic, topic-bound, and so on. One may ask, therefore, what is gained by the extra complexity of an additional null element, *pro*.

The answer is that without the syntactic projection hosting *pro*, we lose the fundamental distinction between OC and NOC adjuncts, namely, predicative and propositional adjuncts. OC adjuncts—whether strict or alternating with NOC versions—are demonstrably *not* dependent on pragmatic principles for their interpretation. An OC PRO may not "consult" discourse; it can only search for an antecedent in the local matrix clause. If OC and NOC adjuncts had exactly the same structure, with PRO the single null element, why this element should behave so differently in the two environments would be mysterious.

On the current approach, however, the answer is straightforward. OC adjuncts contain no "discourse variable." PRO itself is not a variable; rather, it is an operator-variable chain, producing a predicate. Predicates must be syntactically saturated; hence, they are impervious to discourse. NOC adjuncts, on the other hand, harbor a "discourse variable"—namely, *pro*—projected above the PRO chain. It is in virtue of this variable that discourse holds sway over the reference of PRO. Thus, syntactic complexity—to a minimal degree—is fully warranted by the shape of the data. A complete understanding of NOC must incorporate both syntactic and pragmatic assumptions, dispensing with neither one. For a summary of the case against conflating OC and NOC, see section 14.5.

The preceding discussion has shown that the traditional view of adjunct control—mostly generalized from the behavior of temporal adjuncts—is far from accurate. In fact, when we consider the full range of data, two empirical generalizations stand out.

(237) *Properties of adjunct control in adult grammar*
   a. Temporal adjuncts allow either OC by the local subject or NOC.
   b. Temporal adjuncts, under restricted conditions, allow object control and extrasentential control—both as NOC varieties.

This updated picture of the adult grammar of adjunct control has obvious implications for studies of child grammar. If these two generalizations characterize the target grammar, then children who accept adjunct control by some antecedent *other* than the local subject cannot be charged with any deficiency in grammatical knowledge. Adults accept non-local-subject control of adjuncts, and children accept it. The extent of the discrepancy between children's and adults' grammars has been overestimated, not because the child data have misrepresented children's knowledge (but see Gerard et al. 2018) but because the adult data have misrepresented adults' knowledge. The analytic question here is not why children "depart" from the adult grammar in accepting such interpretations at all (they do not), but why they *over*accept them—if indeed they do—in contexts where adults reject them. As I will show, this reorientation of the analytic question radically deflates much of the theoretical machinery formerly recruited to explain the "gap" between children's and adults' knowledge of control. At the same time, it narrows the true gap down to very specific pragmatic deficits that are independently observed at the relevant ages.

12.1 Children's Performance on Adjunct Control

In this section, I will briefly look at the major relevant findings, though because the acquisition literature is vast, I will inevitably gloss over many details. I will then consider the three main developmental accounts offered to explain the divergence between children's grammar and adults' grammar. Finally, I will show how the present analysis points toward a very specific account of this divergence—one free of the difficulties facing the others.

Probably the finding most often replicated is that children between 3 and 5 years of age and occasionally even older accept object control into temporal adjuncts where adults normally do not—for example, in (238).

(238) Cookie Monster touches Grover after jumping over the fence.

Object control is often allowed, or even preferred, by many children at this stage. This result has been obtained through various methodologies: acting out the understood meaning of the sentence (Goodluck 1981, 1987, 1998, 2001, Hsu, Cairns, and Fiengo 1985, Lust et al. 1986, Hsu et al. 1989, McDaniel and Cairns 1990, McDaniel, Cairns, and Hsu 1991, Goodluck and Behne 1992, Cairns et al. 1994); judging the grammaticality of the sentence in the context of a given (displayed) meaning (McDaniel and Cairns 1990, McDaniel, Cairns, and Hsu 1991, Cairns et al. 1994); providing a truth value judgment of the sentence in the context of a given (displayed) meaning (Broihier and Wexler 1995, Adler 2006, Gerard 2019); providing a referential judgment on PRO (Janke and Bailey 2017); selecting a picture appropriate for the understood interpretation (Janke and Perovic 2017, Janke 2018a); and coloring in a picture corresponding to the understood interpretation (Gerard et al. 2017, Gerard et al. 2018).

Some of these studies have been designed in a way that restricted the available choices of antecedent for PRO to either the subject or the object alone. For example, only two puppets, identifying the matrix subject and object, are offered to act out the sentence; or only two pictures are displayed to choose from or to color in, illustrating the actions corresponding to subject or object control construals. Obviously, extrasentential control cannot be detected in these experimental designs. A number of studies, however, specifically probed for the option of extrasentential control of the temporal adjunct. They all found that children at this developmental stage are quite tolerant of this option when the intended referent of the extrasentential antecedent is made clearly salient. Extrasentential control has been attested with preposed adjuncts (Lust et al. 1986, Goodluck 1987) and with final adjuncts (McDaniel, Cairns, and Hsu 1991, Cairns et al. 1994, Broihier and Wexler 1995, Janke 2018b; the last one studied older children).

In accepting object control and extrasentential control of adjuncts, children are no different than adults, as stated in (237b). Nonetheless, the *extent* of these NOC options differs dramatically between the two. As demonstrated in section 11.3, object control of temporal adjuncts is rarely acceptable for adults. In contrast, children between 3 and 5 years of age freely allow it, and often favor it over subject control. They also accept extrasentential control more liberally, a point to which I return below.

Do children ever *exclude* subject control? Hsu, Cairns, and Fiengo (1985), McDaniel, Cairns, and Hsu (1991), and Cairns et al. (1994) have all claimed that there is a substantial subgroup of children who indeed lack subject control at a certain stage. From the standpoint of the present analysis, this would be doubly surprising: not only would it imply that these children pass through a stage in which their grammar possesses NOC but not OC, it would also imply that their NOC derivations, for some mysterious reason, cannot generate subject control (that NOC derivations do, for adults, is demonstrated in section 14.2). However, the logic of Economy of Projection dictates just the opposite asymmetry (this point is elaborated in chapter 13). Furthermore, the grammatical devices employed in OC most likely develop before those employed in NOC, for it is well-known that pragmatic knowledge of reference and point of view develops quite late.[1] Given these considerations, a strictly object control developmental stage for temporal adjuncts would be extremely puzzling.

Indeed, the reality of such a stage has been called into question by Broihier and Wexler (1995). As they correctly point out, act-out experiments cannot establish this stage, as they are only capable of revealing a preference among explicitly presented choices. A strictly object control child should *reject* subject control and extrasentential control—but act-out tasks cannot detect rejection responses. Relatedly, the existence of a "mixed subject/object control stage" is dubious, for there is no positive evidence that children ever *disallow* extrasentential control. Using data from a forced picture selection task, Janke (2018b) has argued that both older children and adults employ a "mixed" subject/object control grammar, excluding extrasentential control; but we will see that her data too do not support the claim (see note 3 of chapter 5 for the parallel issues that arise in Janke and Bailey 2017).

The evidence from grammaticality judgments for a strictly object control stage, on the other hand, is rather sparse and rests on very low rates (McDaniel and Cairns 1990, McDaniel, Cairns, and Hsu 1991, Cairns et al. 1994). Broihier and Wexler's (1995) own study (14 children between 3;10 and 5;5 years of age, truth value judgment task) found no strictly object control child: 6 children only accepted subject control (as adults would with a local human subject), and 8 children accepted either subject, object, or extrasentential control.

Preference for object control may well be real for some children, but preferences do not reliably track grammatical knowledge. Indeed, Lust et al. (1986) documented consistent parallels between children's choice of antecedent for PRO in a nonfinite temporal adjunct and their choice of antecedent for an overt pronoun subject in a finite temporal adjunct. Given that the latter choice is pragmatically regulated, it is natural to conclude that the former is too, insofar as it falls under NOC.

Gerard et al. (2018) argue that children's low rates of subject choice in previous act-out experiments are largely due to extragrammatical factors—specifically, high task demands that interfere with control resolution. While I agree that task demands may have affected the reported results, I do not think they can substitute for a genuinely linguistic explanation.[2] Let us review the issues.

Gerard et al. (2018) conducted two experiments. In the first one (34 children, 4;0–5;3), using a truth value judgment task (TVJT) with adjunct control stimuli, they found that some children accepted only subject control, 1 child only accepted object control, and most (20 out of 34) accepted either. Overall, subject control was accepted 63% of the time.

Their second experiment (32 children, 4;0–5;3) involved a coloring book task. In this design, children hear a test sentence and then see, on a touchscreen, two pictures connected by an arrow (representing the temporal order). One picture depicts the main clause action and the other depicts the adjunct action. In the latter picture, the two characters corresponding to the matrix subject and object appear with an object to be colored. The child is to choose which object to color on the basis of the understood control relation. For example, in *Dora washed Diego before eating the red apple*, the second picture depicts both Dora and Diego holding apples. Coloring Dora's apple reveals a subject control construal, while coloring Diego's reveals an object control construal.

In this task, children's performance increased to 85% subject control responses, which Gerard et al. take to be nearly adultlike. Notice that like the act-out design (and unlike the TVJT), the coloring book task can at most reveal preferences within grammatical knowledge, not its actual scope. There is no way of telling how many of the trials that elicited subject control responses were, in fact, ambiguous for the children. Thus, the increase in subject control responses from the TVJT to the coloring book task is completely expected.

Nevertheless, Gerard et al. capitalize on the claim that their results are significantly different not only from those of TVJT experiments but also from those of act-out experiments: "The current study used the coloring book task, which has the same limitation of the act out task of revealing only one interpretation at a time, but for which children showed a much more adultlike pattern of behavior overall" (2018:16). This point is debatable, however, since the criteria for classifying children's responses as "subject control," "object control," or "mixed" are not constant in the literature. It may well be that Gerard et al.'s "subject control" children are a mixed group of some with the adult grammar and some with a subject preference. Recall that of the 14 children in Broihier and Wexler's (1995) study, 6 were already responding like adults; they were set aside, unlike in Gerard et al.'s study.

Moreover, even by the pure criterion of subject response percentage, Gerard et al.'s results (85%) are not different from those of *all* previous studies. Goodluck and Behne (1992) found a similar rate of subject control responses—88%—in act-outs with transitive main clauses. The vast variability in children's performance on adjunct control between ages 3 and 5 has been repeatedly documented in the literature; it may well be that the performance of the children in Gerard et al.'s experiment simply approached the upper limit. Thus, the claim that previous studies underestimate children's knowledge due to task demands is not fully warranted.

Suppose, however, that we agree on the facts. What task demands, according to Gerard et al. (2018), interfere with children's processing of adjunct control? They discuss two such factors: the operational steps required in the act-out task, and the cognitive load associated with temporal ordering of events.

Gerard et al. observe that in the act-out design, the child needs to plan and execute two actions: main clause action and adjunct action. The coloring task, however, involves selecting the right color and coloring. "If this difference affects how well the representation of the test sentence is maintained in memory," they write (2018:21–22), "then children's behavior will be different in the different tasks, independent of their grammars." Surely, however, short of independent evidence that this difference *does* (not just *might*) affect control interpretation, this is an untested hypothesis. Moreover, nothing in this processing explanation predicts the tight referential correlations between PRO and overt pronouns in past experiments, or the overwhelming effect of pragmatic salience on the rates of non-subject-control responses (see the next section).

Gerard et al. further suggest that in act-out experiments, children need to hold the order of events in memory while they resolve the control dependency, again a potential source of processing load. This claim is further defended in Gerard 2019. Yet it is known that 3- to 5-year-old children have no difficulty in understanding the meaning of the temporal subordinators *before* and *after* (a point established independently, and also in the very same act-out experiments, as a control condition). Why would a cumulative effect arise between the temporal relation and the control relation? Perhaps it does, but one would like to see independent evidence for interference between these two quite different conceptual relations.

Notably, Gerard (2019) found that eliminating event ordering from the task somewhat increased adultlike responses, but nonadultlike responses—specifically, object control—were still nonnegligible, occurring 25% of the time. This suggests a deeper cause than task-related processing load. Indeed, temporal ordering of events in itself is not likely to be a crucial factor, as the way children act out *simultaneous* adjuncts, headed by *when* (Lust et al. 1986, Goodluck 2001) and *while* (Adler 2006), is not discernibly different from the way they act out those headed by *before* and *after*.[3] Gerard (2019) suggests that the difficulty may arise simply from representing multiple events, whether simultaneous or not. Yet representing multiple events is a component of all the tasks involving control between main and embedded clauses, regardless of specific design, including coloring, and including *complement* control, which children largely master by the age of 3 to 5. That aspect alone does not single out act-out tasks in adjunct control as being inordinately difficult. I conclude that the increased rates of object control in children's performance reflect a genuine lacuna in children's linguistic *competence*.[4]

Next, consider extrasentential control. As mentioned above, this option has rarely been tested directly in children. Even when pragmatic salience of potential controllers has been manipulated as an experimental variable, the characters whose salience was manipulated were normally the matrix subject or object, not external antecedents (though see Janke 2018a for an exception). In Lust et al.'s (1986) study (101 children, 3;1–7;11, act-out task), a mere 2.5% of the children's responses picked out an extrasentential controller. However, the authors correctly point out that "the most natural response in the act-out task as administered here appears to be not to generate spontaneous reference to an additional doll not named in the stimulus sentence, especially if one or more of the named dolls are possible referents grammatically" (1986:274–275n7). Interestingly, though, they found that even within this narrow dataset, extrasentential control was more frequent with preposed adjuncts than with final adjuncts. I return to the significance of this finding below.

A very different picture emerged in a study by Goodluck (1987) (12 5-year-olds, 12 6-year-olds, act-out task). Goodluck tested examples like the following.

(239) a. After jumping quickly over the fence, the pirate is very scared.
       b. The pirate hits the engineer after jumping up and down.

Of the 5-year-olds, 62.5% selected extrasentential control in preposed adjuncts, and of the 6-year-olds, no less than 94.5% did so. Final adjuncts elicited much less extrasentential control: 7% at 5 years and 4.17% at 6 years.

Clearly, NOC is a robust option for these children, much more than it is for adults (regrettably not tested in this study). Although the experimental setup contained dolls unmentioned in the test sentences, they were not pragmatically cued in any way. Still, they comprised the majority of control choices for preposed adjuncts, and a nonnegligible minority for final adjuncts. It is very unlikely that an adult population would exhibit a similar response profile.

Goodluck (1987) conducted a smaller follow-up experiment to find out what factors facilitated NOC in the first study. It turned out that the choice of a nonaction main predicate (like *be scared*), the absence of a matrix object, and the predominance of optional coreference stimuli (with pronominal subjects) in the test set were all relevant factors. When transitive action predicates were tested and the number of optional coreference stimuli was reduced, extrasentential control dropped to zero. Goodluck concluded that children's responses to adjunct control stimuli are highly sensitive to the experimental setup and the context in which stimuli are presented. Surely this conclusion holds in general of the findings in the acquisition literature on adjunct control. The upshot for the present investigation is somewhat different, however: it is only in virtue of harboring a NOC derivation that temporal adjuncts are capable of displaying this context sensitivity. Complement control (often compared with adjunct control in the relevant studies) is systematically immune to these effects. Curiously, this theoretical point is usually missed, with adjuncts being strictly analyzed under OC despite their context sensitivity.

Extrasentential control in final adjuncts has also been documented in 3- to 5-year-old children. Of the 20 children who took part in McDaniel, Cairns, and Hsu's (1991) grammaticality judgment task, 5 indicated that anyone could be performing the action described in a final adjunct.[5] Cairns et al. (1994) later performed a longitudinal study using both act-out and grammaticality judgment methodology. The 15 children who took part (3;10–4;11 at the beginning of the study) were tested three times, at 3-month intervals. Of these, 6 allowed extrasentential control in final adjuncts throughout the experiment, and 3 more allowed it at the first session only.[6]

In Broihier and Wexler's (1995) study (14 children, 3;10–5;5, TVJT), 6 out of 14 children exhibited the adult pattern. Each of the remaining 8 children accepted either subject, object, or extrasentential control, to varying degrees. On average, extrasentential control was accepted 57% of the time. Once again, these NOC rates clearly exceed what adults (or indeed, the other 6 children in the experiment) would accept.

Finally, Adler (2006) (30 children, TVJT) studied the change in extrasentential control across three groups of 10 children, mean ages 3;7, 4;5, and 5;5.

She found that adultlike responses increased continuously with age: for example, 35% (youngest group), 20% (middle group), and 5% (oldest group) acceptance of extrasentential control with *before*-adjuncts. Similar patterns resulted with *after*-adjuncts and *while*-adjuncts.[7]

To summarize the acquisition findings, two discrepancies between adult and child grammars stand out.

(240) In developing their grammar of adjunct control, children (roughly between the ages of 3 and 5) pass through a stage in which
    a. Object control is accepted significantly more than in the adult grammar, and
    b. Extrasentential control is accepted significantly more than in the adult grammar.

These two discrepancies form the explananda in the realm of adjunct control acquisition. Below I consider how they are addressed by the main theoretical proposals in this area, and eventually present my own account.

I should mention that the empirical description in (240) is not uncontested. In particular, Janke (2018b), using a picture selection methodology, found that children and adults tolerate object control equally and that neither population accepts extrasentential control. Let us look at these findings.

In Janke's first experiment (76 children between 6 and 11, and 15 adults), participants were asked to select one of two pictures that matched the interpretation of sentences with adjunct control (each picture depicted the main action and the embedded action). The sentences were presented either in isolation (241a), following a weak pragmatic lead-in to the object's referent (241b), or following a strong one (241c).

(241) a. Harry tapped Hermione while feeding the owl.
    b. Let me tell you something about Hermione. Harry tapped Hermione while feeding the owl.
    c. Hermione is looking after the birds. Hermione takes out the food. Harry tapped Hermione while feeding the owl.

It was found that even without a pragmatic lead-in, children and adults occasionally select object control (11.1% and 13.4%, respectively), and with a weak one adults do so to a greater extent (9.6% and 18.9%, respectively). A strong pragmatic lead-in drastically increased object control rates to 40.6% (children) and 51.1% (adults), replicating the pattern reported for adults in Janke and Bailey 2017 (see (7)). Janke found no significant difference in the tolerance of children and adults to object control in temporal adjuncts, certainly not in the direction of children having greater tolerance.

However, absence of evidence is not evidence of absence. Importantly, the children studied by Janke (6–11 years old) are much older than those who took part in the studies surveyed above (usually ranging between 3;0 and 5;6 years). In fact, according to most of these studies, by age 6 children converge on the adult grammar of adjunct control. Hence, the finding that the older children do not really differ from adults is anything but surprising. Rather, the novelty in Janke's study is the finding that object control in temporal adjuncts is a robust phenomenon even in the standard adult grammar, and is crucially tied to topicality. This point has been extensively discussed in section 11.3, where I also provided arguments against Janke's OC analysis of object control in temporal adjuncts and in favor of the NOC analysis.

Janke's (2018b) second experiment (43 children, 7;3–11;2; 14 adults) challenges (240b). In that experiment, strong pragmatic cueing was directed toward an extrasentential antecedent, as in (242).

(242) Ron is preparing for a competition. Ron practices in the air. Hermione held the balloon while flying the broom.

Unlike in the first experiment, here the pragmatic lead-in had no effect. Children selected subject control between 96% and 99% of the time, and adults did so 100% of the time. Janke concludes that "temporal adjunct control is not a NOC relation" (p. 383). But this conclusion is premature in light of the methodological concerns raised above about act-out and forced (picture) selection designs. When presented with two potential interpretations (or depictions thereof) for a sentence, local subject control vs. extrasentential control, speakers select the one they *prefer*; they do not thereby imply that the alternative interpretation is *excluded*. The preference for local human subject control is overwhelming, for reasons unpacked in section 11.4 (see table (230)), explaining these results. In addition, unlike in the previous experiments the matrix object is not a semantically suitable controller in examples like (242), lowering the competition with the subject.

Furthermore, the older age of the children in Janke's study may well place them beyond the point at which the discrepancy in (240b) is detectable. Just as they are similar to adults with respect to object control into adjuncts, they are similar to adults in their tolerance for extrasentential control (namely, hardly tolerant). This finding does not impinge in any way on the robust manifestation of extrasentential control documented in younger children (Goodluck 1987, McDaniel, Cairns, and Hsu 1991, Cairns et al. 1994, Broihier and Wexler 1995, Adler 2006).

12.2 NOC Properties in the Child Data

Janke (2018b) follows Janke and Bailey (2017) in analyzing object control into temporal adjuncts as a species of OC, obtained under c-command in a strictly right-branching VP-structure. In section 11.3, I presented two arguments against this analysis and in favor of a NOC analysis, based on adjunct stranding under VP-ellipsis and on control by prepositional objects. Do the child data provide evidence to support this view?

In fact, object control of adjuncts in children displays a number of characteristic NOC properties, emerging from the large body of work on the topic. I will mention three such properties.

First and foremost is the systematic observation that the availability of object control readings is keyed to the topicality of the object. The more salient the referent of the object in the preceding context, the more likely it is to be selected (or allowed) as a controller for the adjunct. This finding has been replicated through different methodologies (Lust et al. 1986, Cairns et al. 1995, Janke and Bailey 2017, Janke 2018b); an important observation is that subject PRO and subject pronouns in parallel adjunct environments (differing only in finiteness) display a similar pattern of sensitivity to pragmatic salience (Lust et al. 1986, Cairns et al. 1995). Given that the reference of the relevant pronouns is resolved by discourse mechanisms like topic linking, it is reasonable to conclude that a similar process underlies the resolution of object-controlled PRO in temporal adjuncts. By contrast, as these studies have repeatedly shown, the reference of OC PRO in complements is insensitive to these discourse properties.

As discussed in section 11.3, it is extremely unusual for a syntactic dependency to be licensed or ruled out on the basis of a notion like topicality, not to mention the latter's gradient character, which would require the licensing itself to be correspondingly gradient. It is also striking that no discourse effects are reported for local subject control, which is standardly taken to be the default. A simple distinction in type—syntactic OC for subject control, pragmatic NOC for object control—explains this asymmetry with no further ado.

A second finding of the acquisition literature that supports the NOC analysis of object control is that it is found more frequently in preposed adjuncts than in final ones. Lust et al. (1986) found that while preposed adjuncts yield fewer subject control choices than final ones, the opposite holds of object control choice: this is *enhanced* in preposed adjuncts. Recall that it is a general feature of alternating OC/NOC adjuncts that they are more tolerant of NOC in clause-initial than in clause-final position (Kortmann 1991, Williams 1992, Kawasaki 1993, Landau 2013, Green 2018).

At the end of section 6.3.2, I proposed that the relative ease of NOC in this position is somewhat of an illusion. NOC itself is just as grammatical in clause-final position. It is OC by the subject that is less accessible in the clause-initial position, the reason being the lack of surface c-command between the subject and the adjunct; as a result, the NOC derivation receives higher processing resources and is perceived as more accessible. The adult grammar overcomes the processing problem with the OC derivation by LF movement of the subject and the mechanism of "suspended saturation" (see (136)). Moreover, I suggested that the derivational complexity of suspended saturation might be beyond the computational resources of young children. This would leave them with only a NOC derivation, resulting in even higher rates of non-local-subject control.[8] These higher rates are revealed both in object control into preposed adjuncts, as shown above, and in extrasentential control, climbing above 90% in the latter case (Goodluck 1987). This co-patterning is yet another strong indication that object control into temporal adjuncts falls together with NOC.

The third finding of the acquisition literature that supports the NOC analysis of object control concerns the little-discussed topic of control by preposi-tional objects. Before discussing these data, I will present my own account of children's performance on adjunct control; then it will be clear why they con-tribute to the NOC analysis.

12.3   Existing Grammatical Accounts

Now that the empirical picture is clarified, we can proceed to the theoretical account of children's performance on adjunct control. Before presenting my own account, I will briefly introduce the three main existing *grammatical* approaches.[9] These approaches have been extensively discussed and evaluated in the past, so I will limit myself to the core ideas, referring to problematic aspects when necessary. I will discuss the third approach ("nominalization") more extensively, as its predictions are closest to those of my approach, and as it seems superior to its predecessors.

Overall, it should be borne in mind that these proposals have been formu-lated and developed against the backdrop of an exaggerated perception of the discrepancies between the child and adult data. Given our current state of knowledge, it will be seen that these accounts are not so much falsified as sim-ply unnecessary.

Account 1: Variable attachment hypothesis (Goodluck 1981, Hsu, Cairns, and Fiengo 1985, Hsu et al. 1989, Janke 2017, 2018a, Janke and Bailey 2017, Janke and Perovic 2017). On this account, object control into temporal adjuncts is an instance of OC just as subject control is. The two options arise from the possibility of attaching the adjunct low in the VP or at the S level. The Minimal Distance Principle (MDP) selects the closest c-commanding DP as controller—object or subject, respectively. In the 1980s accounts, it was assumed that before they apply the MDP, children rely on strategies—"first NP" (leading to strict subject control) and then "closest NP" (leading to strict object control, including prepositional objects). When the MDP activates, children discard prepositional objects as controllers (for lack of c-command). Then, for a while, children alternate between subject and direct object control, reflecting variable attachment of the adjunct. Finally, they select high attachment and converge on the adult grammar (strict subject control). In the more recent incarnation of this account by Janke and her colleagues, low attachment is an option available to adults and children alike, and is only chosen under strong pragmatic pressure (see (211)).

The main empirical problem with this account is the characterization of object control into temporal adjuncts as OC—against all the evidence presented here that it is genuinely NOC. The main theoretical problem in the early versions is the radical discrepancies posited between child and adult grammars, violating the Continuity Hypothesis; in addition, it is not explained how and why the child shifts from one stage to the next—from a linear strategy to a c-command one, and from variable attachment to S-attachment only (for pertinent discussion, see Wexler 1992, Broihier and Wexler 1995).

Account 2: Coordination + Variable attachment hypothesis (McDaniel and Carins 1990, McDaniel, Cairns, and Hsu 1991, Cairns et al. 1994, Adler 2006). This account supplements the previous one with an initial stage in which the adjunct is coordinated with, rather than subordinated to, the main clause; presumably, at this early stage the child has yet to learn the lexical properties of prepositions like *before/after* that dictate a subordination analysis. Because the coordinated "adjunct" is not c-commanded by the "main" clause, the MDP fails to apply and NOC (including extrasentential control) results; different strategies may then favor subject or object control, for different children. After subordination is mastered, the rest of the development proceeds as in Account 1.

While object control in the initial, coordination stage is analyzed as NOC, similarly to the present account, it is later analyzed as OC into a low-attached adjunct; the empirical objections to Account 1 then carry over. Theoretically, an even greater discrepancy is assumed between the child and adult grammars, as the child first misanalyzes all subordinated adjuncts as coordinated clauses. Yet all the pertinent experiments independently test children's semantic knowledge of the relevant temporal prepositions. It is far from clear how this knowledge can be represented in coordination rather than subordination.

In addition, in the relevant experiments children provided similar judgments on preposed nonfinite and finite adjuncts (Lust et al. 1986, Goodluck 1987), indicating that their grammar generates such constructions; yet on the conjunction analysis, such adjuncts should be excluded, as conjuncts cannot be preposed by themselves (*_And Mary danced, John sang_). See Wexler 1992 for further critical comments.

Account 3: Nominalization (Carlson 1990, Wexler 1992, Broihier and Wexler 1995, Goodluck 1998, 2001). On this account, children do not have PRO available until a certain maturational stage. To make sense of nonfinite adjuncts before this point, children analyze them as nominalizations, being "fooled" by the morphological ambiguity of the English gerund. An even later stage introduces a null temporal operator that is needed to fully represent temporal adjuncts as adults do. Throughout the time that children employ the nominalization analysis, NOC is allowed (consistent with various strategies) because nominalizations do not project a syntactic PRO that can be controlled.

Empirically, this account comes closest to the present proposal in grouping all of children's "nonstandard" productions and interpretations of adjunct control under NOC. It is also possible that it generates interpretations that are indistinguishable from characteristic NOC interpretations with PRO, although this is less obvious (on this subtle issue, see Landau 2013:208–213). Yet the nominalization analysis raises a number of problems.

First, Wexler's (1992) syntactic assumptions concerning the adult grammar are untenable. PRO is said to be unavailable due to a "Proto Case Filter" that rules out any NP without case. The assumption is that PRO lacks case in the adult grammar, but this is not true (Landau 2006 and references therein). In addition, Wexler argues that temporal adjuncts are constructed with a null temporal operator, also assumed to be unavailable to children. Yet that operator cannot be part of nonfinite adjuncts even in the adult grammar, as these fail to exhibit its signature embedded reading (_John kissed Mary before he said he did_ vs. _John kissed Mary before saying he did_; see Geis 1970, Larson 1987). Wexler (1992:290n30) recognizes this problem but does not solve it. Further problems with the operator-based account are discussed in Adler 2006:117. In general, on the plausible view that PRO is just an instance of a minimal pronoun (Herbeck 2015, Landau 2015, McFadden and Sundaresan 2018), assuming its late maturation would entail the undesired consequence that other instances of minimal pronouns (bound pronouns, reflexives, resumptive pronouns, and even _pro_) should mature late.

Second, the nominalization analysis cannot extend to the temporal subordinators *when* and *while*, although they exhibit exactly the same pattern of late acquisition, with overacceptance of NOC, as *before* and *after* do (Lust et al. 1986, Goodluck 2001, Janke and Perovic 2017, Janke 2018b). A nominal complement violates the c-selectional requirements of the former, requirements already known to children at the relevant age (Sellar 1999).

(243) a. *John kissed Mary when/while the dance.
      b. John kissed Mary before/after the dance.

One would be forced to assume that only in the context of gerunds do children exceptionally allow *when/while* to select a nominal. Indeed, this is just what Goodluck (2001:506) assumes for *when*, concluding that "the child actively form[s] structural hypotheses about the input in a manner that is not narrowly guided by knowledge of the lexicon of the language." This strikes me as a defeatist position for acquisition research, best avoided if possible.[10]

Third, the nominalization analysis does not easily extend to infinitival adjuncts, for their morphological shape cannot be mistaken for a noun. The RatC subordinator *in order* does not select a nominal; furthermore, no null operator is involved in generating the adjunct. Thus, none of the motivating ingredients of nominalizations are present in this case. Nonetheless, children display similar, if not more extreme, delay effects in mastering RatC control (Hsu, Cairns, and Fiengo 1985, McDaniel and Cairns 1990, Cairns et al. 1994).

The nominalization analysis does account for one challenging finding: children accept an agentive reading of a *by*-phrase inside an active intransitive adjunct (244a–b), even though adults accept that reading only in an overtly marked nominal adjunct (244c) (adults interpret the *by*-phrases in (244a–b) as locative). This would follow if children also analyze the adjuncts in (244a–b) as nominal (Goodluck 2001; 20 children, 4–6 years old, act-out).

(244) a. Snowy pushes Leo before dancing by Ellie.
      b. Snowy pushes Leo when dancing by Ellie.
      c. Snowy pushes Leo before some dancing by Ellie.

However, a default child preference for interpreting *by*-phrases as agentive (Fox and Grodzinsky 1998) may account for this pattern. In fact, Goodluck (2001) must have recourse to this preference anyway, to explain why children *favor* the agentive readings over the locative ones in (244a–c) (78%, 68%, and 67% agentive readings, respectively). This preference may lead to "local analysis" that disregards thematic requirements of the bigger structure; it also explains Goodluck's striking finding (2001:502n14) that some children even acted out an agentive construal of the *by*-phrase inside an active complement

(*Leo tells Ellie to jump by Snowy*); how knowledge of object control is compatible with this interpretation is not clear.

Goodluck (2001:507n18) argues against this alternative explanation, pointing out that the children did well in the pretest on the locative meaning of *by*-phrases. But the pretest items were unambiguous simple clauses with overt subjects (e.g., *Elli jumps by Snowy*), and even there the children only displayed 74% success. The inherent weakness of act-out results is the impossibility of distinguishing knowledge from preference. Goodluck may be right in claiming that children *know* both uses of *by*-phrases; nevertheless, children *act* in accordance with their preferences, and when faced with a control adjunct, where the agent is not overtly expressed, they might simply assign the agent role to an overt *by*-phrase by default.

It would be useful to further probe children's responses to stimuli like (244a–b) at ages 3–6. It may turn out that these responses reflect extragrammatical strategies, rather than nonadultlike syntactic analysis. I leave this issue for future research.[11]

12.4 The Proposal: Impoverished Pragmatic Knowledge

To account for the acquisition data, I propose that children overapply NOC in temporal adjuncts. More precisely, they admit NOC interpretations that in the adult grammar are suppressed by the co-presence of a dominant, distinct OC reading. Framing the issue in these competition-based terms will prove highly beneficial. Specifically, as stated in (240) and repeated here, two discrepancies between adult and child grammars stand out.

(245) In developing their grammar of adjunct control, children (roughly between the ages of 3 and 5) pass through a stage in which
    a. Object control is accepted significantly more than in the adult grammar, and
    b. Extrasentential control is accepted significantly more than in the adult grammar.

It is noteworthy that quite a few of the earlier studies that *officially* took adjunct control to be OC, in practice recognized (often in footnotes) that adults also accept, to varying degrees, nonlocal-subject control in these adjuncts. Thus, these authors sensed that the gap between children and adults is, in fact, much smaller than what the standard theory at the time authorized.

For example, Lust et al. (1986:273) note that absolutive adjuncts do not obey strict OC, and later observe the same for temporal adjuncts: "Exceptions to the claim of obligatory control by main clause subject have been noted . . .

for example, *When walking down the street, it started to rain.* Another example is *After explaining it, they got the idea that I ordered the department heads not to talk*" (1986:274n4). Goodluck (1987:261) observes that extrasentential control is "perhaps not surprising, or a large deviation from the adult competence, given that adults permit external reference for temporals in (marginally-grammatical) sentences where there is no suitable referent for the temporal subject inside the sentence (as in, e.g., *After skiing quickly, hot chocolate tastes good*)." This description is largely true, although too restrictive, since extrasentential control is occasionally allowed even across a suitable sentence-internal referent (see below).

McDaniel and Cairns (1990:324n1) mention that some adults also accept either subject or object control into temporal adjuncts (just like children in their "mixed" stage). Cairns et al. (1991:319) report that some adults accept control by a prepositional object (as in *The lion stands near the elephant before climbing up the steps*); I return below to the relevant child data regarding this construction. In a revealing footnote (1991:321n17), Cairns et al. then struggle to explain how it is possible for some adults, presumably possessing a stable grammar, to exhibit subject-or-object control, which, according to their analysis, only arises in children as a transitory stage between "object grammar" and "subject grammar." The puzzle is resolved on the present account, where both children and adults possess a single, stable grammar, in which certain adjuncts alternate between OC and NOC; the difference lies solely in what NOC amounts to (see below).

Indeed, the intuition that children and adults employ the *same* grammar of adjunct control, and that children simply broaden the purview of NOC, has been made explicit at least once in the past, in Goodluck 1987:261: "Whatever rules and/or structures are available to the adult in interpreting such sentences may be used more widely by the child and enter into the external reference responses children gave to temporals." Goodluck and Behne (1992) proposed that children attach the adjunct correctly but, unlike adults, allow NOC in this configuration. Although they offered no further analysis, I believe this is just the right idea (or almost right—since adults too enjoy the NOC option), but Goodluck abandoned it in later works (in favor of the nominalization analysis). It is instructive to see why:

There is a conflict between assuming that there is an arbitrarily interpreted PRO as the subject of the adjunct clause, and correct knowledge of attachment of the adjunct to the main clause IP node (i.e., within the c-command domain of the subject). It is generally assumed that PRO_{arb} in adult grammars is characterized by the absence in the sentence of any c-commanding NP that could act as a controller, which will not be the case if children know the correct attachment of the adjunct clause. (Goodluck 2001:497).

The key assumption here is that c-command by the matrix subject inexorably leads to OC by that subject. Because there is independent evidence that children do not err in the attachment height, NOC (or PRO_{arb}) cannot be licensed.

But we now know that the key assumption is false: NOC *does* arise under a c-commanding subject; see the evidence in (173), (174), and (179). The reason that c-command by the subject is not decisive is that the source of NOC is different: it is the semantic type of the adjunct. A propositional adjunct will license NOC even when c-commanded by the subject, simply because it is already saturated and does not interact with the matrix subject at all (see section 2.2). With this piece in place, there is no reason to abandon the appealing initial hypothesis: children and adults alike produce and interpret temporal adjuncts via two routes, OC and NOC. Children's adjuncts are internally structured and are externally attached exactly like adults' adjuncts are. Children differ only in the extent to which they allow NOC, as stated in (245).

We finally come to the central question: *why* do children overapply NOC in adjuncts? Recall that section 11.4 ended with the conclusion that in the adult grammar, NOC itself is somewhat dualistic: the antecedent must be either a salient topic or a salient logophoric center (see (229)). Both topicality and logophoricity are discourse-based grammatical concepts. If young children do not fully master these concepts because they take longer to develop, specifically maturing after syntactic principles are in place, then children's performance on constructions that depend on these concepts will be nonadultlike.[12]

Indeed, the late development of pragmatic knowledge is already a cornerstone of the field (see note 1 in this chapter). Yet we should look for something stronger: independent evidence that in the same age range at which children overapply NOC in adjuncts, they have not yet mastered topicality and logophoricity. Only then will the hypothesis that the adjunct data are naturally related to these pragmatic delays rest on firm grounds.

The evidence exists and is quite revealing. First, consider the acquisition of logophoricity. Studies comparing children's knowledge of syntactic reflexivity and logophoric reflexivity have consistently found a lag between them: children know that syntactic (argumental) reflexives require a local c-commanding antecedent, but for a substantial period of time they do not properly apply the pragmatic felicity conditions on logophoric reflexives (Sigurjónsdóttir and Hyams 1992, Avrutin and Cunningham 1997, Hestvik and Philip 2001, Coopmans et al. 2004, Sigurjónsdóttir 2013, Su 2017). Strikingly, just as in the adjunct control case this incomplete pragmatic knowledge is expressed as *over*acceptance of sentences and interpretations that are rejected in the adult grammar.[13]

For example, Avrutin and Cunningham (1997) have found that while children are nearly adultlike on sentences like (246a) with non-c-commanding antecedents, accepting them only 12% of the time on average, they diverge from adults on sentences like (246b), accepting them 53% of the time on average. Note that *herself* is logophoric only in (246b), where it occupies a nonargument position (Reinhart and Reuland 1993).

(246) a. [The woman near the girl$_i$] covered herself$_i$.
      b. [The woman near the girl$_i$] drew a circle around herself$_i$.

This particular finding has a very close counterpart in the acquisition of adjunct control, where children overaccept prepositional objects as controllers (see (249)): in both cases, the child's notion of "logophoric antecedent" is too coarse to exclude certain nominals that lack the qualifying properties to be appropriate binders or controllers for adults. In a similar vein, Su (2017) found that preschool children acquiring Mandarin overaccept extrasentential antecedents for the logophor *ziji* in contexts where adults confine themselves to a sentence-internal antecedent. This mirrors the increased rates of extrasentential adjunct control in children, (245b).

Regarding the acquisition of topicality, the picture is somewhat more complex, because the manifestations of this concept in the grammar are so diverse. Whether a given referent may count as a topic depends on first-person beliefs as well as the ability to incorporate the beliefs of others into one's linguistic system. Children are known to have difficulties with "nonshared assumptions," as evidenced, for example, in their overuse of definite articles (see Schaeffer and Matthewson 2005 and references therein) and null subjects at early stages (Hyams 2011, Hughes and Allen 2013, Valian 2016). In the same vein, children between 3 and 5 years of age are insensitive to first mention as an index of high accessibility when linking pronouns to discourse antecedents (Arnold, Brown-Schmidt, and Trueswell 2007), again reflecting an egocentric bias.

At the same time, it has been reported that as early as age 2;6, children know the pragmatic condition (discourse givenness) on topic fronting (De Cat 2009). Nevertheless, they overuse pronominal forms in situations where the selected topic is not uniquely identifiable by the interlocutor, suggesting that their pragmatic system is still more egocentric than the adult one. The source of this limitation may be their "reliance on the visual context as the main domain of reference," as De Cat (2011:853) proposes; or it may be something else.

It is noteworthy that the extensive literature on the acquisition of information structure reveals much less consistency and agreement than the literature on the acquisition of logophoricity (see Dimroth and Narasimhan 2012 and Höhle, Berger, and Sauermann 2016 for overviews). This is not surprising, in a sense, given the manifold ways in which information structure interacts with the grammar. From the present perspective, it is possible to relate the gradual development of NOC in adjunct control to the gradual development of topic-sensitive grammatical devices. However, the relation will inevitably remain loose until research offers a sharper understanding of the precise features of topicality that young children do not fully master, and how these features play out both in adjunct control and outside of it.

One appealing possibility, suggested by Adler (2006:156), is that children fail to distinguish between the discourse-level topic and the sentence-level topic. For adults, the two need not converge. For example, when I say *Mary's husband is seriously ill. She bought some pills today*, the topic of this discourse is Mary's husband, or maybe his illness, but the topic of the second sentence is Mary; hence, a pronominal subject is licensed. Adler suggests that children blur this distinction, perhaps by equating the sentence-level topic with the discourse-level one, or by failing to update the current sentence-level topic for each incoming sentence.[14] The result is that their pool of "topic-worthy" potential antecedents is larger than the adult pool, which is restricted to the sentence-level topic. This would indeed account for the broader range of NOC interpretations allowed by children. Because the distinction between sentence-level and discourse-level topics is not expressed morphologically or syntactically, and relies purely on subtle understanding of the dynamics of communicative situations, it is not available to children at the outset and takes time to mature.

If children do not fully or even partially master the concepts of topicality and logophoricity by age 5, how would their production and comprehension of adjunct control constructions be affected? By assumption, their core grammar is adultlike. This means that they know that temporal subordinators select either predicative or propositional nonfinite clauses; they know that the former yields OC and the latter NOC; and they know the attachment sites necessary for these adjuncts to be properly composed and interpreted. What they lack, however, is a reliable "monitor" of [top] and [log] levels for any given antecedent. These specifications act as filters on potential antecedents; in their absence, the filters are gone and any nominal, in principle, may qualify as a NOC antecedent.

To visualize the difference between adults and children, let us evaluate the "worthiness" of each type of controller for each group, using the processing model in (230). Because all the child data involve human (or humanized) characters, I leave out the case of inanimate control.[15]

(247) *Adults: Controller-worthiness scale*

	Local [+human] subject	Local [+human] object	Nonlocal [+human] DP
OC-worthy	+	–	–
NOC-worthy: [log]	+	[+**log**]: + (weak) [–**log**]: –	[+**log**]: + (weak) [–**log**]: –
NOC-worthy: [top]	+	[+**top**]: + (weak) [–**top**]: –	[+**top**]: + (weak) [–**top**]: –

A local human subject is the most strongly favored controller, being selected under OC, and being an optimal NOC controller thanks to its high topicality (by default) and logophoric perspective. Other nominals may only control via NOC, and only if they reach some minimal level of salience on either the topicality or the logophoricity scale (where "minimal" is understood very loosely to be a subjective, context-sensitive measure). A DP with no status on these scales does not stand a chance against the local human subject—hence the overwhelming preference for this choice in the adult grammar.

In young children, the internal computation is simplified. The NOC measures are not developed yet. Without them, NOC is unrestricted: any antecedent may provide reference for the free variable (*pro*) at the edge of the propositional adjunct, and children may resort to any strategy whatsoever to assist them in fixing that reference.

(248) *Children (ages 3–5): Controller-worthiness scale*

	Local [+human] subject	Local [+human] object	Nonlocal [+human] DP
OC-worthy	+	–	–
NOC-worthy	+/–	+/–	+/–

Table (248) represents the extreme condition of a child completely uninformed about NOC measures. This is of course a very rare, perhaps unattested scenario, but it is useful as a theoretical starting point to which subsequent development can be compared. Actual children in actual linguistic situations may assign different ranks of [top] and [log] to different nominals. In fact, because these concepts are underdeveloped, nonadult behavior is expected. For example, a child may take the object to be more topical than the subject, or a contextual antecedent more salient in logophoric status than the subject, without any explicit indication (of the sort required by adults) that this is so. These choices provide much opportunity for NOC to emerge in the child data in situations where OC would suppress it for adults; the local human subject would be no more worthy overall than the alternatives. This is, then, how the child-adult asymmetries in (245) arise.[16]

Notice that the grammatical "vacuum" under the NOC possibility invites processing *strategies* to step in; for example, "first DP" or "closest DP" will yield subject and object control, respectively, both as instances of NOC, as already suggested in some of the works cited above. Similarly, children's processing *limitations* may produce nonrandom biases.

One such limitation, especially pronounced in children, is similarity-based interference. Gerard et al. (2017) have shown that when the matrix subject and object match in features, the rate of subject control choices made by children (3;11–5;3 years) is lower than when they mismatch: 75% → 60% for gender, 76% → 64% for number. They explain this as a special case of similarity-based interference, in which a nongrammatical intervener (the matrix object) is mistakenly selected as the antecedent of a target (PRO) instead of the grammatical antecedent (the matrix subject) when the two are "too similar" for the processor to keep apart. Gerard et al. suggest that "at high decay rates, the structural information about the main clause may no longer be available by the time that the retrieval mechanism is deployed in the adjunct clause, especially if children are less competent than adults at encoding the structural information in the first place" (2017:11).

Importantly, this processing effect cannot wholly replace a grammar-based account. Even in the mismatch condition, children's rates of subject control responses were significantly lower than adults'.[17] On the present account, this is not surprising, because a local human subject does not enjoy any decisive advantage as a NOC antecedent for children as it does for adults—*regardless* of its (dis)similarity to the object in terms of features. In other words, the logic of children's performance has two steps: first, due to immature pragmatic knowledge, subject control is *less* favored in children than in adults; second, due to processing limitations, object control is (sometimes, in match conditions) *more* favored in children than adults. The latter ingredient complements the former in a full model of performance.

The proposed pragmatic account naturally accommodates the significant variability among children and across experiments, a point often noted but not really explained by any of the syntactic approaches. Both topicality and logophoricity are gradient notions (unlike high/low attachment or nominal-ization). The accessibility of a given nominal as a controller reflects its status on both scales—an additive effect that makes judgments on NOC so variable. While previous accounts like Goodluck and Behne's (1992), Wexler's (1992), Broihier and Wexler's (1995), and Goodluck's (1998, 2001) all attribute the observed variability to absence of control, they offer no positive analytic tools for tracking the sources of this variability. By using the *same* pragmatic con-cepts that underlie the adult competence as an explanation for children's "deviations," the present analysis places both children's and adults' compe-tence on the same continuous plane and avoids the unpleasant need to explain how the child "recovers" from "incorrect" grammatical analyses.

It is important to keep in mind that children between 3 and 5 years old entertain two derivational routes in adjunct control—OC or NOC—just like adults. The only difference lies how they calibrate these two options. Evi-dence for the fact that children do not simply treat adjunct control as NOC is the recurring finding that by and large, they prefer local subject control to any other option. Another piece of evidence is the clear difference between their responses to OC/NOC "hybrid" constructions, like adjuncts, and their responses to pure NOC constructions, like clausal subjects. These were directly compared by Adler (2006) (30 children, 3–6 years, TVJT), who found that extrasentential control was accepted even more liberally in gerundive subjects. Importantly, every child who was nonadultlike in responding to temporal adjuncts was nonadultlike in responding to gerundive subjects, but not vice versa; two-thirds of the children reached adult level in responding to adjuncts before reaching it in responding to subjects. This finding immediately follows from the fact that responses to the temporal adjunct conditions are "mixes" of OC and NOC, while responses to the gerundive subject conditions are just NOC. Therefore, the delay in the latter is more pronounced.

As the child grammar develops, the concepts of topicality and logophoricity are fleshed out. Evidence for growing sensitivity to topicality was discussed above (see Lust et al. 1986, Cairns et al. 1995; and regarding older children, see Janke and Perovic 2017, Janke 2018b). Is there evidence for children's increasing sensitivity to logophoric status?

The answer is yes. The final set of data in this chapter addresses this issue. It involves control by prepositional objects, an option often ignored or simply left unanalyzed, whereas in fact its internal structure is far from random and lends itself to an analysis in the present terms.

Consider (249a–c), where the matrix clause contains a locative PP, a simple PP, and a *by*-phrase PP, respectively.

(249) a. The lion jumps over the bear after climbing up the ladder.
      b. The lion pushes on the bear after climbing up the ladder.
      c. Daisy is hit by Pluto before doing some reading.

Hsu, Cairns, and Fiengo (1985) found considerable rates of prepositional object control (POC) in these cases: on average, 34% for type (249a), 47% for type (249b), and 30% for type (249c). These averages, however, conceal a great difference between the youngest children (at 3;2), where POC is generally at its peak, and the oldest ones (at 8;3), where it is very low. Still, POC remained a thorny problem for Hsu, Cairns, and Fiengo, since they analyzed the "object control stage" in terms of OC under c-command. Prepositional objects do not c-command the adjunct PRO, and thus POC should never reach such high rates, even among children. Although subject control was preferred with PP objects more than it was with direct objects, it was far from exclusive; in fact, until age 6;6, children *favored* POC over subject control in sentences of type (249b).

Control by the passive *by*-phrase was further studied in Goodluck and Behne 1992 (13 4-year-olds, 16 5-year-olds, and 13 6-year-olds; act-out). On average, 55% of children's choices displayed *by*-phrase control (and the rest, subject control), with the 6-year-olds making this choice at a higher rate (71%) than the 4- and 5-year-olds (48% and 52%, respectively). Goodluck and Behne describe these responses as "errors," but evidently they are not, since even adults frequently accept adjunct control by the implicit passive agent, as documented throughout chapter 5. Goodluck (1998) (24 children, 4–5 years, act-out) found similar rates of *by*-phrase control (44% and 57%, depending on whether passive sentences were included in the training set or not).

McDaniel, Cairns, and Hsu (1991) report some apparently confusing results with POC. They tested four children (4;1–4;10 years, judgment task) on sentences (250a–b).

(250) a. The lion stands near the elephant before climbing up the steps.
      b. Grover gives a sponge to Bert before falling into the water.

All four children accepted POC (by *Bert*) in (250b) but only one accepted POC (by *the elephant*) in (250a). The authors observe that some adult participants also accepted these sentences under the POC reading. Finally, they point out that completely discarding the c-command condition to allow POC here will overgenerate possessor control (as in *Grover squeezed Bert's sponge before jumping over the gate*), which no adult or child appears to accept. They leave these data as an open problem.

How can we make sense of this array of findings? Starting from the assumption that POC is simply NOC, we are led to trace the subtle empirical distinctions to the relative strength of the NOC components: topicality and logophoricity. The former does not seem relevant; there is no reason to believe that the prepositions *on*, *near*, *by*, and *to* register different degrees of topicality on their objects. Logophoricity, however, seems much more relevant. How prominent and integrated into the event the mental perspective of a participant denoted by some prepositional object is, crucially depends on the semantics of the preposition. Consider the following scale as a first approximation.

(251) *Logophoric scale of semantic roles*
      agent ≫ experiencer ≫ addressee ≫ recipient ≫ theme ≫ location

Agents are the prototypical logophoric centers in virtue of harboring both intentionality and the most prominent mental perspective over the event. Note that these are purely conceptual properties, holding equally of subject agents and *by*-phrase agents. Next come experiencers, whose mental perspective is deprived of intentionality. Following them are addressees (= recipients of mental content) and recipients of physical objects. The former are more prominent precisely because they acquire the mental content delivered by the agent and thus assume their own mental perspective over the event. Theme and location follow, with the theme being somewhat more prominent simply because it is necessarily involved in the agent's actions and intentions, while the location is incidental.

This scale provides an approximate fit to the POC data reported above. In most studies, the highest rates of POC were indeed found with *by*-phrase agents (249c); recipient POC (250b) was more acceptable than theme POC (249b). The lowest rates were found with locative POC (249c)/(250a). Recall that in the presence of inanimate subjects, even adults accept POC, as shown in (215), repeated here.

(252) a. Sometimes it snowed on us while camping at Trout Camp.
      b. The welcome drinks were sent to us while waiting for the check-in.

The outstanding difference between children and adults is that children accept POC to a much greater extent. In particular, they also accept it in the presence of a human local subject. The reason is that (at the relevant stage) they still grapple with the intricacies of the scale of logophoricity. Although they often rank agents above goals and themes on that scale, they fail to do so as systematically as adults do; they will have achieved adult level only when they have fully internalized the dynamics of shifting perspectives in discourse. Thus, POC may coexist with subject control, just as object control does, for as long as children enrich and calibrate their pragmatic knowledge, until it reaches the adult level of sophistication.

The present account, which locates children's nonadultlike performance on adjunct control in their impoverished pragmatic knowledge, makes specific predictions for future experimental work. On this account, we expect to find a tight correlation between individual children's level of pragmatic development and their performance on adjunct control. More specifically, it should be possible to determine, by independent measures, how well a child masters the notions of topicality and logophoricity, and then to check how well these two index the child's accuracy in adjunct control.

An interesting question is whether the two pragmatic concepts weigh equally in this process or whether one is more dominant than the other. Present knowledge suggests that logophoricity is less developed in young children than topicality, but this is yet to be confirmed experimentally. Of particular interest is the question of how children deal with (nonhumanized) inanimate controllers: do they process them only through OC (like adults) or do they overgeneralize NOC to them? No existing study has tested this question with children. Yet these as-yet unknown results bear important implications both for the general theory of control and for our broader understanding of the developing grammatical systems in the child's mind. Hopefully, future psycholinguistic research will address these issues and produce illuminating results.

13 Deriving the Default Status of Predicative Control

A key question raised in section 2.2, but as yet unanswered, is why s-selection appears to work asymmetrically.

(253) *S-selection in nonfinite adjuncts*

	Adjunct's head s-selects	Propositional variant
Strict OC adjuncts	Property	−
OC/NOC adjuncts	Property/Proposition	+

Whether strict NOC adjuncts exist is doubtful (see chapter 8). Assuming not, the asymmetry consists in how controlled adjuncts are mapped in the semantics: they *always* map to properties, and *sometimes* to propositions. This predicative default is also reflected in certain developmental findings, to which I turn below.

Of course, such a state of affairs is not logically necessary—hence an interesting design feature of language, if true. Grammar could have worked the other way round, with a propositional denotation always being available and a property denotation being restricted. In such a hypothetical language, all controlled adjuncts would allow NOC and only a subset would also allow OC. Yet typological evidence strongly suggests that such a language does not exist, as I discuss below.

To illustrate: As noted in section 5.1, Williams (2015) and Williams and Green (2017) analyze control into RatCs as purely NOC and never syntactic. As shown there, this is false, even on the basis of Williams's own "remote control" test, but the question now is why it *must* be false—that is, why any adjunct that displays NOC must also display OC. Once again, the generalization is empirical. A strict NOC adjunct would consistently allow human controllers but would not allow inanimate ones. Moreover, the lexical entry of the P head would be simplified to s-selection of a proposition only, removing the potential ambiguity.

The question of why linguistic inventories choose predicative control as default is conspicuously reminiscent of the question of why predicative control (= OC) is selected as the default reading *in specific utterances.* They are still different, though. The former question is about s-selectional properties of P heads, applying at the level of lexical entries, whereas the latter is about processing preferences applying at the sentence level and beyond. The former is about the expressive range of the grammar; the latter is about biases *within* that range. These biases have been studied extensively in Kortmann 1991, Kawasaki 1993, Lyngfelt 1999, Adler 2006, Landau 2013, 2017, Duffley and Dion-Girardeau 2015, and Green 2018. Below I will argue that there is a deep, nonaccidental relation between the two senses or levels of "default."

Before developing an answer to the question of what makes predicative adjuncts the default, let me point out that the question is indeed pressing and real. It turns out that the facts of English reflect a general, possibly universal pattern. In an extensive typological study, sampling 110 languages from all major language families and areas, Stassen (1985) examined clausal adjunction (and coordination) in an effort to uncover implicational universals regulating the grammatical expression of these constructions. Two aspects that he documented, which are particularly relevant here, involve the option of hosting a lexical subject in the adjunct and whether or not the main clause and the adjunct share a subject (i.e., subject control).

Stassen's terminology requires some explication. "Deranking" describes using some dependent form of the predicate ("deranked" from the standard, finite form), which cannot head an independent clause. Most often, the term describes nonfinite verbs in subordinate adjuncts. "Conditional deranking" describes deranking that is conditioned by subject identity with the main clause, namely, subject control (i.e., without subject identity, some languages may not resort to nonfinite adjuncts). "Absolute" refers to an adjunct containing its own lexical subject, a situation also described as "non-identity of subjects." The latter term does *not* cover NOC, which Stassen in fact does not report at all (not surprisingly, as even in well-studied languages NOC is often overlooked).

With these clarifications in place, we can turn to Stassen's conclusions.

Languages which permit the deranking of predicates under non-identity of subjects will always allow deranking to take place in cases of subject-identity, but the converse does not hold. Alternatively, we may state as a universal fact of natural language that there are no languages in which deranking under non-identity of subjects is possible while at the same time deranking under identity of subjects is forbidden. Apparently, conditional deranking is, somehow easier to execute than deranking under non-identity of subjects. Hence, given the plausible principle that one can perform a difficult task only if one has mastered all the easier ones, it is only to be expected that the possibility of absolute (i.e., non-identity) deranking will necessarily imply the ability to achieve deranking under identity of subjects. . . . This possibility of conditional deranking under identity with a non-subject is rather marginal in natural languages. As far as I know, no language permits this type of non-subject identity on conditional deranking while at the same time forbidding conditional deranking under subject-identity. On the other hand, there are numerous languages which permit conditional deranking only if the identity relation holds between two subjects. (Stassen 1985, 85–86, 88)

Two implicational universals are stated here—both exceptionless, on Stassen's account. Using familiar terminology, they can be restated as follows.[1]

(254) *Stassen's implicational universals for nonfinite adjuncts*
U1: A lexical subject is possible in the adjunct → subject control is possible
U2: Object control is possible in the adjunct → subject control is possible

In fact, both universals follow from the PVC, repeated here.

(255) *The Propositional Variant Criterion (PVC)*
For a clausal adjunct $[P [PRO \ldots]]_W$:
a. W has no propositional variant ⇔ W is predicative ⇔ W displays strict OC
b. W has a propositional variant ⇔ W is either predicative or propositional ⇔ W displays OC or NOC

Consider U1. An adjunct with a lexical subject is propositional. By (255b), when its subject is controlled, either OC or NOC will be allowed. Both will license subject control. U2 also follows, on the crucial assumption, defended at length in chapter 11, that object control in alternating adjuncts is an instance of NOC. Once again, this implies that the adjunct is propositional and so subject control will be licensed, either via NOC or via OC. Stassen makes clear that the implications are unidirectional. Indeed, subject control in itself does not guarantee the possibility of a lexical subject in the adjunct: if the adjunct belongs to the strict OC category, being inherently predicative it will not tolerate a lexical subject. Even propositional adjuncts may resist a lexical subject when they are nonfinite, due to idiosyncratic restrictions (e.g., *while/when*-gerunds in English).

Notice, incidentally, that these results further corroborate the NOC analysis of object control in alternating adjuncts. If object control in temporal adjuncts were derived via a *different* mechanism than NOC—say, by direct predication—then the striking alignment of U1 and U2 would remain accidental. It is only in virtue of the NOC analysis that a common source can be established for the two environments: object control and "absolute" (lexical subject) both utilize the propositional variant of the adjunct.

What we would now like to uncover is the deeper logic behind the asymmetry built into the PVC, which accounts for the distribution of s-selection in table (253). At the level of s-selection, we find the following implication.

(256) For a nonfinite clause S:
P can select a propositional S → P can select a predicative S

(256) accounts both for the PVC and for Stassen's universals. When the subject of S is PRO, we obtain the implication "NOC is possible → OC is possible." The question is why.

Note, first, that (256) does not apply to finite clauses (or, in Stassen's terms, it only applies to "deranked" clauses). Clearly, finite adjuncts exist in any language that have no controlled counterparts, let alone predicative OC counterparts.[2]

(257) a.   Mary cried as/because she missed her sister.
b. *Mary cried as/because missing/to miss her sister.
c.   The car broke as/because it was too old.
d. *The car broke as/because being/to be too old.

Second, (256) cannot be reduced to some functional pressure toward more expressive grammars. Indeed, OC can express dependencies with inanimate antecedents, which NOC cannot. However, this does not imply any reduced expressive power, for the propositional variant can always be recruited to express the desired meaning via pronominal coreference with an inanimate antecedent—as in (257c). What we are interested in finding out is why, in no language L, is there is a hypothetical P, call it GOBE, that has the following distributional profile (the gerund stands for any nonfinite form L uses in adjuncts).

(258) a.   John$_i$ jumped [GOBE Mary/he$_i$ fell down].
b.   The keys$_i$ disappeared [GOBE they$_i$ dropped out of the bag].
c.   Diane$_i$ couldn't understand it. The keys disappeared
[GOBE PRO$_i$ placing them in the top drawer].
d. *The keys$_i$ disappeared [GOBE PRO$_i$ dropping out of the bag].

The adjuncts in (258a–c) are all propositional: the first two with lexical subjects, the third displaying NOC (i.e., long-distance control). Yet a predicative adjunct, which requires unambiguous OC, is, by hypothesis, unattested (258d). Expressivity is not at stake, given that the intended reading is delivered in (258b). Redundancy avoidance is not at stake either, given that such finite/nonfinite redundancies are widespread (*The keys$_i$ disappeared after they$_i$ dropped out of the bag, The keys$_i$ disappeared after dropping out of the bag*). If I am correct in assuming that natural language has no GOBE-headed adjuncts, then (256) represents a nontrivial truth that calls for explanation.

My approach to this puzzle focuses on the developmental stage when adjunct control is acquired by the child. Specifically, consider the input. The most conservative assumption is that the vast majority of utterances with non-finite adjuncts of the OC/NOC class that the child is exposed to exhibit local human subject control, as in (259); indeed, this picture emerges from Gerard's (2020) corpus study. These sentences, in principle, lend themselves either to OC or to NOC analyses.

(259) Susan went to sleep after eating her dinner.

On the OC derivation, a predicative adjunct attaches to Voice'. This results in a complex predicate with two bound variable positions, which are bound by the external argument in Spec,VoiceP as it saturates the complex predicate (see (133)). *Eating her dinner* and *went to sleep* share the same subject – namely, *Susan*. On the NOC derivation, a propositional adjunct attaches to VoiceP and modifies the main event directly (see (132)). The subject of this propositional adjunct (= NOC PRO) is a free variable that "searches" for a prominent logophoric antecedent. The most prominent one is the matrix subject, so *Susan* is picked out as the subject of *eating her dinner*.

The two derivations converge on the same interpretation. The question is, which one will the child opt for?

I suggest that *Economy of Projection* (EoP) holds the key to the puzzle.[3] Recall that a propositional adjunct structurally includes a predicative adjunct as a subconstituent (a key feature of the TTC).

(260) a. *Predicative adjunct:* $[_{PP} \text{ P } [_{FinP} \text{ PRO}_i \text{ Fin } [_{TP} \text{ PRO}_i \ldots]]]$
      b. *Propositional adjunct:* $[_{PP} \text{ P } [_{CP} \textit{pro} \text{ C}_{[+log]} [_{FinP} \text{ PRO}_i \text{ Fin}$
        $[_{TP} \text{ PRO}_i \ldots]]]]$

The idea of EoP is that all else being equal, a more minimal structure is favored over a less minimal one (Chomsky 1991, Safir 1993, Grimshaw 1994, Bošković 1996, Speas 2006). "All else being equal" primarily refers to semantic equivalence: if two structures generate the same meaning, project the more minimal one. This, I suggest, explains why the predicative adjunct is immediately projected when a speaker encounters sentences like (259). Because the OC and NOC derivations generate the same meaning (= local subject control), the grammar automatically opts for the OC derivation, which represents the structure of the adjunct more minimally. Thus, the grammar defaults to (260a).

As with any economy account, EoP requires carefully spelling out the equivalence class of competing derivations. While semantic equivalence is a necessary condition on the members of this class, it is not sufficient. Thus, *John is bald* does not block the less minimal structure of *John is bald and two plus two are four*, although the two sentences have the same intension. Economy comparisons are limited to derivations drawing on identical lexical resources. The term "lexical" is crucial, as it allows a certain divergence in non-truth-conditional functional material. In the present case, a complementizer and a null pronoun are present in (260b) but not in (260a), yet these functional elements do not affect the semantic equivalence of the two derivations (under the local subject control reading). Hence, they compete, and the more minimal one wins.

By contrast, nonfinite-finite pairs like *Jack ate after sleeping / Jack ate after he had slept* do not qualify as equivalent for economy comparisons, because they do differ in interpretation, albeit in a subtle way, along the strict/sloppy reading divide. For example, (261b), with *he* referring to Jack, is compatible with Mike working hard before sleeping (if that happened after Jack's sleeping), but (261a) is not.

(261) a. Only Jack worked hard before sleeping.
      b. Only Jack worked hard before he slept.

It is independently known that the LF representations of variable binding and covaluation do not compete with or block each other; see the discussion of (288) below. For this reason, a nonfinite adjunct cannot block a finite adjunct even when the two produce the same referential choice for the adjunct's subject.

It is noteworthy that economy considerations are frequently invoked in developmental accounts of language acquisition, the general assumption being that children favor more economical grammatical analyses over less economical ones. Specifically for EoP, it has been suggested that functional projections are avoided unless forced by positive input that cannot be analyzed otherwise (Roeper and de Villiers 1995, Radford 1996, Thráinsson 1996, Rizzi 2000, Roeper and Rohrbacher 2000, Zeijlstra 2007). For example, Thornton and Tesan (2013) explain young children's nonadult productions of negative sentences by the assumption that they start out assigning the negative marker (*no/not/don't*) an adverbial status, rather than a head status, because the former analysis avoids the more complex structure involving NegP. The present proposal is very much in the same spirit: using EoP to identify default parameter settings or early syntactic (mis)analyses.

An objection raised against standard applications of EoP (and other economy calculations) is their global character—the need to compare distinct derivations (even if restricted to a narrow reference set, defined by semantic equivalence). It is possible, however, to obtain the effect of EoP in the present case without invoking globality. Suppose that a target semantic interpretation launches the syntactic derivation—that is, the grammar constructs a derivation to deliver the target interpretation. Suppose that interpretation involves local subject control of an adjunct. Then, once the FinP of the adjunct is completed, nothing demands further projection of the CP layer. The grammatical derivation can directly proceed to merge FinP with the P head of the adjunct and adjoin the resulting PP to the matrix clause. Local subject control will be guaranteed by predication. Because nothing demands projecting the CP, it is avoided. Strictly speaking, the propositional variant is not even constructed in parallel (for comparison), so globality is not invoked. Of course, this can only work if the target interpretation is indeed obtained via the shorter derivational path. If it is not, this path will be discarded in favor of a longer path that does deliver the desired meaning.

At around the same initial stage, our hypothetical child is exposed to further input. Part will consist of examples of local control by an inanimate subject, as in (262a) (although probably at low rates); these data will obviously strengthen the OC derivation, being underivable by NOC. However, another part (presumably available very early on) will consist of simple finite adjuncts headed by the same P, as in (262b).

(262) a. The balloon exploded after touching the fire.
       b. The monkey got angry after the raccoon had stolen the coconut.

Data like (262b) unambiguously indicate that *after* can s-select a proposition. Therefore, the child already knows, very early on, that *after* can s-select either a property or a proposition. Note that actual NOC examples with these adjuncts, which are indeed rare and hard to come by (see (88b), (89b), (90a), (98e)), are not required in order to secure the inference that a propositional variant exists; simple finite adjuncts suffice. Indeed, Gerard's (2020) corpus study indicates that temporal adjuncts in the linguistic input to children occur far more frequently in their finite form than in their nonfinite form, and that NOC is only rarely attested in the latter.

Crucially, the propositional possibility in no way cancels the predicative possibility. The two can happily coexist as long as nothing in the input falsifies the predicative option. Moreover, data like (262a) *prove* it to be indispensable. Recall also that the finite variant does not block the nonfinite one (due to lack of semantic equivalence).

Because the key trigger for postulating a propositional variant is the appearance of a finite version of the adjunct in the input, we predict that the absence of such a version will delay the acquisition of a NOC variant. Thus, the PVC predicts a certain developmental sequence among adjunct-introducing prepositions. Those that occur early on with finite clauses, like *before/after/while*

(Gerard 2020), will also display NOC properties early on in acquisition (and to a greater extent than they do with adults—for the pragmatic reasons discussed in section 12.4). In contrast, those that do not occur with finite clauses at all, like *without*, will be confined to the predicative (OC) default for much longer—essentially, until the rather uncommon nonfinite occurrences with lexical subjects are encountered (e.g., *He sneaked in without anyone noticing*). Indeed, precisely this split was reported in Adler 2006: while children displayed nonadultlike NOC responses to temporal adjuncts, they displayed adultlike responses to *without*-adjuncts at the youngest age (i.e., rejecting extrasentential control).[4]

This is, then, how the asymmetry in table (253) and the implication in (256) arise. Speakers will never be discouraged from positing a predicative entry for locally controlled adjuncts, as it is the most economical syntactic analysis. On the other hand, they will only posit a propositional entry in response to positive evidence (usually in the form of finite adjuncts, but occasionally in the form of nonfinite or nominalized clauses with lexical subjects). The outcome is that *all* nonfinite adjuncts will be associated with a predicative entry, but only those with propositional variants will be supplemented with a propositional entry.

If the primary status of a predicative adjunct in the adult language (and in typological patterns) is rooted in the acquisition sequence, we may expect to find supporting evidence in developmental data. One piece of evidence was mentioned above: the split between temporal adjuncts and *without*-adjuncts in the child data, pointing to the earliness of the predicative variant. In fact, we expect children to pass through a grammatical stage where they assign only a predicative entry even to temporal adjuncts. This stage is likely to be quite short, given that evidence for a propositional entry (like (262b)) is readily available, so we may get a partial glimpse of it only with some children.

In fact, McDaniel, Cairns, and Hsu (1991) have identified a peculiar developmental stage that appears to fit just this profile; they dub it the Adverbial Coreference Requirement (ACR). Out of 20 children in their first study, 12 displayed an ACR grammar (ages 4;0–5;4, mean 4;7), and out of 14 children in their second (longitudinal) study, 3 displayed it (1 between 4;6–4;9, 1 between 4;9–5;2, and 1 at 5;3).

A child displaying the ACR grammar requires coreference between a matrix DP and some embedded position in the adjunct—either PRO or some pronoun. On the basis of coreference judgments elicited from the children (following a training session in this kind of task), McDaniel, Cairns, and Hsu characterize the ACR grammar as manifesting the following distribution of grammaticality judgments.

(263) *Judgments in the ACR grammar*
    a.   Grover$_i$ tells Cookie Monster$_j$ that [he$_{i/j/k}$ will climb up the tree].
    b.   Grover$_i$ pats Bert$_j$ [before he$_{i/j/*k}$ climbs up the steps].
    c.   The zebra$_i$ touches the elephant$_j$ [before the gate bumps him$_{i/j/*k}$].
    d.   The zebra$_i$ touches the lion$_j$ [before PRO$_{i/j/*k}$ drinking some water].
    e.   The lion$_i$ pats the zebra [before PRO$_{i/*m}$ tickling him$_{j/k}$].
    f. ?*Bert hits Cookie Monster [before Grover/I/she jump(s) over the fence].

First, ACR children know that pronouns can be free, and they allow this option in complements (263a). Nevertheless, in finite adjuncts a pronoun must corefer with a matrix argument (263b–c). Children actually split between subject and object antecedents (so the "i/j" indices represent different grammars), matching their preferences regarding control of PRO (263d) (as discussed in chapter 12). Strikingly, a pronoun inside an adjunct may be free if and only if PRO is bound (263e). Finally, adjuncts with lexical subjects and no coreference with the matrix clause (263f) are "ungrammatical in most cases or uncertain" (McDaniel, Cairns, and Hsu 1991:309). Note that non-ACR children (sometimes younger than ACR ones) do not display any of these peculiarities; that is, they never require pronouns to be bound and they accept adjuncts with no referential link to the matrix clause.

To accommodate this developmental stage, McDaniel, Cairns, and Hsu revise the theory of control in three ways. First, they define "control" rather abstractly, as obligatory coreference between any embedded position and the closest c-commanding matrix DP. Second, they distinguish two parameter values: Infl-to-Infl control, which underlies "switch reference" systems in Native American and Aboriginal Australian languages, leading to coreference (or anti-coreference) between the embedded and matrix subjects; and argument-to-argument control, as in English, which allows any matrix argument to be the controller. Third, they propose that ACR children exceptionally analyze temporal adjuncts in English as falling under the generalized control condition (bearing [+CR] (i.e., [+coreference]) on their head).

These assumptions raise nontrivial difficulties, both theoretical and developmental. Twenty years later, Cairns (2013:275) candidly remarked: "A satisfactory explanation for the ACR was never formulated and it remains an interesting, but mysterious phenomenon." We may therefore ask whether the present approach offers a natural explanation.

In fact, the paradigm in (263a-f) lends itself to a simple formal description: for ACR children, *before*-adjuncts are necessarily predicative, regardless of finiteness. Predicates must have an open position for the λ-bound variable, explaining the mandatory occurrence of either controlled PRO or a bound pronoun.[5] This mandatory presence of a bound pronoun is a familiar feature of other constructions with predicative clauses, such as prolepsis (see section 14.4.5), left-dislocation, and certain kinds of copy raising (Landau 2011).

(264) a. We've heard of Bill$_i$ that many museums are now buying his$_i$/*the paintings.
   b. This gentleman$_i$, I truly appreciate his$_i$/*the comments.
   c. Your building$_i$ sounds like you hate everyone *(in it$_i$).

Similarly, certain adjectival constructions require an embedded gap for the null operator to bind (Landau 1999).

(265) a.   The soup$_i$ is ready [Op$_i$ [PRO$_{arb}$ to eat t$_i$]].
   b.   The soup$_i$ is ready [Op$_i$ [for you to eat t$_i$]].
   c.   The soup$_i$ is ready [Op$_i$ [t$_i$ to be eaten]].
   d. *The soup$_i$ is ready [Op$_i$ [PRO$_{arb}$ to eat the appetizers]].
   e. *The soup$_i$ is ready [Op$_i$ [for the appetizers to be eaten]].

A null operator chain may terminate in a trace or a pronoun, or be formed with PRO itself, as in predicative nonfinite adjuncts. At LF, all these structures are interpreted as predicates of type <e,<s,t>>, satisfying the selectional requirement of the adjunct's head, *before*$_{[pred]}$. The adjuncts in (263c–d), for example, have the structures in (266a–b).

(266) a. [$_{PP}$ before [$_{CP}$ Op$_i$ [$_{TP}$ the gate bumps him$_i$]]]
   b. [$_{PP}$ before [$_{FinP}$ PRO$_i$ [$_{TP}$ t$_i$ drinking some water]]]

In the adult grammar, alternating OC/NOC adjuncts are either predicative or propositional. Indeed, on the current proposal, this is just what makes them alternate between the two options. To account for ACR children, then, we need only assume that they lack the propositional entry: the ACR stage is a pure reflection of the default grammatical choice, rooted in EoP as discussed above. It is interesting to see that at this stage, children do not distinguish finite from nonfinite versions of the adjunct and uniformly treat both as predicative. This further supports the proposed unified semantic treatment (see chapter 6). Focusing on *before*-adjuncts, adults and ACR children differ as follows.[6]

(267) *Adult vs. ACR grammar of* before-*adjuncts*
   a. ⟦*before*$_{[prop]}$⟧ = λp$_{<s,t>}$.λq$_{<s,t>}$.λe.**before**(p,q)(e)
   b. ⟦*before*$_{[pred]}$⟧ = λP$_{<e,<s,t>>}$.λQ$_{<e,<s,t>>}$.λx.λe.**before**(P(x),Q(x))(e)
   c.

	Head of nonfinite adjunct	Head of finite adjunct
Adult grammar	*before*$_{[pred]}$ / *before*$_{[prop]}$	*before*$_{[pred]}$ / *before*$_{[prop]}$
ACR grammar	*before*$_{[pred]}$	*before*$_{[pred]}$

It may look problematic that children master the more complex lexical entry of *before*[pred] before that of *before*[prop]. This is not a real problem, though, since both entries share their substantive core, the temporal relation **before**. At the same age, children already produce and understand complex predications like *He looks sad*, which invoke the same mechanism of argument sharing that *before*[pred] does. The crucial factor at this stage is EoP, which by default favors the predicative structure over the propositional one when instances of local control are encountered. Children quickly grow out of the ACR stage upon encountering propositional adjuncts with lexical subjects. Although these occur only in the context of finite adjuncts, the children's revised lexicon now contains *before*[prop]. This head can then be employed with nonfinite adjuncts; the result is NOC.[7]

Note that I have assigned either *before*[prop] or *before*[pred] to finite adjuncts in the adult grammar. Why not assume just the propositional variant? What is the evidence for a predicative finite adjunct? Unlike in nonfinite adjuncts, where the predicative option is necessary to express inanimate control, in finite adjuncts it is redundant with the propositional option, given inanimate pronouns (e.g., *The cake$_i$ was eaten immediately after it$_i$ came out of the oven*). Nevertheless, there may be indirect evidence that it still exists. Consider the strict/sloppy ambiguity under narrow ellipsis of the complement of the temporal P, exemplified in (268) for Hebrew.

(268) Dani$_i$ higi'a lifney še-hixrizu alav *pro$_i$*,
      Dani arrived before that-announced.3PL on.3SG

      aval Yosi higi'a axrey ___.
      but Yosi arrived after

      'Dani arrived before they announced him, but Yosi arrived after (that).'

The sentence is ambiguous, meaning that Yosi arrived either after they announced Dani or after they announced Yosi. The sloppy reading does not necessarily indicate ellipsis (surface anaphora), for it is well-established that deep anaphors also support it (see Merchant 2013a for evidence), and temporal prepositions easily license such deep anaphoric complements, whose content is deictically retrieved. Regardless of the syntactic analysis of the gap following *after*, though, we may take the presence of a sloppy reading as evidence that there exists a property-denoting antecedent for that gap. Thus, the clause 'they announced him' must have not only a propositional but also a predicative representation, with a null operator binding the object pronoun. This supports the idea that the predicative variant is never lost. More strikingly for Hebrew, this variant exists even though temporal prepositions in this language do not select nonfinite complements. This means that the predicative variant is selected as default independently of finiteness, simply because it expresses coreference with the local matrix subject more economically (using a smaller structure).

If the adult grammar allows $before_{[pred]}$ to take finite clauses, then a major puzzle concerning the developmental path of ACR children is avoided. These children need not "unlearn" any "wrong" setting in their grammar (a constant worry when the target language is a superset of the child's language). Instead, they simply have to expand their grammar to include the propositional variant of the adjunct, headed by $before_{[prop]}$, and they may well do so for both nonfinite and finite adjuncts. We thus see that acquisition data provide support not only for the OC-NOC duality of adjunct control and the distinct roles of topicality and logophoricity in mastering it (chapter 12), but also for the fundamental asymmetry that makes the predicative adjunct the default—in acquisition, in typological distribution, and in real-time processing.

As a final note, I should point out that the developmental data gathered after McDaniel, Cairns, and Hsu 1991 somewhat obscures this neat picture. Cairns et al. (1994) and Cairns et al. (1995) discovered that children display considerably more variation regarding the paradigm in (263). While some stick to the ACR pattern, others extend it to complements, requiring a coreferential pronoun in (263a), or even in the presence of a controlled adjunct PRO as in (263e). More puzzlingly, they allow adjuncts without any pronoun, as in (263f). Despite the latter finding, Cairns and her colleagues renamed the relevant stage "Pronoun Coreference Requirement" (PCR), reflecting its neutrality between adjuncts and complements. Children as old as 9 years were found to display PCR grammars. Most importantly, Cairns et al. showed that a contextual bias toward a specific referent significantly increases the rate of accepting this referent as antecedent either for a pronoun or for an adjunct PRO. In other words, the PCR effect is sensitive to pragmatic context.

The question, then, is whether the PCR analysis genuinely subsumes and improves over the ACR analysis. If it does, then the developmental data do not bear on the present issue, which is the primacy of the predicative adjunct over the propositional adjunct. Indeed, if children simply *prefer* an embedded coreferential pronoun, however strongly, rather than *requiring* it (and only in predicative clauses), then the whole phenomenon lies outside syntax.[8]

The data are not sufficiently sharp, unfortunately, but I believe they still support a separate *grammatical* analysis for the ACR, supplemented by an independent *pragmatic* preference for embedded coreferential pronouns (the PCR). A number of observations point in this direction. Possibly the strongest argument in its favor is the persistent discrepancy (noted by Cairns and her colleagues) between the strength of the coreference requirement in adjuncts and its strength in complements. The 1991 study (represented in (263)) found a sharp dichotomy: complements never required pronominal coreference, adjuncts did. In the 1994 study, 94% of the children classified as PCR required pronominal coreference in adjuncts but only 63% required it in complements.

Only in the 1995 study was no significant difference found between the two environments (less than 6% violations of the PCR in complements); this study, though, ranged over older ages than the previous ones (4;6–6;10 in one experiment and 7;0–9;10 in the other). It may well be that the onset of the ACR stage precedes that of the PCR stage, and that the latter continues for a while after the former has ended. Indeed, the 1995 study found that within the older group of children, the non-ACR children (6 out of 33), who allowed sentence-external antecedents for pronouns in adjuncts 33% of the time, were still "weak PCR" for complements, allowing external reference for pronouns in complements only 12% of the time.

A second reason to seek a grammatical rather than pragmatic account for the ACR is its tight correlation with OC. In all three studies, children in the earliest "no control" stage never manifested the ACR. That is, a grammar in which adjunct PRO is exempt from OC is also a grammar in which embedded pronouns are exempt from the ACR. Conversely, most children who shifted to the OC stage also shifted at the same to time to the ACR. These correlations are naturally understood if OC and the ACR in adjuncts share an underlying mechanism, which they do on the current analysis—namely, predication.

In this chapter, I address a number of issues left open in the preceding discussion. Some will receive a more systematic treatment than others; the purpose will be not so much to present definitive answers as to flag interesting avenues for future research. Throughout, the leading question will be what light the present theory can shed on the rich empirical terrain of adjunct control.

Section 14.1 addresses a type of control that is occasionally associated with adjuncts—"event control." I will show that the term has been used too broadly but does, in fact, capture a genuine class of cases that should be accommodated. Section 14.2 returns to the "overlap zone" in diagram (43) and investigates whether local NOC exists (answering positively, on the basis of evidence from ellipsis). Section 14.3 revisits a peculiar restriction on NOC in RatCs that was first observed in the 1980s and was taken up again in Landau 2017; I revise the latter analysis in light of some problematic data. Section 14.4 briefly lays out several points where crosslinguistic variation seems to occur in the distribution or interpretation of controlled adjuncts. Given the sparsity of relevant data, this section hardly scratches the surface of this topic, and simply points to some key research questions. Finally, section 14.5 returns to the fundamental dichotomy running through this entire work—the OC-NOC split—and asks what has remained of it. It then summarizes the empirical and theoretical reasons that still motivate preserving this dichotomy, even if it is occasionally clouded in the "messiness" of actual judgments.

14.1   Does Event Control Exist?

Building on observations by Quirk et al. (1985) and Kortmann (1991), Fischer and Flaate Høyem 2019 (F&FH) discuss a special class of adjuncts that predicate some informational property of the matrix *event*. These adjuncts appear as bare predicates—participles or infinitives in English, German, and Norwegian ((269a) is from F&FH 2019:10, (269b) is from Kortmann 1991:73, (269c) is from the internet).[1]

(269) a. [As a last step], Peter waxed the floor.

b. [Unknown to Mr. Mori], the other big trading houses were also putting together a consortium.

c. The economy gained 20,000 jobs in February, [PRO indicating that the nation's 10-year economic expansion has potentially hit a speed bump].

F&FH assimilate these cases to standard OC, the only difference being that the controller is not a DP but an event variable. Assuming an Agree-based theory of OC (Fischer 2018), they propose that the event variable on the matrix verb is a syntactic feature that percolates to the V′ projection, from which it c-commands any adjunct to VP; Agree between this valued variable and PRO supplies the latter with the necessary event interpretation.

I believe that something like event OC is real, but its scope is narrower than what F&FH assume, and the mechanism is different. First, there is little motivation to posit PRO inside bare predicates like the adjuncts in (269a–b), lacking any clausal structure. Clearly, the interpretive result can be achieved without the mediation of PRO, so evidence for PRO must be *syntactic*. Such evidence normally consists of effects like partial/split control, independent case valuation, or licensing of subject-oriented adjuncts, but nothing of the sort is attested in these bare predicates. In fact, F&FH show that the case of the DP in German *als* 'as'-predicates is parasitic on the matrix ACC or NOM—which makes an intervening PRO redundant, if not problematic.

Second, to allow c-command by the event variable, F&FH assume that initial adjuncts must reconstruct to a VP-internal position. As illustrated earlier in (172), this implication is false in the general case of sentence-initial OC adjuncts. Bare event predicates are similar in showing no evidence of reconstruction. In fact, they must scope over negation, which follows if they *cannot* reconstruct.

(270) a. As a tribute to John, they didn't invite his ex-wife.

   = *Their not inviting John's ex-wife was a tribute to him.*

   ≠ *It's not the case that they invited John's ex-wife as a tribute to him.*

b. Finally acknowledged by many, Trump's environmental policy isn't rational.

   = *It's acknowledged by many that Trump's environmental policy isn't rational.*

   ≠ *It's not acknowledged by many that Trump's environmental policy is rational.*

One also wonders whether event variables should be reified as projecting indices, and furthermore, what it means for an event *variable* to be *valued* for the purposes of Agree. (On other difficulties with the Agree-based theory, see chapter 10.)

I would like to suggest a different approach. As a starting point, consider the following example from F&FH 2019:8.

(271) [As a friendly favor] and [PRO to give him$_i$ the opportunity to meet a nice girl], John$_i$ was introduced to Mary.

F&FH observe that the infinitive here must be event-controlled, as it is conjoined with a clear-cut event predicate (the first conjunct). From this they infer that PRO in the infinitive denotes the matrix event. Notice, however, that the construction is perfectly acceptable with an unambiguously human PRO (272a–b). In fact, the second conjunct can be overtly propositional with a lexical subject (272c–d).

(272) a. [As a friendly favor] and [PRO$_i$ to see her dream come true], Mary$_i$ introduced John to her roommate.
       b. [As a friendly favor] and [PRO to avoid any embarrassment], this party had no exes.
       c. [As a friendly favor] and [in order for George to prepare for the final exams], his roommate left him the apartment for the weekend.
       d. [As a friendly favor] and [after they had breakfast with her], Anne's neighbors drove her to town.

The infinitive displays local subject control in (272a) and pragmatic control in (272b). In neither case can PRO be construed as referring to an event. And in (272c–d), there is not even a PRO to refer to an event. Yet all four adjuncts support an event-modifying reading. How can that be?

One clear implication is that event modification is *independent* of event control and can be realized through other means. These other means, perhaps, are general enough to account for other cases of "event control." For the cases at hand, a simple treatment suggests itself. The clause-containing PP adjuncts in (271)–(272) are propositional modifiers of type $\langle\langle s,t\rangle,\langle s,t\rangle\rangle$. Assume that *as*-phrases are of the same type. Thus, the adjunct *as a friendly favor* denotes a function that applies to a set of eventualities and returns those eventualities in it that count as a friendly favor. Combined by generalized predicate modification, the conjunction in (272b) would intersect the main proposition with the proposition $\lambda e.e$ *is a friendly favor and is an event brought about by x to avoid any embarrassment*, where x is the NOC antecedent of PRO. The conjunction in (272d) would intersect the main proposition with $\lambda e.e$ *is a friendly favor and temporally follows the event of their having breakfast with her.* The effect of "event control" is a by-product of the fact that the same event variable is shared in all these operations. Yet neither "event control" nor an event-denoting PRO is invoked at any stage, and in fact, these would yield anomalous readings in (272a–b).

There is still a residue for which event control seems to be the only available analysis: (269c), and in general, adjuncts with causative verbs, in particular "informational" predicates (*indicating, suggesting, implying, confirming, refuting*, etc.). Although these predicates can apply to humans, they need not, and commonly they refer to facts or events.

(273) a. It rained heavily, confirming my worst expectations.
    b. There was nobody around, suggesting an informer had warned them in advance.

Given that NOC requires a human subject, these adjuncts must be OC adjuncts— namely, predicative adjuncts of type $\langle e,\langle s,t\rangle\rangle$. The question then is how the matrix event saturates the open position of PRO.

An important clue is F&FH's observation that this class of adjuncts can be paraphrased with appositive relative clauses.[2]

(274) a. It rained heavily, which confirmed my worst expectations.
    b. There was nobody around, which suggested an informer had warned them in advance.

In his insightful analysis of these constructions, Potts (2002) proposes that appositive *which* ranges over individuals. In order for *which* to apply to the main clause proposition, that proposition must be type-shifted into a "nominalized proposition" (Chierchia 1985, Chierchia and Turner 1988). In Potts's ontology, if proposition p denotes the set of worlds W, then the nominalized p is the plural individual whose subparts are all and only the worlds in W. Both the syntax and the semantics of *which*-appositives provide ample support for this individual guise of propositional arguments. In fact, the striking parallels between DPs and CPs have inspired some researchers to pursue a completely uniform semantic treatment in which the two categories map to a single semantic type (Liefke and Werning 2018).

Insofar as type shifting of propositions to individuals is called upon in (274), it seems natural to invoke it in (273) as well. If propositions are already a kind of individual with no recourse to type shifting, the two cases become one. "Event control" simply reduces to standard control by individuals. The control relation in (273), then, is run-of-the-mill predication between TP and its sister adjunct.

14.2 In Defense of Local NOC

At a number of points throughout this work, I have suggested that OC and NOC readings (of alternating adjuncts) may coexist, and while the OC reading is often favored for a variety of processing reasons, it does not strictly exclude the NOC reading. Recall the following distribution from chapter 3.

(275) *Extensional relation between OC and NOC readings*

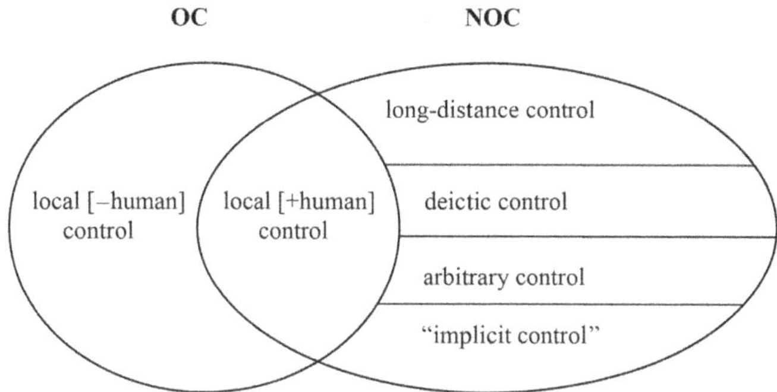

That a coherent, local OC reading does not necessarily block a pragmatically supported nonlocal NOC reading has been illustrated by examples like (2)–(7) in chapter 1. What is still unclear is whether the overlap area—local [+human] control—indeed supports two derivations: one in which PRO in the adjunct clause is a λ-abstractor, associated with the matrix subject by predication, and another in which PRO is linked to a free logophoric variable. This question is far more difficult to settle, as in this case the two derivations yield identical interpretations. The table in (276) presents the analytic picture.[3]

(276) *Nonfinite vs. finite adjunct: Local [+human] subject control*

	Predicative adjunct	Propositional adjunct
Bill$_i$ had slept 5 hours [before he$_i$ took the exam].	+	+
Bill$_i$ had slept 5 hours [before PRO$_i$ taking the exam].	+	?

If the "?" in the table turns out to be "+", the OC/NOC alternation in adjuncts will be seen to be fully productive and unrestricted within the grammar. Furthermore, s-selection and c-selection will be seen to be truly independent, in that either finite or nonfinite adjuncts map to either properties or propositions.

If "−" is established instead, the implication will be that within a restricted domain—namely, *when they yield nondistinct interpretations*—OC does block NOC. Resolution of this issue is of considerable theoretical interest, for it arises in much the same form within binding theory as well, to which I return later in this section.

Although nondistinct, OC and NOC by the local matrix subject are obtained by different grammatical mechanisms: predication—a local relation—in OC, and logophoric anchoring—a nonlocal relation—in NOC. This contrast underlies the familiar strict/sloppy reading test: under OC, PRO must receive a sloppy interpretation, while under NOC it allows either strict or sloppy readings. The prediction for adjunct control is clear: in ellipsis environments, an elided predicative adjunct should force a sloppy reading (= control by the local subject), whereas an elided propositional adjunct should allow a strict reading (= control by a nonlocal subject).[4] Past work has claimed that only the sloppy reading is attested with temporal adjuncts (Hornstein 2003, Boeckx, Hornstein, and Nunes 2010:87) and with RatCs (Green 2018:138). I believe that is inaccurate. Although the sloppy reading is strongly favored (by the same processing biases that favor local over nonlocal control), it is not forced. Indeed, under the right pragmatic conditions, the strict reading emerges.

In the following examples, English speakers accept (to varying degrees) the strict reading of PRO in the elided adjunct (temporal clause in (277a–c), RatC in (277d)).

(277) a. Bill felt much better after quitting his heavy drinking. His family did too.
         [*His family felt much better after he quit his heavy drinking.*]
      b. Ann and her douchebag partner Paul are talking about their first baby.
         Ann: You know, I was so nervous before having the epidural.
         Paul: Yeah, I remember. Well, I wasn't.
         [*I wasn't so nervous before you had the epidural.*]
      c. Clearly, Father Taylor glows with enthusiasm when preaching about Eternal Torment, but nobody in the congregation does.
         [*Nobody in the congregation glows with enthusiasm when Father Taylor preaches about Eternal Torment.*]
      d. Tom lied about his age in order to be admitted to Lakeside School. His parents cooperated; they did too.
         [*They lied about his age in order for him to be admitted to Lakeside School.*]

How is the ellipsis site resolved in these examples? Simplifying somewhat, standard criteria of semantic parallelism demand that the missing VP, together with the adjunct, be semantically equivalent to the antecedent VP. The strict reading can only arise in the ellipsis site if the elided adjunct is propositional. But then its correlate in the antecedent must also be propositional. Because this correlate displays local subject control, we conclude that this reading can arise via a propositional adjunct, namely, via NOC.

More explicitly, following the compositional format in (133), a predicative analysis of the correlate adjunct in (277d) looks as follows.

(278) *Predicative RatC analysis for (277d)*

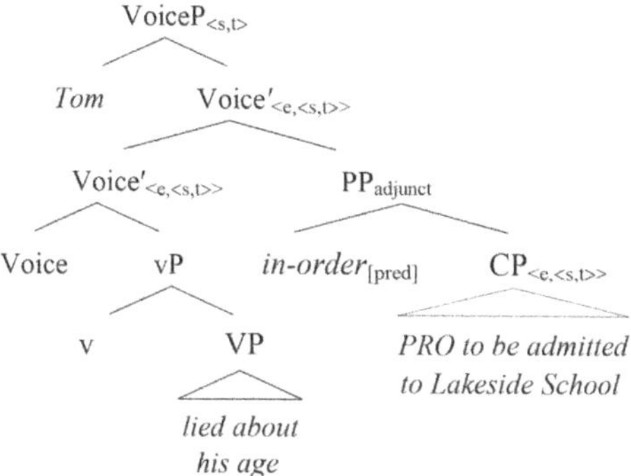

Movement of *Tom* to the subject position abstracts over the external argument position; the resulting one-place predicate then serves to check semantic parallelism with the elided VP. I use *Rat* below to refer to the rationale modification relation: *Rat(p,q)* holds iff p provides the rationale for q. The index z refers to *Tom* but is not bound by it, to allow the strict reading of *his age*.

(279) *Denotation of the antecedent VoiceP in (278)*
$\lambda x.\lambda e.\text{Rat}(\llbracket\text{PRO to be admitted to Lakeside School}\rrbracket$ (x),
$\llbracket\text{lie about z's age}\rrbracket$ (x))(e)

It can now be observed that once this denotation is applied to the subject of the elided VP in (277d), a sloppy reading for PRO is obtained (unproblematically, the pronoun *his* can still be read strictly): *Tom's parents lied about his age in order for them to be admitted to Lakeside School*. Thus, the predicative analysis fails to deliver the observed strict interpretation of PRO, here and in the other cases of (277).

Compare the propositional analysis and its predictions for ellipsis.

(280) *Propositional RatC analysis for (277d)*

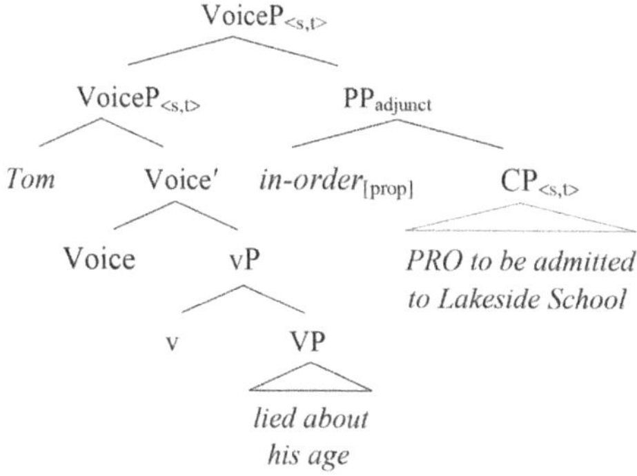

By the assignment function g, *his* refers to Tom. By logophoric NOC, PRO refers to Tom as well. In (281), these two variables are indexed y and z, respectively, such that $g(y) = g(z)$. After movement of *Tom*, the VP denotation is as follows.

(281) *Denotation of the antecedent VoiceP in (280)*
    $\lambda x.\lambda e.$Rat($\llbracket PRO_z$ to be admitted to Lakeside School$\rrbracket$,
    $\llbracket$lie about y's age$\rrbracket$ (x))(e)

Applied to the subject of the elided VP, this denotation yields the desired strict interpretation: *Tom's parents lied about Tom's age in order for Tom to be admitted to Lakeside School.*

These facts, then, establish that the overlap in diagram (275) is real: local control by a human subject can be obtained either by OC or by NOC. To finish off this part, we should verify that unambiguous OC adjuncts *fail* to license strict readings under comparable circumstances. We can test this using the same type of (temporal) adjuncts under an inanimate controller.

(282) a. The storm was over. Electricity$_i$ returned [after PRO$_i$ being cut off
      for 11 hours. Water$_j$ did [~~return after PRO$_{j/*i}$ being cut off for 11~~
      ~~hours~~] too.
   b. Water was cut off for 16 hours, but returned after electricity had
      been cut off for 11 hours.

The subject of the antecedent clause in (282a), *electricity*, cannot control the PRO subject of the elided adjunct; thus, *Water did too* entails that water, not electricity, had been cut off for 11 hours.[5] The intended strict reading, shown in (282b) to be perfectly sensible, is not available in (282a). A similar effect holds with RatCs.

(283) a. The carpets$_i$ were removed from the room [in order PRO$_i$ to be
      dry-cleaned].
      #The furniture$_j$ was [~~removed from the room in order PRO$_{j/*i}$~~
      ~~to be dry-cleaned~~] too.
   b. The furniture was removed from the room in order for the carpets
      to be dry-cleaned.

The elided PRO in (283a) can only be construed as the local subject, *the furniture*, and not as the antecedent subject, *the carpets*. This is so despite the fact that this sloppy interpretation is anomalous (furniture being dry-cleaned) and that the intended strict interpretation is pragmatically natural, as shown in (283b).

The contrast between (277a–d), which allow strict readings under ellipsis, and (282a)/(283a), which do not, neatly aligns with the fundamental distinction between OC and NOC adjuncts—in this case, OC and NOC variants of the same adjuncts. Once we pay attention to the proper conditions under which NOC may be detected, we find it also in environments thought to be solely reserved for OC—namely, environments of local subject control.

This empirical finding has significant implications. First, it is fully harmonious with the proposal in chapter 13 regarding the role of Economy of Projection (EoP) in making the predicative variant of adjuncts the lexical default. The idea there was that grammar construction will always pass through a stage of positing a predicative variant for local subject control, this being more economical, in terms of projection, than the propositional option. This logic extends to particular speech situations as well. With no indication that a propositional variant is needed to parse a given adjunction structure, only the predicative variant will be invoked. The advantage of this economy-based approach is that it allows for a principled class of exceptions—namely, when everything else is *not* equal. The examples in (277) are of exactly that type. The attempted NOC reading goes beyond what OC can provide, and is furthermore pragmatically entrenched. In this situation, economy yields to the novel interpretation.

The above argument in defense of local NOC was based on interpretive distinctions between OC and NOC that arise in rather intricate scenarios. Is there any evidence that local NOC occurs even when it is semantically indistinguishable from OC? Findings from the processing of adjunct control indeed support this conclusion (Parker, Lago, and Phillips 2015). As part of a larger study of "facilitatory interference" during retrieval of an antecedent for PRO in adjuncts, Parker, Lago, and Phillips examined the effect of the [±human] property on acceptability judgments.[6] In particular, they compared the ratings that 24 adult speakers assigned to sentences like (284a–b), on a 7-point Likert scale (1 = least acceptable, 7 = most acceptable).

(284) a. The doctor was certified after [PRO debunking the hypothesis].
     b. The discovery was certified after [PRO debunking the hypothesis].

A significant difference was found between cases of local human subject control (like (284a)), which received a mean rating of 6.09, and local nonhuman subject control, like (284b), which received a mean rating of 4.81. Importantly, in simple predications without control, human and nonhuman subjects were rated equally. Parker, Lago, and Phillips interpreted this contrast as evidence for a "weak constraint," operative in adjunct control, favoring human over nonhuman controllers.

A natural way of "unpacking" this preference is to analyze it in terms of the abstract processing model presented in (230), repeated here.

(285) *Controller-worthiness scale (a processing model)*

	Local [+human] subject	Local [–human] subject	Nonlocal [+human] DP	Nonlocal [–human] DP
OC-worthy	+	+	–	–
NOC-worthy: [+log]	+	–	+	–
NOC-worthy: [+top]	+	+ (weak)	+ (weak)	+ (weak)

The two left-hand columns display the processing advantage that local human control has over local nonhuman control. Notice that the difference is confined to the NOC derivation. If local subject control had only been mediated through OC in the grammar, there would have been no difference between these two columns; OC could simply be established without consulting NOC. The evidence from processing, however, suggests that the grammar does distinguish among local subject controllers on the basis of the [±human] property, indicating that NOC is activated simultaneously with OC.

Regrettably, the argument is less than fully compelling. It is possible that the lower acceptability of (284b) is due not to nonhuman control per se, but to the fact that the sentence admits another reading—namely, NOC by some unspecified participant (possibly the matrix agent). That such ambiguities arise in the presence of a matrix inanimate subject was illustrated in (169) and can also be seen in (286).

(286) Peter was so frustrated. His message never registered [even after PRO imposing itself/himself upon the rest of the team].

The participants in Parker, Lago, and Phillips's study were only asked to provide acceptability ratings, regardless of interpretations. It is possible that some of them, in fact, only rated the NOC reading, delivering an (understandably) lower rating than they would assign to the OC reading. Others may have vacillated between the two readings, delivering a low rating just because of this uncertainty. Clearly, one would like to see pure OC and NOC interpretations compared for acceptability, as in the following pair.

(287) a. The doctor was certified after [PRO developing the treatment].
    b. The treatment was certified after [PRO being administered to mice].

An advantage of (287a) over (287b) would provide striking support for the dual theory of adjunct control developed here. On the other hand, absence of evidence (for a contrast) would not necessarily be evidence for absence. Perhaps the processor does engage in the NOC derivation only under a pressing need (e.g., obtaining a novel, pragmatically supported interpretation). If so, (287a) would be parsed as OC only, just like (287b), with no perceived difference in acceptability. Any result here would be informative and revealing about the workings of OC and NOC during real-time processing.

I would like to end this discussion with some remarks on the parallels that emerge between control theory and binding theory vis-à-vis the issue of grammatical competition.

Consider these representative cases of binding.

(288) a. *John$_i$ likes him$_i$.
      i. [λx.x likes x](j)   *binding*
     ii. [λx.x likes j](j)   *covaluation*
    b. John likes his math teacher, and Ben does too.

While Condition B of binding theory rules out (288a-i), it has nothing to say about (288a-ii), where the name and the pronoun "corefer" by virtue of being assigned the same referential index. Following Reinhart 1983, Grodzinsky and Reinhart (1993) formulated Rule I to address this issue. The idea was that covaluation between two positions is blocked if variable binding between them is possible and yields the same interpretation. Because the same interpretation is indeed obtained in (288a-i) and (288a-ii), the latter was said to be blocked by Rule I (and the former, of course, by Condition B).

This view faced a number of problems, chief among them that sentences like (288b) are ambiguous between the strict and sloppy readings, suggesting that binding (in the antecedent clause) does not always block covaluation even when the two strategies are semantically equivalent. In the revised system presented in Reinhart 2000, 2006, Rule I is weakened to allow covaluation when binding conditions are not violated. Because Condition B does not rule out (288b)—unlike (288a)—covaluation is permitted even if the same interpretation results. The "no sneaking in" rationale holds that semantics and pragmatics may not sneak in interpretations that are ruled out in the syntax.

Binding is analogous to OC, and covaluation is analogous to NOC. The finding that the grammar tolerates the coexistence of OC and NOC derivations in local subject control is consistent with the fact that OC is allowed, and so nothing new is "sneaked in." In truth, the opposite finding—that local OC blocks local NOC—would have introduced a curious discrepancy between the ways in which binding and control are handled at the interfaces.

What about nonlocal NOC? This is unproblematic, just as "exceptions" to binding conditions are. Intuitively, no competition arises when the two strategies yield distinct interpretations. For control, EoP does not apply; for binding, Rule I does not apply.

(289)　a. This happens especially frequently when [PRO$_{arb}$ trying to reach numbers in New York.

　　　b. Strangely, the candidates talked avidly when we$_i$ asked them where they were from, but they hesitated [after PRO$_i$ asking them about their work].

　　　c. [Who is this man?]—He$_i$ is Ralph$_i$.

　　　d. The suspect claims that he was at the opera at the time of the murder. But if it is true, only he$_i$ (himself) saw him$_i$ there.

In (289a–b), the NOC readings are distinct from the OC readings. While in (289a) the OC reading is anomalous, this is not required to license NOC, as (289b) demonstrates. Semantic distinctness is sufficient.[7] Likewise, Conditions C and B are violated in (289c) and (289d), respectively, yet covaluation is permitted precisely because it yields an interpretation distinct from variable binding ((289c) does not assert that Ralph has the self-identity property and (289d) does not assert that only the suspect has the self-seeing property).

　　The purpose of these remarks is certainly not to advocate for a unified theory of binding and control; the differences are too deep and far-reaching for any such attempt. Rather, the idea is to highlight the similar ways in which competition between two strategies—one syntactic or at least LF-visible, and the other pragmatic, related to reference tracking in discourse—plays out both in the binding module and in the control module. Finding such parallels across empirical domains is a promising sign that a fundamental design feature of language is at work.

14.3　The Jaeggli-Roeper Generalization

In section 5.1, I established that RatCs display either OC or NOC and provided empirical tests to tease them apart. While OC into RatCs is just like OC into other adjuncts, NOC into RatCs is subject to a specific semantic restriction: the controller must be not only a logophoric center but also an *initiator* in Farkas's (1988) sense—that is, stand in the RESP(onsibility) relation to the matrix eventuality. Although Farkas was mostly interested in the semantics of complement control, she suggested that RatC control is regulated by the same concepts (see Farkas 1988:38).

(290)　*RatC control according to Farkas (1988)*

　　　In a RatC construction, where S_m, S_e are the matrix and embedded eventualities, respectively, and the subject of S_e is PRO, the controller of PRO is the individual i such that

　　　a. RESP (i, S_m) (= i brings about S_m intentionally), and

　　　b. In bringing about S_m, i intends to bring about S_e.

Farkas cited (291a–b) to illustrate that whenever RESP (i,S_m) is not satisfied, because S_m is not the sort of eventuality that can be intentionally brought about, a RatC construction is semantically anomalous.

(291) a. #John resembles his father in order to annoy his grandmother.
     b. #The weather has been good lately in order to please the tourists.

Although Farkas did not recognize that RatCs can be licensed via the OC path, in which case the controller need not be an initiator (see (72)), her characterization of NOC controllers in terms of the RESP relation was an important step forward—in particular, the understanding that the notion of *initiator* is broader than, and not reducible to, the notion of a grammatical agent.[8]

Curiously, though, Farkas said nothing about the role of PRO in relation to S_e. The system in (290) specifies two relations: a binary relation between i and S_m, and a ternary one among i, S_m, and S_e. PRO itself is not semantically restricted in any way. This is indeed curious because in her discussion of *complement* control, Farkas pays considerable attention to the semantic role of PRO. Indeed, that role lies at the center of her theory of control shift (e.g., *He promised her to take the exam* vs. *He promised her to be allowed to take the exam*). I will return to this asymmetry at the end of this section and suggest that in RatC control too—specifically, in NOC—the semantic role of PRO is also crucially implicated.

The relevant facts were noticed in Jaeggli 1986 and Roeper 1987, and have received hardly any attention since, except in Español-Echevarría 2000 and Landau 2017. The latter is the basis of the present discussion, although I will modify some of its conclusions. Jaeggli and Roeper observed that "implicit agent control" (really NOC, assuming the conclusions of chapter 3) fails when the infinitive is passivized. ((292) is from Jaeggli 1986:617 and (293) from Roeper 1987:278.)

(292) a. *The report was carefully prepared [PRO to be congratulated by the
        board of directors].
     b. *The structure of DNA was investigated [PRO to be awarded the
        Nobel Prize].

(293) a. A vote was taken [PRO_i to elect a president].
     b. *A vote was taken [PRO_i to be elected president].
     c. $John_i$ took a vote [PRO_i to be elected president].

In Landau 2017, I restated these findings in terms of the OC-NOC distinction.

(294) *The Jaeggli-Roeper Generalization (JRG)*
     An active RatC allows OC or NOC; a passive RatC imposes OC.

Recall from section 5.1 that sentences like (292a–b) and (293b) are redeemed if turned into remote control (bisentential) constructions, as in (295) (from Green 2018:147). The reason is that the RatC is no longer an adjunct falling under the jurisdiction of the JRG. The very fact that NOC succeeds in these constructions (OC cannot traverse sentence boundaries) indicates that what makes (292a–b)/(293b) ungrammatical is the unavailability of NOC.

(295) a. The ship was sunk. The goal was to be promoted.
     b. A vote was taken. The goal was to be elected president.

There is reason to believe that the JRG is not a quirk of English alone. Spanish and Hebrew exhibit a similar pattern: a passive PRO can be controlled by the matrix subject (the (a) examples) but not by the matrix implicit agent, which can only control via NOC. ((296) is from Español-Echevarría 2000:98.)

(296) *Spanish*
    a. Juan hundió el barco para ser recompensado por la reina.
       Juan sank the boat for be.INF rewarded by the queen
       'Juan sank the boat in order to be rewarded by the queen.'
    b. *El barco fue hundido para ser recompensado por la reina.
       the boat was sunk for be.INF rewarded by the queen
       'The boat was sunk in order to be rewarded by the queen.'

(297) *Hebrew*
    a. roš-ha-memšala ha-populist horid misim
       head-the-government the-populist lowered taxes
       kedey le'hibaxer šenit.
       in.order to.be.elected second.time
       'The populist prime minister lowered taxes in order to be elected for the second time.'
    b. *misim hurdu kedey le'hibaxer šenit.
       taxes lowered.PASS in.order to.be.elected second.time
       'Taxes were lowered in order to be elected for the second time.'

As Lasnik (1988) observes, not only embedded passives but also other types of predicates, like that in (298c), hamper the possibility of NOC in RatCs.[9]

(298) a. John sank the ship [PRO$_i$ to be promoted].
     b. *The ship was sunk [PRO to be promoted].
     c. *The ship was sunk [PRO to become a hero].

Citing (299a–b) as support, Español-Echevarría (2000) proposes to augment (290) with a semantic condition on PRO, to the effect that it must be assigned the agent role in the RatC.

(299) a. *The book was written [in order PRO to become rich].
     b. The book was written [in order PRO to make money out of it].

However, the very same objections to the adequacy of "agent" in picking out the *controller* of a RatC apply in the case of PRO. Participants who are not grammatical agents yet have the capacity to bring about an eventuality—that is, *initiators*—are acceptable as referents of NOC PRO in RatCs. In fact, even acceptable NOC examples with passive PRO (contrary to the JRG) are found in situations where it is clearly understood as an initiator of the embedded eventuality. ((300a–b) are from Williams 2015:299 and Duffley 2014:192, respectively, and (300c–f) are all attested on the internet.)[10]

(300) a. The king's ship was sunk [just PRO to acquire notoriety].
     b. When a bail bonds company is used in California, only 10% of the total bail amount is paid [in order PRO to be released].
     c. Everything will be done [in order PRO to become famous].
     d. The things that are done [in order PRO to be seen by and get the attention and admiration of people] will not get a reward by the Lord.
     e. The lack of evidence will not make things any easier for him as there is no information about the ladder, and no photographs were taken [in order PRO to be able to assess the condition of the ladder].
     f. A priority admission deadline is the last day completed application files must be submitted [in order PRO to be admitted in time for the start of your intended semester].

How much "control" (in the nonlinguistic sense) an individual has over certain eventualities is open to interpretation; the boundaries of "initiator" as an empirical category are somewhat fuzzy. Green (2018:146–147) dismisses the relevance of the initiator concept on the basis of the contrast between (293b) and (300a), arguing that this concept does not explain why the passive PRO in the former cannot count as an initiator. But in fact, sometimes passive PRO does count as such, as in (300b,d,f). Decontextualized examples make poor testing grounds. Moreover, election being a collective process, it is somewhat more difficult to construe a single voter as responsible for the results of the election in (293b).

In light of these considerations, I suggest that RESP is the relevant notion for describing the restriction on embedded predicates in RatCs under NOC. This restriction applies *in addition to* the general restriction that Farkas (1988) has identified, namely, that there must be an initiator to the matrix eventuality. We can separate the different conditions as follows.

(301) *Conditions on RatC constructions*

In a RatC construction, where S_m, S_e are the matrix and embedded eventualities:

a. $\text{Rat}(S_m, S_e)$

b. $\exists i \, [\text{RESP} \, (i, S_m)]$

If the subject of S_e is NOC PRO:

c. $\text{PRO} = i$

d. $\text{RESP} \, (\text{PRO}, S_e)$

(301a–b) replicate Farkas's (290a–b); note that the intentional/teleological implication is encoded in the **Rat** relation (as in (279)). These two conditions characterize any RatC construction, controlled or not, OC or NOC. For NOC, (301c) identifies the initiator of the matrix eventuality as the controller, again in line with (290). The novel part is (301d), which accounts for the JRG, its extensions as well as the "exceptions." Whenever PRO is not in a RESP relation to the embedded eventuality, the grammar can only resort to OC by the local subject; this is the source of all the anomalous readings observed in the ungrammatical examples cited above. Strictly speaking, sentences like *The ship was sunk to be promoted* are not ungrammatical (i.e., the grammar generates them). Rather, they are forced to receive an anomalous OC reading on pain of NOC being filtered out by (301d).[11]

As observed in Landau 2017, although the JRG was originally understood as a fact about the interaction of matrix and embedded passivization in RatC constructions, its ultimate explanation—here, (301)—does not make any reference to passive. This is because passive itself, or more precisely, "implicit agent control," is but one instance of NOC on the present approach. Indeed, we have already seen that embedded passivization is neither necessary ((298c), (299a)) nor sufficient (300b,d,f) to block NOC.

The same is true of matrix passivization. That it is also not sufficient to block NOC is shown in (300a–f). To see that it is not necessary, we simply have to look at nonpassive matrix contexts that make the NOC reading sufficiently salient and distinct from the OC reading. One such context, already shown to be available to RatCs in (73), is copular clauses.

(302) a. The door is open to greet passing neighbors.

b. The painting was on the wall in order to check how it would be received.

As with Jaeggli's and Roeper's examples, embedded passivization renders such examples ungrammatical. Note that it is general world knowledge that makes the embedded eventualities (*to be greeted . . .* , *to be asked . . .*) unlikely to be within the power of the participant denoted by PRO.

(303) a. *The door is open to be greeted by passing neighbors.
     b. *The painting was on the wall in order to be asked how much it cost.

We further expect RatC constructions involving *two* copular clauses to manifest the same sensitivity to the initiator relation, but crucially only under NOC. (304a) is a NOC example found on the internet (accessed 18 March 2019). Notice that neither the matrix predicate nor the embedded one selects an agent, yet both head eventualities that bear the RESP relation—to the controller and to PRO, respectively—in accordance with (301).[12]

(304) a.   The nozzle itself is just the right size [in order PRO to be able to apply the correct amount of lubricant].
     b. *The nozzle itself is just the right size [in order PRO to be the best gardener in the neighborhood].
     c.   The nozzle itself is just the right size [in order PRO to be useful for your oil pump].

NOC fails in (304b) because "being the best gardener in the neighborhood" is an individual state property, for which one cannot be causally responsible. In contrast, "being able to apply the correct amount of lubricant" is a transitory property that (given the size of the nozzle) can be viewed as within one's causal potential. RESP also fails to hold between PRO in (304c) (= the nozzle) and the state of being useful for an oil pump; an inanimate object cannot be an initiator. Crucially, this is harmless (and irrelevant) because PRO in this last example is linked to the controller, the matrix subject, by OC, and OC is not subject to (301c–d).

Finally, it should be clear that initiators are a proper subset of logophoric centers; in addition to bearing a mental perspective on the reported eventuality, they harness the causal capacity to bring it about. We thus expect to find a certain discrepancy between potential NOC controllers for RatCs and NOC controllers for other adjuncts. In particular, logophoric *non*initiator antecedents should make possible controllers, for example, in temporal adjuncts but not in RatCs. Experiencer arguments seem to fit this description: they are clearly logophoric centers, but are not causally implicated in actuating the eventuality.

That experiencer objects may control into a variety of adjuncts has already been shown in section 11.2. Examples (201a–b), repeated here, illustrate it with absolutive adjuncts.

(305) a. [PRO$_i$ sitting quietly here], the memory stirred him$_i$.

     b. [PRO$_i$ driving to Chicago that night], a sudden thought struck me$_i$.

Next, consider the minimal pairs (306a–b) and (306c–d). To facilitate the NOC reading, the matrix subject is inanimate and the adjunct is preposed. As (306e–f) verify, the matrix and embedded eventualities in and of themselves are compatible with the **Rat** relation; hence, the deviance of (306b,d) is solely due to the failure of NOC.

(306) a.   [Before PRO$_i$ starting to work], the alarm bell startled John$_i$.

     b. *[In order PRO$_i$ to start working], the alarm bell startled John$_i$.

     c.   [Despite already PRO$_i$ giving up eating meat], the lecture shocked the audience$_i$.

     d. *[In order PRO$_i$ to give up eating meat], the lecture shocked the audience$_i$.

     e.   [In order for John$_i$ to start working], the alarm bell startled him$_i$.

     f.   [In order for the audience$_i$ to give up eating meat], the lecture shocked them$_i$.

These facts indicate, once again, that the notion of initiator is not reducible— neither to agent, nor to logophoric center.

Acquisition studies seem to support the conclusion and the general point that RatC control involves extra semantic complexity. Recall from chapter 12 the finding that children often select the matrix object as controller for temporal adjuncts (see (245a)) before they internalize the default subject control choice of adults. This was shown to be a consequence of impoverished pragmatic understanding of the underlying notions of topicality and logophoricity. Now, the evidence suggests that control in RatC adjuncts takes even longer to master. By the time children discard object control in temporal adjuncts, some of them still employ it in RatC adjuncts (Hsu, Cairns, and Fiengo 1985, Cairns et al. 1991, Cairns et al. 1994). This points to delayed understanding of the underlying concepts responsible for selecting the subject as the RatC controller. Crucially, it is not the OC path that is deficient in children, but the NOC one. To master the NOC derivation of RatCs, children must master not only topicality and logophoricity, but also the RESP relation implicated in (301b,d). As long as they do not fully master it, they will lack sufficient knowledge of what it is that makes subjects better *initiators* than objects, leading to a prolonged period of object control responses to RatC adjuncts.

To sum up: The OC/NOC alternation is robustly attested in RatC constructions, as it is with other adjuncts in this category. In addition, RatCs display some specific properties related to the intricate concepts of purpose and causal efficacy that are inherent in the semantics of the subordinator *in order*.

These properties restrict the range of predicates that may be modified by a RatC, whether controlled or not. They further restrict the range of predicates that may occur inside the RatC itself when it is subject to NOC. The RESP relation provides a more accurate description of these properties than previous alternatives that were couched in grammatical voice or agenthood, but it too requires further elaboration.

14.4 Dimensions of Variation

In this section, I briefly address four issues that arise from crosslinguistic comparison of adjunct control constructions: finiteness of adjuncts, nuances in modificational relations, potential extension of the notion of initiator, and variable availability of NOC variants across speakers. I show that the present analysis can naturally accommodate such variation, although much of the empirical work remains to be carried out. Finally, I discuss at greater length how "topic control" can be fully integrated into the TTC on the basis of the present findings from NOC.

14.4.1 Finiteness

One obvious point of crosslinguistic variation, which indirectly affects control possibilities, is the inventory of nonfinite adjuncts each language affords. Synonymous prepositions may display distinct selectional properties across languages. Thus, both *before* and *after* in English take either a nonfinite or a finite complement; in Russian, the counterpart of *before* can take an infinitive but the counterpart of *after* cannot; in Swedish, the opposite holds (the counterpart of *after* takes an infinitive, the counterpart of *before* does not); and in Hebrew, both can take only finite complements. Similarly, *without* in English takes only a nonfinite complement, but its counterparts in German and Dutch take either a nonfinite or a finite complement.

In languages with a clear finite-nonfinite distinction, only the nonfinite forms will be subject to control. Put differently, finite clauses will necessarily be propositional, with null subjects displaying typical *pro*-drop behavior.

14.4.2 Nuances in Modificational Relations

A virtual terra incognita in current research on adjuncts in general and controlled ones in particular is how P heads of adjuncts in different languages choose to carve out the semantic space of modificational relations. As a case in point, consider goal clauses in Polish. As mentioned in note 2 of chapter 4, these clauses alternate with RatCs according to whether or not the complementizer *żeby* occurs.

(307) Filip$_i$ pojechał   [(żeby)   kupić   bilety].
      Philip   went   in.order   buy.INF   tickets
      'Philip went (in order) to buy tickets.'

Huettner (1989:40) characterizes goal adjuncts as follows: "The main clause describes a kind of (possibly abstract) motion towards the goal expressed in the infinitive." The "(possibly abstract)" part is important, for English allows goal clauses in sentences like (308a–b), where the action in the main clause does not proceed along any spatial dimension, but is still conceived as being goal-oriented.

(308) a. He fought to rescue the girl.
      b. She studied to become a doctor.

As it happens, Polish has no accurate counterparts to (308a–b). The complementizer *żeby* is required in these contexts, forcing a RatC reading (Anna Bondaruk, pers. comm.).

(309) a. Walczył   *(żeby)   uratować   dziewczynę.
         fought.3M.SG   in.order   to.save   girl
         'He fought in order to save the girl.'
      b. Studiowała   *(żeby)   stać   się   lekarzem.
         studied.3F.SG   in.order   to.become   REFL   doctor
         'She studied in order to become a doctor.'

Thus, it seems as though goal clauses in Polish are restricted to modifying *physical* motion verbs—(307) but not (309a–b)—a subset of the admissible environments for English goal clauses.[13] This restriction can be naturally added to the denotation of the f_{Goal} relation introduced in (124). Whether Polish or English represents the common case, whether other restrictions apply to f_{Goal} in other languages, whether any principled system underlies the observed variation—all these are unexplored questions, whose answers depend on extensive crosslinguistic documentation, currently altogether lacking.

14.4.3   Broader Relevance of "Initiator"

In sections 5.1 and 14.3, I have demonstrated that the notion "initiator," originally from Farkas 1988, plays a central role in the interpretation of RatC constructions—both in the modification relation itself, and in restricting the referential options of the controller and PRO under NOC. An interesting question is whether this notion plays a similar role in other adjunct control constructions. Answering this question in full is beyond my present goals, partly because the data are murky. Some preliminary observations are nevertheless pertinent.

Recall the conditions of RatC control.

(310) *Conditions on RatC constructions*
   In a RatC construction, where S_m, S_e are the matrix and embedded
   eventualities:
   a. $\text{Rat}(S_m, S_e)$
   b. $\exists i\, [\text{RESP}\, (i, S_m)]$
   If the subject of S_e is NOC PRO:
   c. $\text{PRO} = i$
   d. $\text{RESP}\, (\text{PRO}, S_e)$

(310a–b) are clearly specific to the **Rat** relation and are not expected to apply
beyond its domain. What about (310c–d)? In Landau 2017, I suggested that
these conditions do hold of temporal adjuncts, in light of the contrast between
(311a) and (311b). Green (2018:39–40), however, cites the acceptable examples
given in (311c–d) as evidence that NOC in temporal adjuncts is not absolutely
blocked by embedded passives (note that (311d) is ambiguous between the OC
and NOC readings).

(311) a.   The robbers filled their bags [while PRO being caught on camera].
      b.   *The bank was robbed [while PRO being caught on camera].
      c.   That Gatorade was a vision [after PRO being worked to exhaustion
           by my coach today].
      d.   Chickens taste better [after PRO being forced to eat celery].

On the one hand, the initiator concept is not expected to apply to temporal
adjuncts, whose meaning does not involve causation or intentionality. On the
other hand (as Green himself admits), NOC is more difficult to obtain in
nonagentive temporal adjuncts. The reasons may involve poorly understood
pragmatic biases. How other adjuncts (in the alternating class) behave is an
unexplored topic. Example (115d), repeated here, might suggest that telic
clauses are exempt from (310c–d).

(312) There's a lot of tension building up throughout the film, [only PRO to
       be let down by the final twist].

The controller here is not the initiator of the matrix eventuality, and PRO
itself is not in a RESP relation with the embedded eventuality. However, consider the following examples of justification clauses.

(313) a. John_i brought us all wine and chocolate [for PRO_i being voted
           Boss of the Year again].
      b.   *Wine and chocolate were bought [for PRO being voted Boss of the
           Year again].
      c.   [Wine and chocolate]$_i$ were bought [for PRO_i being the best mood
           lifters].

(313b) satisfies (310c) but not (310d): the patient argument of *vote* is not an initiator of the voting eventuality. This effect looks a lot like the JRG effect in examples like (293b).[14] As expected, (313c) is fine even though (310d) is not satisfied, as it falls under OC. Whether it is indeed the workings of the initiator or any other pragmatic constraint that accounts for these contrasts is a topic that deserves investigation.

14.4.4 Availability of NOC Variants

Throughout this work (see especially sections 1.1 and 11.1), I have emphasized that the true scope of NOC adjuncts has been consistently underestimated in the syntactic literature. Part of the reason is a regrettable neglect of pragmatic factors that influence the availability of NOC. But it seems that there is an additional, ineliminable source: some speakers simply do not accept NOC interpretations of certain adjuncts in the alternating category under any circumstances, even granting all the pragmatic support one could hope for. Within the current framework, the grammar of these speakers can be readily described as only permitting predicative variants of nonfinite adjuncts; that is, P heads of nonfinite adjuncts consistently select properties, so that for these speakers all such adjuncts display strict OC. Such lexical variation is not exceptional elsewhere; note that it is also compatible with the point of chapter 13, namely, that predicative variants are the grammatical default.

Suggestive evidence in favor of this account is presented in Herbeck 2020, where the distribution and interpretation of NOC in corpora of spoken Spanish is examined and compared across five different types of nonfinite adjuncts, headed by *al* 'when', *antes de* 'before', *después de* 'after', *para* 'for', and *sin* 'without'. He reports that the adjunct occurring most often with lexical subjects is also the adjunct showing the highest rate of NOC occurrences: namely, the one headed by *al*. This correlation is readily reduced to a single factor in the present system. All the prepositions just mentioned are capable of selecting either properties or propositions, but the actual availability of the (nondefault) propositional variant varies individually. On average, the preposition *al* has the highest ratio of proposition-selecting variants across Spanish speakers. This explains its higher tolerance both to clausal complements with lexical subjects and to NOC complements.[15]

Outside the lexicon, speakers who do permit NOC variants may still differ significantly in the extent to which they do so. Such variation is to be handled by reference to the different ingredients of "NOC pragmatics" in (229), repeated here.

(314) *Pragmatics of NOC*

In a NOC configuration [. . . DP . . . [PRO . . .] . . .] (order irrelevant), DP may control PRO iff

a. DP is [+top] *or* a logophoric center.

b. Default: [+top] $\rightarrow$ [+human].

Variation is expected in both (314a) and (314b); that is, is topicality or logophoricity the prevailing licensor of NOC antecedents, and if topicality counts, how strong is the default preference for human topics as NOC antecedents? It is not implausible to suppose that pragmatic "parameters" exist in this area; this may account for the (apparent) freedom of temporal adjuncts in Turkish to take object controllers (see (219)) as opposed to the evident marginality of this option in English. These matters have barely been described, let alone analyzed, but they will have to be faced sooner or later if we are to gain a full understanding of adjunct control.

14.4.5 Selection for $C_{[+log]}$ or $C_{[+top]}$

In section 11.4, I showed that the controller in NOC may be either a logophoric center or an aboutness topic. Thus, adjunct control subsumes three types of control clauses: predicative (OC), logophoric (NOC), and topic-oriented (NOC). Within the broader context of the TTC (Landau 2015), two of these types also figure in complement control: predicative and logophoric clauses.[16] An intriguing question is whether the third type is ever attested in complements: are there complement clauses that display "topic-oriented" OC? Notice that this is a new question, of a kind that can only arise within a particular formal model—namely, the TTC model—augmented with the selectional theory of adjunct control. Within this model, the existence of such cases is a natural consequence.

There are, in fact, two grammatical constructions that fit this niche. The first is found in Philippine languages, which display a curious duality in the realm of complement control (Schachter 1976, Kroeger 1993, Falk 2006, Landau 2013:111–115). One type has traditionally been called "semantic control" or "actor control": the controllee is systematically the embedded actor, or in Falk's (2006) Lexical-Functional Grammar analysis, the highest argument function, $\widehat{GF}$. Examples (315a–c) are taken from Kroeger 1993:39 (AV = active voice, IV = instrumental voice, DV = dative voice). Notice that PRO is understood as the embedded actor regardless of its case.

(315) a. Binalak   niya-ng   [magbigay PRO$_{NOM}$ ng-pera sa-Nanay].
       PERF.plan.OV 3SG.GEN-COMP   AV.give   GEN-money DAT-Mother
     b. Binalak   niya-ng   [ibigay   PRO$_{GEN}$ sa-Nanay ang-pera].
       PERF.plan.OV 3SG.GEN-COMP   IV.give   DAT-Mother NOM-money
     c. Binalak   niya-ng   [bigyan PRO$_{GEN}$ ng-pera ang-Nanay].
       PERF.plan.OV 3SG.GEN-COMP   DV.give   GEN-money NOM-Mother
       'He planned to give Mother (some/the) money.'

Schachter and Kroeger presented these facts as a challenge to structural control, on the assumption that the voice system in Tagalog tracks grammatical functions. That is, if the *ang*-DP is the subject, then only (315a) features a subject PRO. In Landau 2015:79–80, however, I disputed this description. Following the alternative analysis of the voice system as tracking a clausal topic (Carrier-Duncan 1985, Richards 2000, Pearson 2005), I suggested that (315a–c) all manifest standard control of a subject PRO. The differences among these variants concern which argument is privileged as a topic, an Ā-operation that does not interact with control. In fact, we may well take these examples—at least (315b–c)—to instantiate standard logophoric OC.

The question is whether (315a) should be given a similar analysis; in this example, PRO is both an actor and a topic, making it difficult to tell which property is targeted by the underlying control mechanism. In fact, it seems that topic control must be an available option in the grammar of Tagalog, given that under verbs of orientation ('want', 'hope', 'insist', etc.), control consistently targets the *ang*-DP—namely, the topic—even if it is not an actor. Another kind of nonactor control is attested with embedded nonvolitive mood (where coercion is called upon if the matrix verb requires a volitional action; examples (316a–b) are from Kroeger 1993:97, 95, respectively.)

(316) a. Nagpilit   si-Maria-ng   [bigy-an PRO$_{NOM}$ ng-pera ni-Ben].
       PERF.AV.insist.on NOM-Maria-COMP give-DV   GEN-money GEN-Ben
       'Maria insisted on being given money by Ben.'
     b. In-utus-an ko   si-Maria-ng   [ma-halik-an PRO$_{NOM}$ ni-Pedro]
       PERF.order.DV 1SG.GEN NOM-Maria-COMP NONVOL-kiss-DV GEN-Pedro
       'I ordered Maria (to allow herself) to be kissed by Pedro.'

Falk (2006:76) comes very close to calling these constructions "topic control." He proposes that Lexical-Functional Grammar's SUBJ function consists of two separate functions, $\widehat{GF}$ and PIV(OT). While the former is controlled in (315), it is the latter that is controlled in (316).

The PIV is a kind of sentence-internal topic. Just as a discourse topic (represented in many languages as the grammatical function TOPIC) identifies a single participant as the common thread running through a discourse, the PIV is the common thread running through clauses that make up a sentence. Every clause in a syntactic structure (sentence) will have a PIV. (Falk 2006:76)

In the present terms, Tagalog exemplifies the missing link we expected to find: topic-bound complement OC. PRO in (316) does not pick out an embedded logophoric *role* (AUTHOR/ADDRESSEE); rather, it picks out an embedded discourse function (Topic).[17] Interestingly, the former option *is* available in (315); Tagalog makes full use of the options available to propositional OC, assigning them to different contexts. Possibly, Madurese can alternate between the two options in the same context (Davies 2005). This is a point of parametric variation. Parallel to Falk's suggestion that languages may or may not choose to bundle the PIV and the $\widehat{GF}$ functions together, I propose that languages may or may not choose to license (by selection) $CP_{[+top]}$ as complement of control verbs. A positive choice will open the way to topic control of the kind attested in Tagalog.[18] Once again, in unselected NOC environments, there is nothing to restrict the availability of $CP_{[+top]}$; therefore, it is available alongside $CP_{[+log]}$, accounting for the pragmatic duality of NOC in adjuncts and subject clauses in *all* languages.

Topic control in Tagalog designates as a topic a matrix argument that is a logophoric center (e.g., the experiencer argument of 'want' or 'hope'). Is there a way to tease apart those two roles? Is there a topic-bound construction in which the chosen topic is dissociated from the attitude holder? It seems that such a construction exists, although it is normally not described as "control." Instead, it is called "prolepsis." Consider the following German examples (from Salzmann 2017:2, 5), where the matrix proleptic object and the embedded pronoun coindexed with it are boldfaced.

(317) a. Ich glaube **von ihm**$_i$, dass **er**$_i$ ein ganz guter Trainer ist.
     I believe.1SG of him.DAT that he a quite good coach be.3SG
     'I believe of him that he is a pretty good coach.'

b. Das ist das Stichwort, **von dem**$_i$ ich mich frage
    this be.3SG the keyword of which.DAT I me ask.1SG
    warum der Autor **es**$_i$ nicht mal erwähnt!
    why the author it not even mention.3SG
    'This is the keyword of which I ask myself why the author does not even mention it!'

Prolepsis is quite common crosslinguistically, although the specific range of matrix verbs that allow it varies from language to language. Salzmann's careful study establishes a number of general points concerning its syntax. First, the proleptic object is base-generated in the matrix VP, although it bears no contentful s-selectional relation to its head. Second, the dependency it forms with the embedded pronouns is island-insensitive (as shown in (317b), where a *wh*-island is crossed). Third, the pronoun is not directly bound by the proleptic object; rather, it is bound by a null operator at the edge of the complement clause. Finally, as in the matching analysis of relative clauses, both the pronoun and the operator are merged with lexical NPs that undergo ellipsis under identity with the proleptic object. The derivation is sketched in (318).

(318) *Analysis of prolepsis*

[. . . *believe* [**of DP**$_i$] [$_{CP}$ [$_{DP}$ Op$_i$ ~~NP~~] [$_{TP}$ T . . . [$_{DP}$ **pron**$_i$ ~~NP~~]]]]

From the present perspective, prolepsis is a sort of "hybrid" between predicative and topic-bound OC. Like predicative OC, it is formed by turning the clausal complement into a derived predicate and subsequently predicating it of a matrix argument. The result is obligatory coreference, and indeed, *some* coindexed pronoun is obligatory, although it need not be a subject. Interestingly, unlike in topic-bound OC, the proleptic object is explicitly introduced as an aboutness topic (*believe of X, say about X*). This topicality is independent of any logophoric content and is freely available to inanimate objects, as in (317b). Thus, we may view the null operator in (318) as a topic operator. However, unlike the common type of topic operators (e.g., those entertained in Huang 1984 and Frascarelli 2007), the proleptic operator is discourse-inaccessible: it must be linked to the most local aboutness topic, namely, the proleptic object. This exceptional restriction may simply follow from compositionality: the CP complement in (318) denotes a predicate that must be locally saturated and cannot seek extrasentential antecedents.

Thus, selection for CP$_{[+top]}$ is manifested both in Tagalog-style topic control and in proleptic object constructions, although only the latter completely dissociate topicality from logophoricity. Important questions remain about the ultimate differentiation between these two strategies of forming cross-clausal dependencies, and the present discussion merely scratches the surface. Nonetheless, we can begin to see the contours of a comprehensive constructional typology emerging from the TTC and its present extensions.[19]

(319) *Constructional typology under the TTC*

	Predicative clause [$_{FinP}$ PRO$_i$ Fin [$_{TP}$ ~~PRO$_i$~~ . . .]]	Propositional clause	
		Logophoric [$_{CP}$ *pro* C$_{[+log]}$ [$_{FinP}$ PRO$_i$ Fin [$_{TP}$ ~~PRO$_i$~~ . . .]]]	Topic-bound [$_{CP}$ *pro* C$_{[+top]}$ [$_{FinP}$ PRO$_i$ Fin [$_{TP}$ ~~PRO$_i$~~ . . .]]]
Complement	Predicative OC	Logophoric OC	Topic control (Tagalog)
Adjunct	OC	Logophoric NOC	Topic-bound NOC
Subject	–	Logophoric NOC	Topic-bound NOC

14.5   Are OC and NOC Really Different?

Something curious happened to the fundamental distinction between OC and NOC that underlies this study: it has been gradually eroded. Is it still true that the two processes reign over distinct empirical domains? This has been the picture all along.

(320) *Extensional relation between OC and NOC readings*

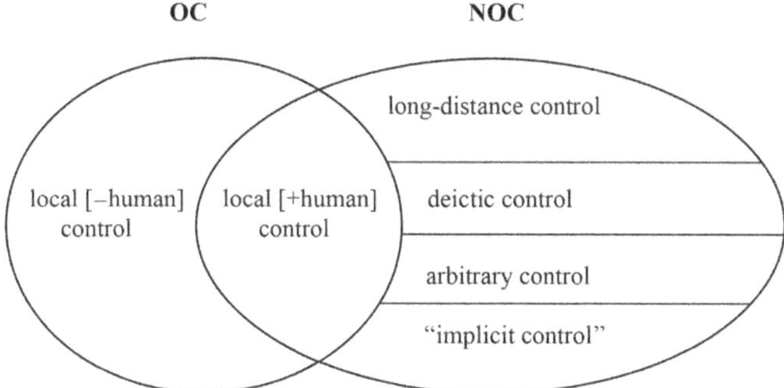

However, is OC *really* needed? As shown in section 14.2, local [+human] subject control is possible under NOC. And as shown in section 11.4, [–human] controllers (local or not) are, under special conditions, also acceptable under NOC. This appears to leave OC with no independent empirical motivation. If NOC has "swallowed up" OC, why continue using these two terms—why assume a dual process? Let us simply assume a unitary phenomenon, called "control," that covers all this ground.[20]

Indeed, the empirical distinction between OC and NOC is no longer straightforward. But the terms have never meant just their empirical extensions; first and foremost, they have stood for different grammatical *mechanisms* of linking PRO to its antecedent. There are plenty of reasons to maintain that distinction, scattered throughout this work. In fact, the reasons are not just theoretical but factual. In this final section, I would like to reiterate the fundamental reasons that warrant the OC-NOC distinction.

First, as the discussion in chapter 4 made clear, there is a class of adjuncts that fall under strict OC. On the selectional theory of adjunct control developed here, they receive a principled account as root modifiers whose semantic type simply cannot give rise to a NOC reading. At least for this class, a unitary theory of control would have to make an exception, somehow stipulating that they lie outside the reach of NOC.

The real issue, however, is the treatment of alternating OC/NOC adjuncts. On the factual level, although it is true that local-subject NOC and inanimate NOC exist, they are highly restricted—and, for many speakers, not available at all. Thus, as a matter of individual mental grammars, OC and NOC often do cut out distinct portions of the "control pie," even for the alternating adjuncts.

A fundamental difference between OC and NOC is the semantic status of PRO: a bound variable under OC, a free variable under NOC. This difference underlies the familiar strict/sloppy interpretation test. If local subject control into adjuncts were just a special case of NOC, we would expect it to allow a strict reading in contexts like (321). This is not what we normally find. Green (2018:139–140) observes that this example "remains true in a situation where Hermione stayed up late in order to help Harry master the summoning charm, but it is false if Ron also stayed up in order to master it himself."

(321) Only Harry stayed up late in order to master the summoning charm.
       = *For no x, x≠Harry, x stayed up late in order for x/*Harry to master the summoning charm.*

Nonetheless, strict readings are possible under special favorable conditions, as shown in (277). Moreover, these favorable conditions selectively exempt [+human] but not [−human] controllers from OC. A local inanimate subject cannot help but use OC, forcing the sloppy reading.

(322) a. Bill felt much better after quitting his heavy drinking. His family
          did too.
          [*His family felt much better after he quit his heavy drinking.*]
       b. The storm was over. Electricity returned after being cut off for 11
          hours. Water did too.
          [*Water$_i$ returned after PRO$_i$/*electricity being cut off for 11 hours.*]

The dual theory naturally explains these facts. Local subject control is obtained by a very strong default (related to Economy of Projection). Overriding this default requires a strong pragmatic bias toward the NOC reading (i.e., construal of PRO as a free variable), but this is only possible if the local subject qualifies as a NOC antecedent by *both* criteria—namely, it is a logophoric center *and* a topic. Inanimate subjects can at most satisfy the second criterion, hence succumb to OC. It is hard to see how a unitary account can derive these facts without replicating the very same distinction it seeks to eliminate.

The phenomenon of remote control, attested in RatCs and temporal adjuncts, also points to an underlying duality of mechanism.

(323) a. George wrote this book in order to get rich.
  b. George wrote this book for a reason. The reason was to get rich.
  c. This book was written in order to be sold to Hollywood.
  d. *This book was written for a reason. The reason was to be sold to Hollywood.

(323a,c) instantiate OC, but (323b,d) cannot, as PRO has no sentence-internal antecedent. Once again, NOC can salvage (323b) but not (323d). Not only do inanimate DPs make very marginal NOC antecedents—the specific semantic conditions on NOC into RatCs (see (301)) disqualifies them in principle. Notice that the contrast cannot be attributed to some semantic dependency between the subject of the first sentence and the noun *reason* (which fails in (323d)); the reason could be external to the subject (conceived by the initiator).

(324) Bill$_i$ will introduce the ambassador to the president for a reason. The reason is to give him$_i$ the opportunity to observe their reactions.

The difference between OC and NOC also shows up in "implicit control."

(325) a. The rain$_i$ washed the stairs [before PRO$_i$ entering the basement].
  b. The stairs were washed by the rain.
  c. The stairs were washed [before PRO entering the basement].

Although the implicit external argument need not be [+human] (325b), it is interpreted as such when controlling PRO (325c). This fact is evidence for a duality of mechanism: OC in (325a), NOC in (325c). NOC controllers must be logophoric centers or highly topical. Because the external argument of a passive construction is clearly not topical (one might say that the passive is a way of "de-topicalizing" it), only the logophoric route is open—hence the [+human] effect seen in (325c).

Once again, a unitary theory will be hard-pressed to explain these facts. Remarking on the contrast in (325), Duffley (2014:163) states that it is "a purely pragmatic phenomenon based on world knowledge of the most likely agent of the action of washing the stairs." However, world knowledge is not relevant here. Even when the actual inanimate causer is overtly expressed in a *by*-phrase, it cannot control the adjunct subject PRO, which must be [+human] (326a); yet it may perfectly antecede a lexical pronoun (326b).

(326) a. #The stairs were washed by the rain before trickling into the gutters.
  b. The stairs had been washed by the rain before it trickled into the gutters.

Next, we saw in section 10.1 that OC and NOC variants differ in their transparency to extraction. While neither one fully admits extraction (due to the Condition on Extraction Domain), there is a clear degradation in the NOC variants.

(327) a. John is well-dressed to greet passing neighbors.
      b. ?Who is John well-dressed to greet?
      c. The door is open to greet passing neighbors.
      d. *Who is the door open to greet?

(328) a. John rewrote his paper after meeting the professor who graded it.
      b. ?Which professor did John rewrite his paper after meeting?
      c. The fate of the paper was unclear after meeting the professor who
          graded it.
      d. *Which professor was the fate of the paper unclear after meeting?

This contrast is particularly challenging to any unitary approach to OC and NOC that trivializes or even wipes out their syntactic differences. If the reference of PRO in *any* adjunct is simply an outcome of the same set of grammatical and pragmatic constraints pitted against each other, it is surely unexpected that the resolution of the process—choice of local or nonlocal antecedent—will interact in any way with extraction from the adjunct. On the present analysis, however, two syntactic differences between OC and NOC are at work: the size of the gerundive clause (FinP vs. CP) and the attachment site of the adjunct (Voice' vs. VoiceP), either or both of which can naturally be held responsible for the observed contrast.

Finally, the developmental evidence presented in chapter 12 points quite clearly to a duality of mechanism in adjunct control. No matter how early they are tested, children always accept local subject control for adjuncts. They may allow or even favor other readings for a short while; for example, if guided by linear proximity or if biased by similarity-based interference, they may prefer object control. Still, they very rarely *reject* subject control. Nonetheless, how tolerant they are to non-local-subject control is much more variable—variability that has long been a puzzle in language acquisition studies. Some children never display any nonadultlike behavior, others allow object control but not external control, and still others allow any interpretation. These variations gradually fade out only after age 5, sometimes later, to converge on the adult grammar. Importantly, their asymmetrical character is rooted in the duality of the grammatical system to be acquired: a syntactic mechanism for OC and a pragmatic procedure for NOC (which already presupposes full mastery of the OC syntax and semantics: predication and semantic composition).

Eliminating the distinction would rob us of the insight it provides into the acquisition sequence.

These seven arguments in favor of the OC-NOC distinction should serve as a proper answer to the skeptic who still wonders why we need a *dual* process of control. I am not familiar with any unitary theory that is able to give a principled explanation for such a rich array of facts, observed at different levels of analysis and grammatical architecture.

15 Conclusion

The study of control, as old as it is, still holds surprises for the willing mind. One especially pleasing surprise is to witness how long-held rigid distinctions give way to subtler understanding, with "forbidden" ties being surreptitiously formed across boundaries thought to be uncrossable not long ago. Consider the complement-adjunct distinction and its repercussions for control. Two deeply rooted convictions (which I used to share) were that complement control, unlike adjunct control, is always OC, and that selection is relevant to complement control, not to adjunct control.

Both convictions turn out to be false. Complement control under verbs of communication displays either OC or NOC (Landau 2020), and adjunct control is heavily shaped by selection, as I have argued here. Interestingly, these convictions were overturned at around the same time, when a better understanding emerged of how selection and control interact—an understanding couched in the predicative/logophoric dichotomy of the TTC.

The way selection plays out in adjunct control is more complex than the way it does in complement control. In complements, selection applies at one level: between the control predicate and its clausal complement. Besides c-selection ([±finite], infinitive or gerund, etc.), s-selection specifies the semantic type of the complement, and certain lexical presuppositions associated with it. If a predicate is selected as complement, the result is predicative control with all of its associated properties (e.g., lack of partial or implicit control). If a proposition is selected as complement, the result is logophoric control with all of its associated properties (e.g., partial control, obligatory *de se* interpretation). All the relevant lexical information is encoded in this relation, between the control predicate and its complement.

In adjuncts, however, selection applies at two levels. First, a P head selects a predicative or a propositional clause as its complement. P heads of strict OC adjuncts opt for the former, while P heads of alternating OC/NOC adjuncts allow either option. At the next level, the PP adjunct as a whole selects the type of matrix eventuality it modifies. Part of this may be expressed as c-selection for particular light v heads ($v_{undergo}$ or v_{do}), but much of it is, again, s-selection: first, selection for semantic type (a predicative or a propositional node within the extended VP), and second, presuppositions pertaining to the modified eventuality (stative or not, agentive or not, perceptual or not, etc.).

While the idea that control is sensitive to selection is not new in itself, the actual extent of its *syntactic* consequences has been largely underestimated. Lexicalist approaches to control (e.g., Sag and Pollard 1991, Růžička 1999, Jackendoff and Culicover 2003) have little to say about the internal structure or external distribution of controlled complements, and nothing to say about controlled adjuncts. In turn, syntacticocentric approaches (e.g., Clark 1990, Larson 1991, Pires 2007, Boeckx, Hornstein, and Nunes 2010, McFadden and Sundaresan 2018) barely note the paramount role of selection in shaping the syntactic structures that they study.

One methodological goal of the present study has been to bridge this gap responsibly: that is, to show that one can be quite precise and formal about certain aspects of selection; couple them with explicit theories of how event structure is syntactically represented and how semantic types are mapped to sentential syntax; and derive from this combination a highly predictive, articulate theory of adjunct control, which has the pleasing feature of enabling many novel empirical discoveries.

The discussion of the interplay between OC and NOC, both across constructions and within the same construction (see chapter 13 and section 14.2), has led to some conclusions of broader significance for grammatical theory. The notion of *competition* was shown to have two distinct senses, grammar-based and processing-based. Economy of Projection is an instance of grammar-based competition: two structures differing in size/complexity compete for the same semantic output. The grammar decides in favor of the smaller/simpler one, and this decision is reflected in two ways. First, the smaller/simpler structure is always available in the grammatical inventory of the language (all NOC adjuncts have OC variants but not vice versa). Second, particular utterance tokens—ones that can potentially be parsed either way to yield a given interpretation—are, by default, parsed as the smaller/simpler structure (local control by a human subject is parsed as OC and not NOC).

By contrast, the reference set of processing-based competition comprises distinct interpretations. The OC reading often trumps a *distinct* NOC reading (leading to the false impression that the grammar does not even generate the latter) for a host of processing reasons: preference for local resolution of gaps, discourse salience of proximate antecedents over distant ones (possibly related to working memory decay), difficulties in simultaneously maintaining multiple logophoric perspectives during online parsing, and so on. None of these preferences is grammatically hardwired, and their relative weights are highly sensitive to context and individual differences. Thus, while no variation is expected in the outcome of grammar-based competition, considerable variation is expected in the outcome of processing-based competition. In addition, careful linguistic manipulation can minimize the impact of these processing preferences to reveal the "dormant" existence of NOC alongside OC interpretations. Similarly, developmental patterns in children are characterized by underdeveloped pragmatic competence, which results in higher rates of NOC acceptance.

Finally, this study has said far too little about crosslinguistic aspects of adjunct control. It is unfortunate that deep and comprehensive analyses in this area are mostly limited to English at present. However, what we already know from other languages has the encouraging character that any expanding linguistic enterprise possesses: a combination of invariant principles with scattered loci of intriguing variation. No doubt, part of the reason for the scarcity of crosslinguistic research lies in the perception that the landscape of adjunct control is either barely mapped out or too chaotic to guide serious language-particular investigations. This perception, I hope, may now be a thing of the past.

Notes

Chapter 1

1. This position is upheld in Manzini 1983 (for modifier adjuncts, though not for extraposed ones), Mohanan 1983, Clark 1990, Hornstein 1999, 2003, Pires 2007, McFadden and Sundaresan 2018, and, in a somewhat weaker form, Fischer 2018. It is also the mainstream view in the acquisition literature, to much detriment (see chapter 12).

2. See Kortmann 1991, Kawasaki 1993, Lyngfelt 1999, Adler 2006, Landau 2013, 2017, Duffley and Dion-Girardeau 2015, and the useful summary in Green 2018:60–71.

3. The Condition B violation under local control in (2b) is not necessary for long-distance control to surface (e.g., replace the adjunct with *after raising issues about their work*).

4. *Herald Tribune*, cited in McCawley 1986–1996.

5. In fact, the adjunct need not be construed in the ellipsis site. The point is that if it is, only local control by *water* is possible.

6. The problem of distinguishing between the two classes of adjuncts is also the primary concern of Green 2018, 2019. Although sharing the motivation and many of the empirical concerns of those works, the present study offers a very different outlook on the problem (see chapter 10 for comparison).

7. Notably different are absolute ("free adjunct") clauses, whose semantic relation to the main clause is very flexible (anterior or posterior temporality, cause, conditional, manner, purpose, contrast, concession, etc.). Kortmann (1991) takes this flexibility to show that no underlying subordinator can be posited, especially because the selected interpretation is so clearly context-sensitive. Yet context sensitivity in no way contradicts strict compositionality, once we allow for underspecified functional elements in the syntactic representation. Consider, for example, how contextual variables restrict the interpretation of quantifiers in examples like *Everybody was amazed* (i.e., not everybody in the world, but everybody *in c* was amazed, for some contextually salient value of c).

 In fact, overt prepositions occasionally manifest such vagueness. If I say *John is with me*, I may mean that John is physically next to me, or that I'm responsible for him (so he should be let in), or that John and I were assigned together as a pair, or that John supports my position, and so on. Vagueness rather than ambiguity seems to be at work here, with the semantic value of *with* being partially open to contextual input. The same *with*—whose core meaning is central coincidence—introduces uncontrolled absolutive adjuncts (*With John being our speaker, our message will definitely get through*). One might assume that the P head of absolutive adjuncts is an underspecified contextual variable, a kind of null *with*, with pragmatic context supplying its value in specific utterance tokens. The inferential processes that enter into the assignment of this value may well be as Kortmann describes them, but they do not affect the syntactic and semantic composition itself. In Stump 1985, the underspecified modificational relation is indeed expressed by a free variable, although one that is introduced syncategorematically rather than lexically. See Zobel 2019 for a purely inferential account of free adjunct modification.

8. Two special cases require further comment. First, there are complex, phrasal adverbial subordinators, which combine paratactically with their CP associate (Blümel and Pitsch 2019). Still, as long as s-selection holds between the PP and the CP, this option requires no special adjustment in the present framework. Second, some subordinating prepositions may have been recategorized as complementizers, for example, *before* and *after* in modern English (Dubinsky and Williams 1995). These may fit into the present framework in either of two ways: (i) embedding the CP under a null P, $[_{PP} \varnothing$ $[_{CP}$ *before/after* $[_{FinP} \ldots]]]$; or (ii) embedding a null C under the temporal one, $[_{CP}$ *before/after* $[_{CP} \varnothing [_{FinP} \ldots]]]$. As long as the proposition-creating head is selected by the modifier-creating head, the semantic composition will proceed unhindered (see section 6.3.2). Bearing these technical adjustments in mind, I will continue to employ the simple [P CP] structure.

9. That adjuncts function as *selectors* is well-established. Thus, manner adverbs (e.g., *loudly*) select events of specific types, evaluative adverbs (e.g., *luckily*) select propositions, often facts, and speaker-oriented adverbs (e.g., *frankly*) select speech acts. See Ernst 2002 for an explicitly selectional theory of the interpretation and distribution of adverbs. Whether *syntactic* selection (c-selection) is needed over and above s-selection is a moot question. Adverbs clearly restrict their hosts (VP and AP, but not NP or PP), but PP adjuncts may attach to just about any predicative category. I will therefore keep to the minimal assumption that the adjuncts discussed in this work (all PPs, by assumption) distribute by s-selection alone. For a c-selectional theory of PP adjuncts, see Zeijlstra 2020.

Chapter 2

1. Although that complement may sometimes be finite; see below.

2. Strictly speaking, the semantic *types* of a property-taking P and a proposition-taking P cannot be the same. However, the semantic *relations* they introduce can be. See the role of g in (125)–(126), section 6.2.

3. Haddad (2017) does claim that Comp-less adjuncts are [+pred] and Comp adjuncts are [−pred]; however, this is a purely syntactic feature for him. In fact, this feature can "override" a semantic proposition and turn it into a syntactic predicate. Adopting the movement theory of control, Haddad assumes that the matrix subject originates as the subject of the adjunct clause (which therefore must denote a proposition). It moves (sideways) to the matrix clause because the adjunct's head is specified [+pred] and movement is said to create a syntactic predicate. Even setting aside the "altruistic" nature of this movement (which does *not* target the adjunct's head itself), the notion

that an open proposition (= the adjunct with a subject trace) can be a syntactic predicate is extremely artificial. By contrast, throughout the present work, predication is
primarily understood as a semantic relation, with syntax perfectly aligned to it, producing λ-abstracts at LF by operator movement.

Chapter 3

1. For extensive discussion of the empirical profile of each type, as well as the relevant references, see Landau 2013:28–38, 230–256. The present chapter draws heavily
on Landau 2017.

2. These are all the nonattitude predicates that trigger what I call "predicative control" in Landau 2015; attitude predicates, which trigger "logophoric control," do
impose the [+human] restriction.

3. This reading is marginal for many speakers because of the default preference for
OC, a well-documented effect (Kawasaki 1993, Lyngfelt 1999, Adler 2006, Landau
2013, 2017, Green 2018).

4. The descriptive literature contains a handful of examples that challenge the
[+human] condition on NOC PRO. (i)–(ii) are cited in Friedrich 1978:241–242 and (iii)
is from Williams 1992:309.

> (i) [PRO$_i$ being stolen], the Bank of England refused to honor the note$_i$.
> (ii) [PRO$_i$ having swelled because of the rains], the workman was unable to remove
> the timber$_i$.
> (iii) [PRO$_i$ having run smoothly for years], it was finally time for my car$_i$ to be
> serviced.

It is perhaps possible to analyze (i)–(iii) as predicative OC adjuncts, fronted from a low
VP-internal position, similarly to other object-controlled adjuncts (cf. structure (130)).
However, in section 11.4 I offer an alternative analysis in terms of "topic control" (see
(122)). More challenging are examples of NOC PRO occurring with weather predicates.
((i)–(iii) are from Quirk et al. 1985:1122, Kortmann 1991:50, and Duffley 2014:181,
respectively.)

> (iv) Being Christmas, the government offices were closed.
> (v) Being Sunday, all banks were closed.
> (vi) Having rained all day long, the hill has become a virtual mud slide.

Kortmann (1991) notes that such examples are extremely rare (none were attested in his
corpus) and suggests that the adjuncts might contain a null expletive (see also Jespersen
1964:313, where these cases are analyzed with dropping of *it*). In section 11.4, I suggest
that these cases, too, should be understood as a special kind of topic control.

Chapter 4

1. Although Green (2019:14) cites the following example. I am not sure that such
metaphorical extensions compromise the general point about selection for an agent.

> (i) Those pants are working hard [PRO to hold in that man's flabby girth].

2. Consider the following contrast in Polish (Bondaruk 2004:221).

(i) Filip$_i$ pojechał [PRO$_{i/*arb}$ kupić   bilety].
     Philip   went   buy.INF   tickets
     'Philip went to buy tickets.'
(ii) Filip$_i$ pojechał [żeby PRO$_{i/arb}$ kupić   bilety].
     Philip   went   so.that   buy.INF   tickets
     'Philip went to buy tickets.'

The complementizer *żeby* has a complex distribution in Polish (Citko 2012). It is obviative with subjunctive and some (desiderative) infinitival complements. With object control verbs, it has no effect on control, but with many subject control verbs its presence allows NOC (while still allowing local control; i.e., it is not obviative). What is relatively clear is that predicative complements (modal, aspectual, and implicative) reject *żeby*, making it a reliable mark of CP-projecting clauses as opposed to FinP-projecting clauses. On this view, the contrast between (i) and (ii) falls nicely out of the present analysis. The infinitive in (i) is a goal clause, hence displays strict OC, which is explained by its predicative nature, correlated with the absence of *żeby*. The infinitive in (ii) is a RatC, hence allows NOC, which is explained by its propositional nature, correlated with the presence of *żeby*. Indeed, the latter can be fronted and the former cannot, just as in English (Anna Bondaruk, pers. comm.). The contrast in Polish is more telling than the one in English because *żeby* is unambiguously a complementizer, directly reflecting clause structure, whereas *in order* is a prepositional element, only indirectly related to the category of its complement. See (26)–(27) for a parallel contrast in Lebanese Arabic.

3. (52a) is from https://thoughtco.com/is-the-aral-sea-shrinking-1434959, accessed 7 December 2020, and (52b) from http://www.amandaheidel.com/the-seed-between, accessed 7 December 2020.

4. https://www.podparadise.com/Podcast/Reviews/1330706945, accessed 7 December 2020.

5. In OPCs, the theme dependency is mediated by an operator that binds an embedded object position (see section 5.2). Nevertheless, I will argue below that both constructions instantiate predication by abstraction. There is a rich literature on the syntax and semantics of purpose clauses in English; see Faraci 1974, Chomsky 1980, Bach 1982, Nishigauchi 1984, Browning 1987, Clark 1990, Jones 1991, Cutrer 1993, and Whelpton 2002.

6. Fischer and Flaate Høyem (2017) claim that direct objects do not c-command low VP adjuncts, hence can only control them indirectly, via little v. Because *indirect* objects do c-command the adjunct and are closer than little v, they take over control in ditransitive/applicative constructions. This claim is falsified by object-controlled SPCs modifying ditransitive VPs.

(i) John built Mary the shelf$_i$ [PRO$_i$ to hold all her art books].
(ii) We bought John$_j$ a puppy$_i$ [PRO$_i$ to keep him$_j$ company].

In fact, SPCs are merged below the direct object; see (130) for the explicit derivation.

Chapter 5

1. Whether there are strictly NOC adjuncts—speaker-oriented adjuncts are an obvious candidate—is an interesting question; I return to it in chapter 8.

2. We may include in this class adjuncts introduced by *without* and *despite*. Notice that (88a–b) directly refute Pires's (2007) claim that gerundive adjuncts introduced by P only display OC. Similarly, his claim that "clausal gerunds in subject position are the only instances of clausal gerunds where NOC PRO properties systematically hold" (p. 180) is false in both directions. As shown throughout this chapter, all gerundive adjuncts in English support NOC. Conversely, certain predicate classes impose OC on their subject gerunds (Landau 2013:41–43).

3. A recent experimental study concludes that "the availability of an external referent for the *ec* [empty category] remains impossible, supporting our classification of final temporal adjunct control as a further type of structurally constrained control" (Janke and Bailey 2017:561). Curiously, the experimental design did not even probe for the possibility of extrasentential control. Subjects were only presented with a choice between subject and object control for the adjunct. The results indicated that priming the object as a topic facilitated object control (see (7)), an interesting finding to which I return in section 11.3, but nothing follows with regard to nonlocal control, which is, in fact, available, as seen in (88), (89b), (90), (92), (93), (96b), and (98e).

4. (94a–c) are respectively from https://nerdeeklife.com/outlander-4x09-birds-and -the-bees/, https://community.babycenter.com/post/a43795168/help_junk_food_is _the_only_thing_i_can_keep_down, and https://www.resetera.com/threads/it-breaks -my-heart-that-we-will-never-get-a-game-like-final-fantasy-xi-again.23194/page-4, all accessed 7 December 2020.

5. Possibly, this is related to the parallel ban on lexical subjects in *wh*-infinitives. There is an ineliminable residue of arbitrariness in any theory of subject licensing, for it is a brute fact that, in many languages, only a proper subset of the nonfinite propositional adjuncts can host a lexical subject. In this respect, little has been learned since the filters of Chomsky and Lasnik 1977.

6. There is an interesting parallel in the domain of gerundive complements. Pires (2007) observes that [–tense] gerunds (those resisting temporal mismatch, (i)) disallow lexical subjects (ii), while [+tense] gerunds allow them (iii).

(i)   *Philip$_i$ tried/avoided last night [PRO$_i$ driving on the freeway this morning].
(ii)   Philip$_i$ tried/avoided [PRO$_i$/*Jane driving on the freeway].
(iii) Last week, Sue$_i$ favored/insisted on [PRO$_i$/Anna moving to Chicago today].

There are good reasons to recast the [±tense] distinction as a [±attitude] distinction, which in turn translates to predicative vs. logophoric/propositional control (see Landau 2015 for discussion). We can then restate Pires's result as follows, along the format of the PVC: for any V that c-selects a gerundive complement X: (i) if V s-selects a predicate, X displays OC; (ii) if V s-selects a proposition, x displays OC or NC (= no control, lexical subject). This echoes Chierchia 1984 but is different in that for Chierchia, *any* OC complement was predicative, whereas for us only those without a propositional variant are; see section 2.2.

7. Examples (99a) and (99b) are respectively from https://www.mmwarburg.de/system /galleries/download/research.mmwarburg.com/Jahresausblick-2019_en.pdf and https:// popula.com/2018/11/06/indiana-los-angeles, both accessed 7 December 2020.

8. Note that the controller is typically understood to be the person from whose perspective the main predication holds: for example, the one who reads in (101b), the one who has the vision in (101c), and the one experiencing the obscuring/highlighting in (101d). Yet in all these cases, this perspective holder cannot be expressed as an argument of the main clause, so is not likely to be grammatically represented as a null argument.

9. Example (102a) is from https://www.facebook.com/speculativephilosophy/posts /the-great-empire-of-the-caliphs-did-not-last-long-for-on-the-basis-presented-by- /2571401772921475.

10. I follow Stromdahl's (2018) name for this type of adjuncts. Green (2018, 2019) names them "response clauses," an unfortunate choice of term, because the response is expressed not by the adjunct but by the main clause (cf. goal/result/stimulus/etc. clauses, where the goal/result/stimulus/etc. is expressed by the adjunct). Moreover, "response" fails to convey the ethical flavor characteristic of these adjuncts.

11. Examples (105a–d) are respectively from https://www.instagram.com/the.lo.down, http://www.woahstyle.com/blog/chic-winter-approved-street-style-outfits-to-copy, https://www.tripadvisor.ca/Restaurant_Review-g33364-d12350115-Reviews-LongHorn_ Steakhouse-Colorado_Springs_El_Paso_County_Colorado.html, and https://www.vox .com/videos/2017/1/30/14382686/jet-fighter-f35-congress-trump, all accessed 8 December 2020.

    Parallel data are reported for Spanish (example from Paz 2019).

(i) Cuba censura   [canción de   Maluma]$_i$ [por PRO$_i$ incitar
     al sexo en grupo].
     Cuba censors   song   of   Maluma for   incite.INF
     the.ACC sex in group
     'Cuba censors song by Maluma for inciting group sex.'

12. https://books.google.co.il/books?id=hN4nii9Fba8C&pg=PA22&lpg=PA22&dq =%22using+statistical+methods+to+radically+speed+up+the+techniques+by+whic h+X-ray%22&source=bl&ots=UXUDPzFiKt&sig=ACfU3U3qLisjHzhFiH_2bb_db VNaq00jOw&hl=en&sa=X&ved=2ahUKEwiy4MXM6b3tAhXDDuwKHbUuBLoQ 6AEwAHoECAEQAg#v=onepage&q=%22using%20statistical%20methods%20 to%20radically%20speed%20up%20the%20techniques%20by%20which%20X -ray%22&f=false, accessed 8 December 2020.

13. https://www.academia.edu/3285375/Treatment_of_Scores_of_Questionable_Valid ity_The_Origins_and_Development_of_the_ETS_Board_of_Review_ETS_Archives _Occasional_Paper, accessed 8 December 2020.

14. (111a–b) are respectively from https://open.library.ubc.ca/cIRcle/collections/73804 /items/1.0389858 and https://desertreefpoodles.com/in-memory, both accessed 8 December.

15. (114a–b) are from http://www.nhgrange.org/secretary%20docs/journals/2017%20 Journal%20of%20Preceedings.pdf and https://www.bbc.co.uk/history/ww2peopleswar /stories/93/a5387493.shtml, respectively. (115a–e) are respectively from https://llgovtech.

co.nz/blog-prototyping-do-they-really-like-your-idea/, https://allafrica.com/stories/2015
07271820.html, https://survivetheark.com/index.php?/forums/topic/232302-547-hours
-played-only-to-realize-everything-gets-stuck, https://www.reddit.com/r/TrueFilm
/comments/2s2nb0/what_have_you_been_watching_110115, and https://www.story
boardthat.com/storyboards/mayarkh/english-comic-pt-2. (116a–b) are from https://
www.investors.com/market-trend/stock-market-today/dow-jones-futures-stock-market
-rally-against-ropes-apple-amazon-netflix-tesla-fall and https://www.abouther.com
/node/16401/lifestyle/travel-food/these-snaps-milky-way-will-leave-you-breathless. All
were accessed 8 December 2020.

Chapter 6

1. I put aside applicative heads and arguments. As it happens, there is no strict OC
adjunct that is controlled by an applicative argument. Control by goals and benefactives (e.g., in OPCs; section 5.2) falls under the general option of NOC.

2. Unaccusative verbs are depicted here with a semantically vacuous Voice projection (encoding morphological information only). Alternatively, they may be pruned to
$vP_{undergo}$.

3. Note that goal clauses are not strictly implicative but do carry real-world entailments (*some* action must be performed toward the stated goal); in that sense, they
resemble *try*-complements (Sharvit 2003). Thus, we can coherently say that John
worked hard to stay out of jail but eventually failed and was put back there.

4. Why selection for property rather than proposition is the default is an intriguing
question to which I return in chapter 13.

5. Except for OPC; see below.

6. The present system takes P heads to be systematically ambiguous between propositional relations (<<s,t>,<<s,t>,<s,t>>>) for NOC variants or property relations (<<e,
<s,t>>,<<e,<s,t>>,<e,<s,t>>>>) for OC variants. It is legitimate to ask whether the sys-
tem can be simplified to one type only. A proposal along these lines (which I owe to
Alexander Williams, pers. comm.) is the following. Suppose that only the propositional relation P exists. The OC adjunct is then derived from the propositional clause
by moving *pro* from Spec,CP to Spec,PP and interpreting it as an abstractor, yielding
an adjunct of type <e,<<s,t>,<s,t>>>. This adjunct can then combine with Voice' (of
type <e,<s,t>>) by Function Substitution (originally the **S** combinator of Curry and
Feys 1958; see Szabolcsi 1983, 1989, Steedman 1987, 1988), effectively identifying the
individual arguments of the two functions and yielding OC. This alternative eschews
the lexical ambiguity of P heads at the cost of enriching the inventory of semantic
rules, but Function Substitution may be required anyway.

    Nonetheless, this alternative analysis raises its own difficulties. First, the machinery
of Categorial Grammar (like Function Substitution) is designed to *replace* syntactic
movement and not to coexist with it (as in this analysis, which appeals to *pro*-movement
as a type-changing operation).

    Second, recall that NOC adjuncts are logophoric in virtue of the semantics associ-
ated with *pro* in their Spec,CP. Deriving OC adjuncts from this source will inevitably
carry over the logophoric semantics—but that is clearly the wrong result: as amply

shown in the text, predicative OC is free of this restriction. If, on the other hand, we allow the P head to take a *non*logophoric, propositional CP complement, a new problem arises: why can this nonlogophoric CP not be used in standard NOC? It seems that only brute stipulation can guarantee that (e.g., a nonfinite, nonlogophoric C *must* trigger movement to its specifier, but a logophoric C need not).

Third, this analysis eliminates the fundamental structural distinction between OC and NOC adjuncts—the idea that the former are smaller (FinP) than the latter (CP). Some evidence for this idea was already presented in (27) and in note 2 of chapter 4, but the main argument for it is presented in chapter 14. The asymmetric distribution of OC and NOC adjuncts (see table (123)), acquisition patterns, and typological evidence all converge on the conclusion that OC variants are available by default, while NOC variants require some additional triggering. The account for this overarching fact that is proposed in chapter 14 capitalizes on the structural difference between FinP and CP, invoking Economy of Projection. If, however, both OC and NOC adjuncts project up to the CP level, that account is lost; if anything, the proposed OC derivation is *more* complex than a NOC one, implicating a movement operation (of *pro*) absent from the latter. Finally, certain extraction asymmetries between OC and NOC adjuncts may plausibly relate to the same structural difference, accounting for the greater difficulty of extraction from NOC adjuncts; see section 10.1 for discussion. Thus, the overall cost of adopting the alternative analysis appears to outweigh its purported benefits.

Chapter 7

1. Note that this does not preclude roots being able to merge with arguments or adjuncts in the syntax. At least s-selection does not rely on formal features. Whether roots c-select their arguments is an open question; see Merchant 2018 for an empirical argument that categorizing heads are responsible for that.

2. For the head of the OPC to mediate all these dependencies, it must be of a super-high semantic type; I leave out the technical details.

3. For the VP-ellipsis examples in (142) and (144), it is important to keep in mind that the adjunct does not *have* to be understood in the elided VP. The point is that it can be, and easily so. Note also that (142d) illustrates subject control OC into a justification adjunct. Object control raises particular issues, addressed in the next section.

Chapter 8

1. On the extreme end of this group we find complete grammaticalization of a few gerundive verbs into conjunctions (e.g., ***concerning*** *this matter,* ***regarding*** *your request,* ***barring*** *unexpected developments*).

Chapter 10

1. Nor are they in complementary distribution in complements (Landau 2020).

2. Recall that on the present proposal, the subject gets to c-command the adjunct only at LF (see (136)).

3. See Dowty 1979, Hitzeman 1997, Lobo 2002, and Artstein 2005 for compelling evidence that sentence-initial temporal adjuncts take scope in their surface position.

4. This conclusion runs counter to Pires's (2007:200n55) suggestion that OC into initial adjuncts necessitates reconstruction. One might argue that the initial adjunct is fronted from a position between the subject and the modal/negation (accounting for both OC under c-command and its wide scope). This, however, would beg the question of why an unfronted adjunct may perfectly scope below the modal/negation.

5. Chomsky (1986a:33) observes that (i) is ambiguous between OC and arbitrary control, arguing that the former corresponds to low attachment of the degree clause and the latter to high attachment (TP-adjunction), outside the c-command domain of the matrix subject. This structural distinction correlates with extraction possibilities; only the former reading survives under extraction from the degree clause (ii).

(i) The crowd$_i$ was too angry [PRO$_{i/arb}$ to hold the meeting].
(ii) Which meeting$_j$ was the crowd$_i$ too angry [PRO$_{i/*arb}$ to hold t$_j$]?

The control-extraction correlation holds quite generally in adjuncts, as we will shortly see, and I will argue that it is indeed indicative of a structural difference in attachment sites. Crucially, however, these data do not warrant the claim that the *arb* reading is associated with TP-adjunction. Parallel to (173), the degree clause can be forced to be c-commanded by the subject and still possess that reading. Note that the intensifier *too* is an NPI licensor itself.

(iii) The crowd was too angry [PRO$_{arb}$ to hold any meeting].
(iv) [Every boyfriend she$_j$ had]$_i$ was too dirty [PRO$_{j/arb}$ to let him$_i$ in the house].

It is also doubtful that these degree clauses support NOC. Vanden Wyngaerd (1994:154–161) points out that such clauses are arguments of the intensifier (*too, enough, rather*, etc.), as they can occur with adjectives that do not normally select infinitives (e.g., *This tie is *(too) bright to wear*). The intensifier selects another argument (often implicit, but in Dutch it can be explicit), which specifies the "evaluator," that is, the person for whom the degree is "too much." It is this evaluator argument (of the intensifier) that controls PRO in the degree clause.

6. For ample empirical evidence against Boeckx and Hornstein's (2007) account, see Landau 2013:242–243. Green inherits from that account the assumption that NOC PRO is a last-resort *pro*, failing to explain its logophoric sensitivity.

7. vP-adjunction in (177b–c) is understood in the cited works as VoiceP adjunction is here, namely, as the topmost adjunction site in the verbal projection.

8. See Landau 2001 for a similar interaction between extraction and the OC/NOC alternation in the domain of extraposed clauses.

9. The choice of the verb *please* in (186d) is unfortunate, as subject control by *the story* is possible in principle. Still, the sentence cannot be read with NOC by the initiator, as (186c) can. I should note that many speakers do not accept any extraction out of adjuncts. I take no position on the absolute acceptability of these examples, and focus only on the degrading effect of NOC.

10. The movement analysis of adjunct OC faces independent problems. Unlike raising complements, nonfinite adjuncts are incompatible with antipronominal

environments, indicating that PRO is a pronoun of sorts, rather than a copy (see Postal 2004:94–102, Landau 2013:16–17 for discussion).

(i)   Lots of things seem to be the matter with your transmission.
(ii) *Lots of things can be the matter with your transmission without being the matter with mine.

11. In fact, it is not clear that the Agree-based theories of Fischer (2018) and M&S (2018) derive the basic fact that arbitrary PRO must be [+human] (originally observed in Chomsky 1981:324–327; see Landau 2013:235–237). Both accounts appeal to "failed agreement" in the sense of Preminger 2014. PRO's features remain unvalued in narrow syntax because no logophoric antecedent is projected above it; Fischer is explicit in restricting PRO_{arb} to "nonattitudinal contexts" (p. 34). But how can "failed agreement" result in a [+human] interpretation? Crucially, Preminger's theory is designed to account for a wide range of scenarios involving default agreement morphology (including weather predicates), with no [+human] feature present. Note that these issues do not arise under the TTC, where *all* NOC clauses are logophoric.

Chapter 11

1. Hasty claims for strict OC in adjuncts may be superseded either by evidence for NOC, as in the cases discussed throughout this section, or by evidence for no control at all. The latter possibility is exemplified by Kissock (2013), who convincingly refutes Haddad's (2009) OC analysis of certain adjuncts in Telugu. Kissock advances a *pro* analysis, but her data are compatible with NOC as well (distinguishing *pro* from NOC PRO is a subtle matter; see section 11.4).

2. Español-Echevarría's (2000) claim that Greek lacks NOC is, ipso facto, refuted by these data.

3. Experiencers may still raise at LF, but adjunct control does not motivate this analysis; see Landau 2010b:chap. 8 for additional arguments.

4. (214a–b) are from http://www.digitaljournal.com/article/235347 and http://robert saunders.org.uk/flies-and-bikes/2018/09/15/astwood-20-15-9-18, both accessed 8 December 2020.

5. I use VP-ellipsis rather than VP-fronting as the latter sounds awkward in spoken English. The structural implications of the two tests are the same.

6. (215a–b) are from http://www.endofthepavement.com/troutCampRiver.html and https://www.tripadvisor.com/LocationPhotoDirectLink-g635527-d2160826-i138311021 -Hard_Rock_Cafe-Batu_Ferringhi_Penang_Island_Penang.html, respectively, both accessed 8 December 2020.

7. (217) is from http://woodschristianhome.info/431-2, accessed 8 December 2020.

8. Note that the last sentence itself involves OC (by *they*) into an initial adjunct; see (170) for more such examples.

9. That PRO and *pro* are underlyingly the same element is, of course, an old idea, with views differing on whether the element is an anaphor (Manzini 1983, Bouchard 1984, Lebeaux 1984), a pronoun (Bresnan 1982, Huang 1989, Petter 1998), or some

minimal variable, valued during the derivation (Holmberg, Nayudu, and Sheehan 2009, Manzini 2009, Landau 2015, McFadden and Sundaresan 2018). What is at stake here is rather a different issue: not whether the two labels reflect a single grammatical element, but whether they even delineate distinct empirical domains.

10. Adler (2006:99) attempts to reduce logophoricity effects to topicality and to demonstrate that they are merely artifacts. She considers the following contrast, based on similar examples in Williams 1992.

(i)   Having just arrived in town, the grand old hotel impressed Bill.
(ii) *Having just arrived in town, the grand old hotel collapsed on Bill.

While Williams accounts for this contrast by reference to the semantic role of *Bill* (experiencer vs. theme), which supports a mental perspective only in (i), Adler argues that it reflects the general accessibility hierarchy for topics: direct objects are more accessible than indirect objects as candidates for topic. However, it can easily be shown that when the syntactic categories are reversed, it is still the experiencer that can control (even as a PP) and the theme that cannot (even as a DP), as discussed in section 11.2. Thus, logophoric status cannot be reduced to topicality.

(iii) Having just arrived in town, the snow really appealed to Bill.
(iv) *Having just arrived in town, the snow totally covered Bill.

11. "Quasi-arguments" (weather and temporal *it*) can also function as OC controllers, unlike pure expletives. This is consistent with the former bearing some minimal semantic content. See Rizzi 1986 for further distributional differences between null quasi-arguments and null expletives. (The contrast in (i)–(ii) is attributed to Richard Kayne in Postal 1974:161n56, 35n3).)

(i) Around here, it always snows [before PRO_i raining].
(ii) There$_i$ can't be peace [without there/*PRO_i being war first].

Consider also (iii)–(iv). (Example (iii) is from Heidi Harley, pers. comm., and the Italian example (iv) is from Alba-Salas 2004:42.)

(iii) It$_i$ is clear that John is guilty [without it/*PRO_i being believed that he is a bad person].

(iv) *Sembrasempre che Eva canti [dopo PRO avere/essere sembrato che balli].
     seems always that Eva sings after have.INF/be.INF seemed that dances
     Lit. 'It always seems that Eva sings after seeming that she dances.'

Given that OC is exempt from the pragmatic conditions constraining NOC, the explanation for (iii)–(iv) must be different from the explanation for (228a–c). On the present analysis, it is straightforward. OC temporal adjuncts are predicates that combine with the main event by a series of functional applications (see (133)). The adjunct clause is turned into a predicate by abstraction over the subject position. When the subject position is not argumental, however, abstraction fails; a variable must have *some* range. Thus, a string like *seeming that she dances* cannot denote a predicate and cannot be semantically integrated.

12. Similar facts obtain in Spanish and German (Jaeggli and Safir 1989); see Landau 2013:235–236 for a summary. Note that example (228b) is not conclusive; we have

already seen that a local human subject strongly suppresses nonlocal NOC interpretations. Nonetheless, expletive PRO is still banned in circumstances favorable to NOC.

(i) *[PRO being obvious that John was late], the ceremony didn't start until 9 p.m.

13. Not just any topic can antecede *zibun*—only one that qualifies as Empathy Focus, or Pivot in Sells's (1987) terms. This may account for the strong [+human] default interpretation, even in the absence of a mental perspective.

14. I use $C_{[+log]}$ and $C_{[+top]}$ instead of $Pers^0$ and $Shift^0$ as the relevant heads of the discourse-related projections, simply to highlight their equivalence in "closing off" the propositional adjunct. The actual labels are not crucial.

Chapter 12

1. For much evidence and discussion, see Chien and Wexler 1990, Avrutin and Wexler 1992, Hyams 1996, Avrutin 1999, Thornton and Wexler 1999, Schaeffer 2000, Batman-Ratyosyan and Stromswold 2002, Schaeffer and Matthewson 2005, and Arnold, Brown-Schmidt, and Trueswell 2007.

2. More accurately, processing will play a role in my account insofar as "weighing" the strength of OC vs. NOC construals is a processing operation. In this operation, however, children are just like adults. What they lack is an informed estimate of the "weakness" of some NOC possibilities, since the underlying pragmatic concepts are still undeveloped (see section 12.4).

3. Object control (under pragmatic priming) was similarly common in Janke and Perovic's (2017) and Janke's (2018b) experiments, which tested the simultaneous subordinator *while* using a picture selection design (presumably free of both processing costs discussed in Gerard et al. 2018). However, the children who took part in these experiments were all age 6 and older, hence outside the relevant age group I focus on here (3–5 years).

4. Other processing effects may still be involved, as Gerard et al. (2017) argue in discussing a separate study; I return to this possibility in section 12.4.

5. Interestingly, in a different session all 5 children chose object control in acting out these sentences, demonstrating the failure of the act-out methodology to faithfully detect grammatical knowledge.

6. It is significant that of these 3 children, none shifted from this NOC stage to a "strictly object control" stage in the next session (as one might expect, given the developmental sequence assumed by the authors). The reason, I suspect, is that there is no such a stage (Wexler 1992, Broihier and Wexler 1995), only a strategy. One child shifted to an object-or-subject control grammar and the other 2 shifted directly to the adult grammar (only subject control).

7. Curiously, children displayed adultlike responses to *without*-adjuncts even at the youngest age (i.e., rejecting extrasentential control). I return to this interesting finding in chapter 13.

8. Note that the local subject may still be selected under NOC, but its "worthinesss" compared with competing antecedents is much reduced.

9. This section focuses on grammatical accounts. Processing accounts, like Gerard et al.'s (2017 2018), are discussed in sections 12.1 and 12.4.

10. Although not discussed in this work, infinitival complements also display some NOC characteristics (e.g., free reference) during very early acquisition, and so the nominalization analysis has been extended to them as well. For example, (ii) is offered as the children's analysis of (i).

> (i) Cookie Monster tells Grover to jump over the fence.
> (ii) Cookie Monster tells Grover about the jump over the fence.

However, while the adjunct-as-nominalization preserves the semantic relation expressed by the subordinating temporal preposition, the complement-as-nominalization radically alters the infinitival original meaning. (i) is interpreted as a directive (transfer of order), but (ii) is interpreted as a communicative (transfer of information). There is no evidence that children fail to grasp the directive sense of (i), and in all likelihood they interpret it no differently than adults. Thus, the nominalization analysis of NOC effects in complements is semantically dubious to begin with.

11. Hyams and Orfitelli (2017:607) suggest that "the presence of an intervening argument . . . blocks the connection between PRO and the matrix subject. As a result, PRO remains 'unlinked,' that is, free in reference, unless it associates with the intervener itself, that is, is object controlled." However, the basic assumption is dubious. First, increased rates of extrasentential adjunct control in children are not limited to sentences with transitive matrix clauses. Goodluck (1987) documents them in sentences without any matrix object like (239a). Second, even matrix PPs often "intercept" control for children, as discussed below with regard to (249)–(250), although these PPs—certainly the nonargumental ones— should cause no intervention on the raising-inspired account of Hyams and Orfitelli.

12. Adler (2006) also attributes children's nonadultlike performance on adjunct control to the lateness of pragmatic development relative to syntactic development. However, following McDaniel, Cairns, and Hsu (1991) and Cairns et al. (1994), she adopts the coordination analysis of NOC in children, which is unnecessary under the present approach.

13. To be fair, there is some disagreement in the literature about whether the evidence weighs in favor of *over*acceptance or *under*acceptance of long-distance binding of logophoric reflexives (see Joo and Deen 2019). I take the former view.

It is a historical curiosity that children's overgeneration of NOC in adjuncts and their overgeneration of logophoric binding—so strikingly alike from the present perspective—were studied, and extensively so, as separate phenomena during the same decade. While the binding facts were framed and understood as a pragmatic delay, the adjunct control facts were explained in terms of syntactic misanalysis. This may reflect the more advanced state of binding theory at the time.

14. In Lexical-Functional Grammar terms, children's NOC is oriented to the TOPIC function instead of the PIVOT function; see (316) in section 13.5.

15. There are no reported studies of how children (before reaching the adult grammar) respond to sentences like (i). However, given that they allow extrasentential control in sentences like (ii) over 50% of the time (Broihier and Wexler 1995), it is very unlikely they will reject it in (i).

(i) The waves were very high before riding the surfboard.
(ii) Gonzo splashed the seaweed before riding the surfboard.

This expectation is consistent with Hsu, Cairns, and Fiengo's (1985) finding that even with two human(ized) matrix arguments, semantic anomaly significantly shifts control from the matrix subject to the matrix object in sentences like (iii).

(iii) The cow pushes the pig all of a sudden after oinking.

16. A straightforward prediction is that constructions for which *only* the NOC analysis is available will display higher rates of extrasentential control, for children and adults alike. Furthermore, the effect of pragmatic highlighting will be more drastic than it is in adjuncts, because no OC variant (which is immune to pragmatic manipulation) exists. Both predictions have been confirmed by Janke (2018a), who studied children's and adults' responses to sentences like *Pouring the water quickly made Luna wet*, which only lend themselves to a NOC analysis. The intermediate status of adjuncts in terms of contextual susceptibility—above the total immunity of complements and below the high sensitivity of subject clauses—confirms their dual OC/NOC nature.

17. Although, crucially, they were still above chance level, which is consistent with *some* adultlike grammatical knowledge of control, as Gerard et al. (2017:10n2) point out. On the present analysis, children at all stages know the OC grammar of adjunct control and are therefore always capable of favoring the local subject as antecedent for PRO.

Chapter 13

1. As noted, Stassen intends these universals to hold of *any* deranking construction—in particular, not just nonfinite ones, and not just in subordination but also in "asymmetric" coordination (where one conjunct features a finite verb and the other verb is "deranked"). Granting that, U1 and U2 are still true as stated.

2. Whether there are semantic relations that universally resist realization as controlled adjuncts is an intriguing question, far beyond the horizon of current understanding. See Reed 2012 for the claim that certain propositional types universally resist realization as controlled *complements*.

3. The relevance of EoP to adjunct control was first observed in Landau 2017. In that work, however, I misapplied the logic of EoP and let it favor OC over NOC even when the two yielded *distinct* interpretations. This error is removed in the present implementation.

4. Adler (2006) attributes this effect to the absence of a plausible "error" of misanalyzing *without* as a conjunction. Solutions appealing to syntactic misattachment or conjunction raise numerous difficulties (Wexler 1992, Goodluck 2001, Gerard 2020); see chapter 12 for discussion.

5. This analysis is possibly challenged by examples in which the pronoun is in the matrix clause and the name is embedded.

(i) Grover touches him$_i$ before Bert$_i$ climbs up the steps.

McDaniel, Cairns, and Hsu (1991) report that 2 of the 3 ACR children in their longitudinal study required coreference between *him* and *Bert* in this sentence, and 1 judged it marginal. It is hard to draw firm conclusions from this unstable pattern, which might not fall together with the judgments reported in the text (note also that the child who disliked coreference in (i) still required it in (263b–c)). If (i) turns out to be of a piece with the rest of the judgments in (263), some method will be required to make the clause [*Bert climbs up the steps*] predicative, by somehow abstracting over a variable associated with *Bert*. It is instructive to look at analogues in prolepsis, where the embedded bound position may host not only personal pronouns but also demonstrative pronouns, epithets, and even full NPs (Salzmann 2017).

6. Assuming that ACR children do not misattach temporal adjuncts, obligatory coreference is expected between the embedded pronoun and the matrix *subject*; yet some of the ACR children imposed coreference with the matrix *object*, as indicated in (263). This must be an effect of an independent pragmatic constraint operative at the same age (the Pronoun Coreference Requirement; see below). In principle, the two subgroups of children should be experimentally distinguishable, a prediction left here for future research.

7. Of course, many children do not evince the ACR stage. These children employ NOC as early as they do OC in adjuncts. Presumably, they move beyond the default, predicative option too soon to be identified as having ACR grammars. What distinguishes the two populations of children is an interesting developmental question.

8. In fact, Cairns et al. (1995) draw the opposite conclusion: "If the responses of the PCR children to sentences with PRO and pronouns are similarly affected by biasing context, we would conclude that the PCR is a grammatical phenomenon." The presupposition here is that adjunct control is wholly grammatical and not pragmatic—a false conception, as amply shown above. Indeed, a strictly grammatical process should be impervious to contextual biases. The fact that adjunct control is sensitive to them plainly indicates that it too has a pragmatic component (specifically, the NOC variant). Cairns et al. reveal their own discomfort with their conclusion in their later statement (p. 13) that "it seems odd to suggest that it [the PCR] is a grammatical phenomenon for children while pronominal reference is a pragmatic phenomenon for adults."

Chapter 14

1. (269c) is from https://mediabiasfactcheck.com/2019/03/08/breaking-u-s-economy -gains-20000-jobs-in-february-indicating-that-the-nations-10-year-economic -expansion-has-potentially-hit-a-speed-bump/, accessed 8 December 2020.

F&FH (2019) include a fourth type of adjunct in their discussion: sentence-final appositive DPs.

   (i) He went to see her at the hospital, [a bad idea].
   (ii) Martin wants to emigrate after all, [a difficult decision].

These seem quite different, though, by F&FH's own observations. First, they cannot be sentence-initial, possibly because they must follow a prosodic hiatus. Second, they scope over any sentence-internal material, *including* the adjuncts in (269). Third, they cannot be coordinated with the latter adjuncts. Fourth (unmentioned by F&FH), they are restricted to root contexts. I assume that these appositive DPs are evaluative expressions introduced in a designated projection (EvalP) at the left periphery of the sentence.

2. This is not strictly true; *which*-appositives are presupposed while event-controlled adjuncts are asserted. This difference, though, is orthogonal to the common feature of a proposition functioning as an individual.

3. Recall from (268) that finite adjuncts may be predicative as well as propositional.

4. The logic here harks back to Chierchia's (1984) classical argument from complement control.

> (i) Ezio began/liked playing the violin, and Nando began it too.   **strict*, √*sloppy*
> (ii) Ezio began/liked playing the violin, and Nando liked it too.   √*strict*, √*sloppy*

The crucial factor is the verb selecting the anaphoric pronoun *it*. Following *begin*, which selects a property, *it* only allows a sloppy reading. Following *like*, which selects a proposition (or a property, according to Chierchia), a strict reading is allowed; see Wurmbrand 2002 for relevant discussion. The elided adjuncts in (277) pattern with *it* in (ii) in supporting a propositional denotation. Note that under VP-ellipsis, control complements do not support a strict reading. This *may* follow from a property denotation for PRO infinitives/gerunds, as Chierchia hypothesizes, or from the lexical interaction with the control verb (an interaction absent with adjuncts). In Landau 2015, attitude control complements are given a propositional denotation.

5. In fact, the adjunct need not be construed in the ellipsis site. The point is that if it is so construed, only local control by *water* is possible.

6. Parker, Lago, and Phillips (2015) refer to "animacy," but all their data are consistent with the narrower property of humanness.

7. Once again, how accessible the NOC reading is in practice, in the presence of a possible OC reading, is a separate matter—a matter of performance, not competence. The grammar generates the NOC structure; factors like logophoric status, topic salience, and distance from PRO affect this accessibility in subtle ways.

8. There is one type of RatC construction, hardly ever discussed, that is exempt from Farkas's RESP condition (290a) (incorporated below as (301b)). In the presence of a matrix modal of necessity, the RatC is construed as a conditional clause. In this context, the RESP condition is voided, as first observed (under different terms) by Faraci (1974:34). I leave out discussion of these cases. See also note 12 below.

> (i) #Ivan was tall (in order) to attract attention.
> (ii) Ivan must/needs to be tall (in order) to attract attention.

9. Lasnik (1988) advocated an "event control" account of (298b–c), but other examples demonstrate that PRO in a RatC under a passive matrix verb need not refer to events.

> (i)   The doors were opened [PRO to enter the room].
> (ii)   The fines were paid [(in order) PRO to avoid further complications].
> (iii) Many theories were proposed [(in order) PRO to understand rationale clauses].

10. Such examples are rare because they require construing a passive event as being initiated by (i.e., within the causal capacity of) the underlying object, which is

more often than not pragmatically implausible. Duffley (2014:193) cites two further "counterexamples" to the JRG (his (181)–(182)), but these, in fact, exhibit OC by the derived subject.

(300c–f) are respectively from https://evoplus.ch/anabolic-steroids-the-big-fraud/, http://jimbomkamp.com/matthew/Matt_5-6P1.htm, https://www.probono.org.za/when -can-an-employer-be-held-liable-for-an-employees-injuries, and https://www.emich .edu/admissions/deadlines.php, all accessed 8 December 2020.

11. One conclusion reached in Landau 2017 is that the **Rat** relation, in itself, does not entail (301c–d); this is evident from OC instances of RatCs that do not satisfy these conditions, like (72). Short of a deeper explanation, then, (301c–d) should be viewed as constructional pragmatic constraints.

12. The modification relation between the two eventualities reflects teleological design rather than purpose. See Kitagawa 1976 for a careful analysis of the different semantic nuances afforded by RatC constructions.

13. I thank Anna Bondaruk for discussion of this point.

14. Note that if this is true, it would also explain the deviance of (109d).

15. Once again, crosslinguistic work only begins to unearth the range of variation. Although Herbeck (2020) found overt subjects and uncontrolled ones (overt or not) with *para*-infinitives in European Spanish, Gómez (2020) reports that only controlled subjects (overt or not) are tolerated with *para*-infinitives in Colombian Spanish. Perhaps *para* is ambiguous between P_{pred} and P_{prop} in the former dialect and only instantiates P_{pred} in the latter (bearing in mind, though, that NOC is underestimated and the differences may amount to distributional frequencies only).

16. Unlike logophoric clauses in adjunct position, those in complement position yield OC because the context of evaluation for the embedded AUTHOR and ADDRESSEE roles is selected to be the matrix context.

17. If the characteristic *de se* reading of PRO under attitude verbs (of which orientation verbs are a subclass) is singularly linked to the embedded AUTHOR/ADDRESSEE roles, as claimed in Landau 2015, we might expect PRO in topic-bound complements to be free of this interpretive restriction. The facts in Tagalog have yet to be determined, but I hesitate to state this as a *prediction*. The exact nature of the topic function activated in control might implicate *de se* on its own. For example, if the controlled topic is related to Empathy Focus, to the Pivot role, or to POV, *de se* may arise independently. These issues clearly deserve further empirical and theoretical development.

18. It seems plausible to link this option to the voice system, which makes it possible to identify which argument the null topic corresponds to by inspecting the verbal morphology (Landau 2015:96n2).

19. The single blank cell in table (319) reflects a specific assumption: namely, that a subject may not be an unsaturated projection, at least not when the predicate is also unsaturated (hence, specification and inversion clauses are unproblematic). For a defense of this assumption in the context of NOC into subject clauses, see Chierchia and Jacobson 1986. This leaves open the challenging cases of subject clauses displaying OC, as with *easy*-predicates and the *rude-of* class (Landau 2013:41). If predication

cannot be the vehicle of OC here, because subjects cannot be predicative, then what is this vehicle? Perhaps nonlocal control into these subject clauses is grammatically well-formed but leads to an interpretive clash with certain lexical presuppositions.

20. My understanding of Kortmann 1991, Lyngfelt 2000, and Duffley 2014 is that the authors all endorse different versions of such a unitary theory; the same principles, in the same components of grammar, apply to so-called OC and NOC constructions. See Landau 2013:255n19 for specific difficulties that arise in Lyngfelt's (Optimality Theory) account due to the unitarity assumption.

References

Adesola, Oluseye. 2005. Pronouns and null operators: Ā-dependencies and relations in Yoruba. PhD dissertation, Rutgers University.

Adler, Allison N. 2006. Syntax and discourse in the acquisition of adjunct control. PhD dissertation, MIT.

Alba-Salas, Josep. 2004. Lexically selected expletives: Evidence from Basque and Romance. *SKY Journal of Linguistics* 17, 35–100.

Arnold, Jennifer E., Sarah Brown-Schmidt, and John Trueswell. 2007. Children's use of gender and order-of-mention during pronoun comprehension. *Language and Cognitive Processes* 22, 527–565.

Artstein, Ron. 2005. Quantificational arguments in temporal adjunct clauses. *Linguistics and Philosophy* 28, 541–597.

Avrutin, Sergey. 1999. *Development of the syntax-discourse interface*. Dordrecht: Kluwer.

Avrutin, Sergey, and Jennifer Cunningham. 1997. Children and reflexivity. In *Proceedings of BUCLD 21*, ed. by Elizabeth Hughes, Mary Hughes, and Annabel Greenhill, 13–23. Somerville, MA: Cascadilla Press.

Avrutin, Sergey, and Kenneth Wexler. 1992. Development of Principle B in Russian: Coindexation at LF and coreference. *Language Acquisition* 2, 259–306.

Bach, Emmon. 1982. Purpose clauses and control. In *The nature of syntactic representation*, ed. by Pauline Jacobson and Geoffrey K. Pullum, 35–57. Dordrecht: Reidel.

Baker, Mark, Kyle Johnson, and Ian Roberts. 1989. Passive arguments raised. *Linguistic Inquiry* 20, 219–251.

Batman-Ratyosyan, Natalie, and Karin Stromswold. 2002. Morphosyntax is easy, discourse pragmatics is hard. In *Proceedings of BUCLD 26*, ed. by Barbora Skarabela, Sarah A. Fish, and Anna H.-J. Do, 793–804. Somerville, MA: Cascadilla Press.

Blümel, Andreas, and Hagen Pitsch. 2019. Adverbial clauses: Internally rich, externally null. *Glossa* 4(1), 19.

Boeckx, Cedric, and Norbert Hornstein. 2004. Movement under control. *Linguistic Inquiry* 35, 431–452.

Boeckx, Cedric, and Norbert Hornstein. 2007. On (non-)obligatory control. In *New horizons in the analysis of control and raising*, ed. by William D. Davies and Stanley Dubinsky, 251–262. Dordrecht: Springer.

Boeckx, Cedric, Norbert Hornstein, and Jairo Nunes. 2010. *Control as movement.* Cambridge: Cambridge University Press.

Bondarenko, Tatiana. 2019. Combining CPs by Restrict: Evidence from Buryat. In *Proceedings of the 14th Workshop on Altaic Formal Linguistics,* ed. by Tatiana Bondarenko, Colin Davis, Justin Colley, and Dmitry Privoznov, 29–36. Cambridge, MA: MIT, MIT Working Papers in Linguistics.

Bondaruk, Anna. 2004. *PRO and control in English, Irish and Polish: A Minimalist analysis.* Lublin: Wydawictwo KUL.

Borer, Hagit. 2005. *Structuring sense.* Vol. 2, *The normal course of events.* Oxford: Oxford University Press.

Bošković, Željko. 1996. Selection and the categorial status of infinitival complements. *Natural Language and Linguistic Theory* 14, 269–304.

Bošković, Željko. 2002. On multiple *wh*-fronting. *Linguistic Inquiry* 33, 351–383.

Bouchard, Denis. 1984. *On the content of empty categories.* Dordrecht: Foris.

Branan, Kenyon, and Abdul-Razak Sulemana. 2019. In Bùlì, covert movement licenses parasitic gaps. In *Proceedings of WCCFL 36,* ed. by Richard Stockwell, Maura O'Leary, Zhongshi Xu, and Z. L. Zhou, 81–90. Somerville, MA: Cascadilla Press.

Bresnan, Joan. 1982. Control and complementation. *Linguistic Inquiry* 13, 343–434.

Broihier, Kevin, and Ken Wexler. 1995. Children's acquisition of control in temporal adjuncts. In *Papers on language processing and acquisition,* ed. by Carson T. Schütze, Jennifer Ganger, and Kevin Broihier, 193–220. Cambridge, MA: MIT, MIT Working Papers in Linguistics.

Browning, M. A. 1987. Null operator constructions. PhD dissertation, MIT.

Cairns, Helen S. 2013. Metalinguistic skills of children. In *Generative linguistics and acquisition: Studies in honor of Nina M. Hyams,* ed. by Misha Becker, John Grinstead, and Jason Rothman, 271–290. Amsterdam: John Benjamins.

Cairns, Helen S., Dana McDaniel, Jennifer Ryan Hsu, Sandra Parsons, and Dahlia Konstantyn. 1995. Grammatical and discourse principles in children's grammars: The Pronoun Coreference Requirement. *CUNY Forum* 19, 27–37.

Cairns, Helen S., Dana McDaniel, Jennifer Ryan Hsu, and Michelle Rapp. 1994. A longitudinal study of principles of control and pronominal reference in child English. *Language* 70, 260–288.

Cardinaletti, Anna. 1990. Subject/Object asymmetries in German null-topic constructions and the status of SpecCP. In *Grammar in progress: GLOW essays for Henk van Riemsdijk,* ed. by Joan Mascaró and Marina Nespor, 75–84. Dordrecht: Foris.

Cardinaletti, Anna, and Giuliana Giusti. 2001. "Semi-lexical" motion verbs in Romance and Germanic. In *Semi-lexical categories: The function of content words and the content of function words,* ed. by Norbert Corver and Henk van Riemsdijk, 371–414. Berlin: de Gruyter.

Carlson, Greg N. 1990. Intuitions, category and structure: Comments on McDaniel and Cairns. In *Language processing and language acquisition,* ed. by Lyn Frazier and Jill de Villiers, 327–333. Dordrecht: Kluwer.

Carrier-Duncan, Jill. 1985. Linking of thematic roles in derivational word formation. *Linguistic Inquiry* 16, 1–34.

Charnavel, Isabelle. 2020. Logophoricity and locality: A view from French anaphors. *Linguistic Inquiry* 51, 671–723.

Chien, Yu-Chin, and Kenneth Wexler. 1990. Children's knowledge of locality conditions in binding as evidence for the modularity of syntax and pragmatics. *Language Acquisition* 1, 225–295.

Chierchia, Gennaro. 1984. Topics in the syntax and semantics of infinitives and gerunds. PhD dissertation, University of Massachusetts, Amherst.

Chierchia, Gennaro. 1985. Formal semantics and the grammar of predication. *Linguistic Inquiry* 16, 417–443.

Chierchia, Gennaro. 1989. Structured meanings, thematic roles and control. In *Properties, types and meanings II*, ed. by Gennaro Chierchia, Barbara Partee, and Raymond Turner, 131–166. Dordrecht: Kluwer.

Chierchia, Gennaro, and Pauline Jacobson. 1986. Local and long distance control. In *Proceedings of NELS 16*, ed. by Stephen Berman, Jae-Woong Choe, and Joyce McDonough, 57–74. Amherst: University of Massachusetts, Graduate Linguistic Student Association.

Chierchia, Gennaro, and Raymond Turner. 1988. Semantics and property theory. *Linguistics and Philosophy* 11, 261–302.

Chomsky, Noam. 1980. On binding. *Linguistic Inquiry* 11, 1–46.

Chomsky, Noam. 1981. *Lectures on government and binding.* Dordrecht: Foris.

Chomsky, Noam. 1982. *Some concepts and consequences of the theory of government and binding.* Cambridge, MA: MIT Press.

Chomsky, Noam. 1986a. *Barriers.* Cambridge, MA: MIT Press.

Chomsky, Noam. 1986b. *Knowledge of language: Its nature, origin, and use.* New York: Praeger.

Chomsky, Noam. 1991. Some notes on economy of derivation and representation. In *Principles and parameters in comparative grammar*, ed. by Robert Friedin, 417–454. Cambridge, MA: MIT Press.

Chomsky, Noam, and Howard Lasnik. 1977. Filters and control. *Linguistic Inquiry* 8, 425–504.

Cinque, Guglielmo. 1999. *Adverbs and functional heads: A cross-linguistic perspective.* New York: Oxford University Press.

Cinque, Guglielmo. 2004. "Restructuring" and functional structure. In *The cartography of syntactic structures.* Vol. 3, *Structures and beyond*, ed. by Adriana Belletti, 132–191. Oxford: Oxford University Press.

Citko, Barbara. 2012. Control and obviation: A view from Polish. Paper presented at SinFonIJA 5, University of Vienna.

Clark, Robin. 1990. *Thematic theory in syntax and interpretation.* London: Routledge.

Collins, Chris. 2005. A smuggling approach to the passive in English. *Syntax* 8, 81–120.

Comrie, Bernard. 1981. *Language universals and linguistic typology: Syntax and morphology.* Oxford: Basil Blackwell.

Coopmans, Peter, Margareet Krul, Esther Planting, Ilse Vlasveld, and Albert van Zoelen. 2004. Dissolving a Dutch delay in the acquisition of syntactic and logophoric reflexives. In *Proceedings of BUCLD 28*, ed. by Alejna Brugos, Linnea Micciulla, and Christine E. Smith, 108–119. Somerville, MA: Cascadilla Press.

Cresti, Diana. 1990. A unified view of psych-verbs in Italian. In *Grammatical relations: A cross-theoretical perspective*, ed. by Katarzyna Dziwirek, Patrick Farrell, and Errapel Mejías-Bikandi, 59–81. Stanford, CA: CSLI Publications.

Culicover, Peter, and Ray Jackendoff. 2005. *Simpler Syntax.* Oxford: Oxford University Press.

Curry, Haskell B., and Robert Feys. 1958. *Combinatory logic, vol. I.* Amsterdam: North Holland.

Cutrer, Michelle L. 1993. Semantic and syntactic factors in control. In *Advances in Role and Reference Grammar*, ed. by Robert D. Van Valin Jr., 167–195. Amsterdam: John Benjamins.

D'Alessandro, Roberta, Irene Franco, and Ángel J. Gallego, eds. 2017. *The verbal domain.* Oxford: Oxford University Press.

Davies, William D. 2005. Madurese control. *K@ta* 7, 1–12.

Deal, Amy Rose. 2017. Shifty asymmetries: Universals and variation in shifty indexicality. Ms., University of California, Berkeley.

De Cat, Cécile. 2009. Experimental evidence for preschoolers' mastery of "topic." *Language Acquisition* 16, 224–239.

De Cat, Cécile. 2011. Information tracking and encoding in early L1: Linguistic competence vs. cognitive limitations. *Journal of Child Language* 38, 828–860.

Dimroth, Christine, and Bhuvana Narasimhan. 2012. The acquisition of information structure. In *The expression of information structure*, ed. by Manfred Krifka and Renate Musan, 319–361. Berlin: Mouton de Gruyter.

Dowty, David. 1979. *Word meaning and Montague Grammar.* Dordrecht: Reidel.

Dubinsky, Stanley, and Kemp Williams. 1995. Recategorization of prepositions as complementizers: The case of temporal prepositions in English. *Linguistic Inquiry* 26, 125–137.

DuBois, John W. 1987. The discourse basis of ergativity. *Language* 63, 805–855.

Duffley, Patrick J. 2014. *Reclaiming control as a semantic and pragmatic phenomenon.* Amsterdam: John Benjamins.

Duffley, Patrick J., and Samuel Dion-Girardeau. 2015. Control in free adjuncts in English and French: A corpus-based semantico-pragmatic account. In *Perspectives on complementation: Structure, variation and boundaries*, ed. by Mikko Höglund, Paul Rickman, Juhani Rudanko, and Jukka Havu, 227–248. London: Palgrave Macmillan.

Ernst, Thomas. 2002. *The syntax of adjuncts.* Cambridge: Cambridge University Press.

Ernst, Thomas. 2007. On the role of semantics in a theory of adverb syntax. *Lingua* 117, 1008–1033.

Ernst, Thomas. 2014. The syntax of adverbs. In *The Routledge handbook of syntax*, ed. by Andrew Carnie, Daniel Siddiqi, and Yosuke Sato, 108–130. London: Routledge.

Erteschik-Shir, Nomi. 1997. *The dynamics of focus structure*. Cambridge: Cambridge University Press.

Español-Echevarría, Manuel. 1998. The syntax of purposive expressions. PhD dissertation, UCLA.

Español-Echevarría, Manuel. 2000. The interaction of obligatory and nonobligatory control in rationale clauses. In *Proceedings of WCCFL 19*, ed. by Roger Billerey and Brook Danielle Lillehaugen, 97–110. Somerville, MA: Cascadilla Press.

Falk, Yehuda. 2006. *Subjects and Universal Grammar*. Cambridge: Cambridge University Press.

Faraci, Robert. 1974. Aspects of the grammar of infinitives and *for*-phrases. PhD dissertation, MIT.

Farkas, Donca F. 1988. On obligatory control. *Linguistics and Philosophy* 11, 27–58.

Fischer, Silke. 2018. Locality, control, and non-adjoined islands. *Glossa* 3(1), 82.

Fischer, Silke, and Inghild Flaate Høyem. 2017. Adjunct control. Handout of a talk presented at the 32nd meeting of the Comparative Germanic Syntax Workshop, NTNU Trondheim.

Fischer, Silke, and Inghild Flaate Høyem. 2019. Event control. Handout of a talk presented at the workshop "Crosslinguistic Variation in Control Phenomena," DGFS 41, University of Bremen.

Fox, Danny. 2000. *Economy and semantic interpretation*. Cambridge, MA: MIT Press.

Fox, Danny, and Yosef Grodzinsky. 1998. Children's passive: A view from the *by*-phrase. *Linguistic Inquiry* 29, 311–332.

Frascarelli, Mara. 2007. Subjects, topics and the interpretation of referential *pro. Natural Language and Linguistic Theory* 25, 691–734.

Friedrich, Wolf. 1978. *Die Infiniten Formen des Englischen*. Munich: Unidruck.

Garrett, Edward J. 2001. Evidentiality and assertion in Tibetan. PhD dissertation, UCLA.

Geis, Michael L. 1970. Adverbial subordinate clauses in English. PhD dissertation, MIT.

Georgieva, Ekaterina. 2018. Non-finite adverbial clauses in Udmurt. PhD dissertation, University of Szeged.

Gerard, Juliana. 2019. The extragrammaticality of the acquisition of adjunct control. Ms., Ulster University.

Gerard, Juliana. 2020. Adjunct control and the poverty of stimulus: Availability vs. evidence. Ms., Ulster University.

Gerard, Juliana, Jeffrey Lidz, Shalom Zuckerman, and Manuela Pinto. 2017. Similarity-based interference and the acquisition of adjunct control. *Frontiers in Psychology*, 18 October 2017. https://doi.org/10.3389/fpsyg.2017.01822.

Gerard, Juliana, Jeffrey Lidz, Shalom Zuckerman, and Manuela Pinto. 2018. The acquisition of adjunct control is colored by the task. *Glossa* 3(1), 75.

Giorgi, Alessandra, and Giuseppe Longobardi. 1991. *The syntax of noun phrases: Configuration, parameters and empty categories*. Cambridge: Cambridge University Press.

Givón, Talmy. 1976. Topic, pronoun and grammatical agreement. In *Subject and topic*, ed. by Charles N. Li, 151–188. New York: Academic Press.

Gómez, Krizzya. 2020. Overt vs. null subjects in nonfinite constructions in Colombian Spanish. Paper presented at the 50th meeting of the Linguistic Symposium on Romance Languages (LSRL), University of Texas, Austin.

Goncharov, Julie. 2016. Binding without Agree. *Syntax-Semantics Interface* 3, 49–72.

Goodluck, Helen. 1981. Children's grammar of complement subject interpretation. In *Language acquisition and linguistic theory*, ed. by Susan Tavakolian, 139–166. Cambridge, MA: MIT Press.

Goodluck, Helen. 1987. Children's interpretations of pronouns and NPs: An alternative view. In *Studies in the acquisition of anaphora, volume II*, ed. by Barbara Lust, 247–269. Dordrecht: Reidel.

Goodluck, Helen. 1998. Children's interpretations of adjunct PRO: New evidence. In *Proceedings of BUCLD 22*, ed. by Annabel Greenhill, Mary Hughes, Heather Littlefield, and Hugh Walsh, 293–302. Somerville, MA: Cascadilla Press.

Goodluck, Helen. 2001. The nominal analysis of children's interpretations of adjunct clauses. *Language* 77, 494–509.

Goodluck, Helen, and Dawn Behne. 1992. Development in control and extraction. In *Theoretical issues in language acquisition*, ed. by Jürgen Weissenborn, Helen Goodluck, and Thomas Roeper, 151–171. Hillsdale, NJ: Erlbaum.

Grano, Thomas A. 2015. *Control and restructuring*. Oxford: Oxford University Press.

Green, Jeffrey J. 2018. Adjunct control: Syntax and processing. PhD dissertation, University of Maryland.

Green, Jeffrey J. 2019. A movement theory of adjunct control. *Glossa* 4(1), 87.

Grimshaw, Jane. 1994. Minimal projection and clause structure. In *Syntactic theory and first language acquisition: Cross-linguistic perspectives*. Vol. 1, *Heads, projections, and learnability*, ed. by Barbara Lust, Margarita Suñer, and John Whitman, 75–83. Hillsdale, NJ: Erlbaum.

Grodzinsky, Yosef, and Tanya Reinhart. 1993. The innateness of binding and coreference. *Linguistic Inquiry* 24, 69–102.

Grohmann, Kleanthes K. 2012. Anti-locality: Too-close relations in grammar. In *The Oxford handbook of linguistic Minimalism*, ed. by Cedric Boeckx, 260–290. Oxford: Oxford University Press.

Haddad, Youssef A. 2009. Copy control in Telugu. *Journal of Linguistics* 45, 69–109.

Haddad, Youssef A. 2017. The Merge condition on adjuncts: Evidence from circumstantial clauses in Lebanese Arabic. In *Perspectives on Arabic Linguistics XXIX*, ed. by Hamid Ouali, 205–226. Amsterdam: John Benjamins.

Haegeman, Liliane. 1990. Understood subjects in English diaries. *Multilingua* 9, 157–199.

Haider, Hubert. 2000. Adverb placement—Convergence of structure and licensing. *Theoretical Linguistics* 26, 95–134.

Haider, Hubert. 2004. Pre- and postverbal adverbials in OV and VO. *Lingua* 114, 779–807.

Han, Chung-hye, and Dennis Ryan Storoshenko. 2012. Semantic binding of long-distance anaphor *caki* in Korean. *Language* 88, 764–790.

Harley, Heidi. 2009. The morphology of nominalization and the syntax of vP. In *Quantification, definiteness, and nominalization*, ed. by Anastasia Giannakidou and Monika Rathert, 320–342. Oxford: Oxford University Press.

Harley, Heidi. 2012. Lexical decomposition in modern generative grammar. In *The Oxford handbook of compositionality*, ed. by Markus Werning, Wolfram Hinzen, and Edouard Machery, 328–350. Oxford: Oxford University Press.

Harley, Heidi. 2013. External arguments and the Mirror Principle: On the distinctness of Voice and v. *Lingua* 125, 34–57.

Hartman, Jeremy. 2008. *Dwarf*-class verbs, theta-theory and argument linking. In *Proceedings of WCCFL 27*, ed. by Natasha Abner and Jason Bishop, 203–210. Somerville, MA: Cascadilla Press.

Haug, Dag T. T., Cathrine Fabricius-Hansen, Bergljot Behrens, and Hans Petter Helland. 2012. Open adjuncts: Degrees of event integration. In *Big events, small clauses: The grammar of elaboration*, ed. by Cathrine Fabricius-Hansen and Dag T. T. Haug, 131–178. Berlin: de Gruyter.

Heim, Irene. 1994. Questions, focus and ellipsis. Class notes for a proseminar in semantics. http://www.sfs.uni-tuebingen.de/~astechow/Lehre/Wien/WienSS06/Heim/HeimQuestionsF94.pdf.

Heim, Irene, and Angelika Kratzer. 1998. *Semantics in generative grammar*. Oxford: Blackwell.

Herbeck, Peter. 2015. Overt PRO in Romance. In *Hispanic linguistics at the crossroads: Theoretical linguistics, language acquisition and language contact*, ed. by Rachel Klassen, Juana M. Liceras, and Elena Valenzuela, 25–48. Amsterdam: John Benjamins.

Herbeck, Peter. 2020. The (null) subject of adjunct infinitives in spoken Spanish. Ms., University of Cologne.

Hermon, Gabriella. 1985. *Syntactic modularity*. Dordrecht: Foris.

Hestvik, Arild, and William Philip. 2001. Syntactic vs. logophoric binding: Evidence from Norwegian child language. In *Long-distance reflexives: Syntax and semantics 33*, ed. by C.-T. James Huang, Gabriella Hermon, and Peter Cole, 119–139. Leiden: Brill.

Hitzeman, Janet. 1997. Semantic partition and the ambiguity of sentences containing temporal adverbials. *Natural Language Semantics* 5, 87–100.

Höhle, Barbara, Frauke Berger, and Antje Sauermann. 2016. Information structure in first language acquisition. In *The Oxford handbook of information structure*, ed. by Caroline Féry and Shinichiro Ishihara, 562–580. Oxford: Oxford University Press.

Holmberg, Anders, Aarti Nayudu, and Michelle Sheehan. 2009. Three partial null-subject languages: A comparison of Brazilian Portuguese, Finnish and Marathi. *Studia Linguistica* 63, 59–97.

Hornstein, Norbert. 1999. Movement and control. *Linguistic Inquiry* 30, 69–96.

Hornstein, Norbert. 2003. On control. In *Minimalist syntax*, ed. by Randall Hendrick, 6–81. Oxford: Blackwell.

Hsu, Jennifer Ryan, Helen S. Cairns, Sarita Eisenberg, and Gloria Schlisselberg. 1989. Control and coreference in early child language. *Journal of Child Language* 16, 599–622.

Hsu, Jennifer Ryan, Helen S. Cairns, and Robert Fiengo. 1985. The development of grammars underlying children's interpretation of complex sentences. *Cognition* 20, 25–48.

Huang, C.-T. James. 1984. On the distribution and reference of empty pronouns. *Linguistic Inquiry* 15, 531–574.

Huang, C.-T. James. 1989. Pro-drop in Chinese: A generalized control theory. In *The null subject parameter*, ed. by Osvaldo Jaeggli and Kenneth J. Safir, 185–214. Dordrecht: Kluwer.

Huang, Yan. 1994. *The syntax and pragmatics of anaphora*. Cambridge: Cambridge University Press.

Huettner, Alison K. 1989. Adjunct infinitives in English. PhD dissertation, University of Massachusetts, Amherst.

Hughes, Mary E., and Shanley E. M. Allen. 2013. The effect of individual discourse-pragmatic features on referential choice in child English. *Journal of Pragmatics* 56, 15–30.

Hyams, Nina. 1996. The underspecification of functional categories in early grammar. In *Generative perspectives on language acquisition*, ed. by Harald Clahsen, 91–127. Amsterdam: John Benjamins.

Hyams, Nina. 2011. Missing subjects in early child language. In *Handbook of generative approaches to language acquisition*, ed. by Jill de Villiers and Tom Roeper, 13–52. Dordrecht: Springer.

Hyams, Nina, and Robyn Orfitelli. 2017. The acquisition of syntax. In *The handbook of psycholinguistics*, ed. by Eva M. Fernández and Helen S. Cairns, 593–614. Oxford: Wiley Blackwell.

Jackendoff, Ray, and Peter W. Culicover. 2003. The semantic basis of control in English. *Language* 79, 517–556.

Jaeggli, Osvaldo. 1986. Passive. *Linguistic Inquiry* 17, 582–622.

Jaeggli, Osvaldo, and Kenneth J. Safir. 1989. The null subject parameter and parametric theory. In *The null subject parameter*, ed. by Osvaldo Jaeggli and Kenneth J. Safir, 1–44. Dordrecht: Kluwer.

Janke, Vikki. 2018a. Discourse effects on older children's interpretations of complement control and temporal adjunct control. *Language Acquisition* 25, 366–391.

Janke, Vikki. 2018b. Who is the agent? The influence of pragmatic leads on children's reference assignment in non-obligatory control. *Journal of Child Language* 45, 442–478.

Janke, Vikki, and Laura R. Bailey. 2017. Effects of discourse on control. *Journal of Linguistics* 53, 533–565.

Janke, Vikki, and Alexandra Perovic. 2017. Contrasting complement control, temporal adjunct control and controlled verbal gerund subjects in ASD: The role of contextual cues in reference assignment. *Frontiers in Psychology* 28 March 2017. https://doi.org/10.3389/fpsyg.2017.00448.

Jespersen, Otto. 1954. *A modern English grammar on historical principles. Part V, Syntax: Vol. 4.* London: Allen and Unwin.

Jespersen, Otto. 1964. *Essentials of English grammar.* Tuscaloosa: University of Alabama Press. (Originally published 1933.)

Jones, Charles. 1991. *Purpose clauses: Syntax, thematics and semantics of English purpose constructions.* Dordrecht: Kluwer.

Jones, Charles. 1992. Comments on Goodluck and Behne. In *Theoretical issues in language acquisition,* ed. by Jürgen Weissenborn, Helen Goodluck, and Thomas Roeper, 173–189. Hillsdale, NJ: Erlbaum.

Joo, Kum-Jeong, and Kamil Ud Deen. 2019. Intrasentential binding and extrasentential binding in child and adult Korean. *First Language* 39, 633–651.

Kawasaki, Noriko. 1993. Control and arbitrary interpretation in English. PhD dissertation, University of Massachusetts, Amherst.

Keyser, Samuel Jay, and Thomas Roeper. 1984. On the middle and ergative constructions in English. *Linguistic Inquiry* 15, 381–416.

Kissock, Madelyn J. 2013. Evidence for 'finiteness' in Telugu. *Natural Language and Linguistic Theory* 32, 29–58.

Kitagawa, Chisato. 1976. Purpose expressions and characterization of volitive NPs. *Linguistics* 182, 53–65.

Klecha, Peet. 2014. Modifying modality. In *Proceedings of NELS 44,* ed. by Jyoti Iyer and Leland Kusmer, 220–232. Amherst: University of Massachusetts, Graduate Linguistic Student Association.

Kortmann, Bernd. 1991. *Free adjuncts and absolutes in English: Problems of control and interpretation.* New York: Routledge.

Koster, Jan. 1984. On binding and control. *Linguistic Inquiry* 15, 417–459.

Kotzoglou, George. 2016. Control in Greek gerunds: Implicit arguments and other factors. In *Selected papers on theoretical and applied linguistics, vol. 21,* ed. by Marina Mattheoudakis and Katerina Nicolaidis, 166–185. Thessaloniki: Aristotle University of Thessaloniki, School of English.

Kroeger, Paul. 1993. *Phrase structure and grammatical relations in Tagalog.* Stanford, CA: CSLI Publications.

Kuno, Susumu. 1975. Super Equi-NP Deletion is a pseudo-transformation. In *Proceedings of NELS 5,* ed. by Ellen Kaisse and Jorge Hankamer, 29–44. Amherst: University of Massachusetts, Graduate Linguistic Student Association.

Kuno, Susumu. 2006. Empathy and direct discourse perspectives. In *Handbook of pragmatics,* ed. by Larry R. Horn and Gregory Ward, 315–343. Oxford: Blackwell.

Landau, Idan. 1999. Psych-adjectives and semantic selection. *The Linguistic Review* 16, 333–358.

Landau, Idan. 2000. *Elements of control: Structure and meaning in infinitival constructions.* Dordrecht: Kluwer.

Landau, Idan. 2001. Control and extraposition: The case of Super-Equi. *Natural Language and Linguistic Theory* 19, 109–152.

Landau, Idan. 2006. Severing the distribution of PRO from Case. *Syntax* 9, 153–170.

Landau, Idan. 2007. Movement-resistant aspects of control. In *New horizons in the analysis of control and raising,* ed. by William D. Davies and Stanley Dubinsky, 293–325. Dordrecht: Springer.

Landau, Idan. 2010a. The explicit syntax of implicit arguments. *Linguistic Inquiry* 41, 357–388.

Landau, Idan. 2010b. *The locative syntax of experiencers.* Cambridge, MA: MIT Press.

Landau, Idan. 2011. Predication vs. aboutness in copy raising. *Natural Language and Linguistic Theory* 29, 779–813.

Landau, Idan. 2013. *Control in generative grammar: A research companion.* Cambridge: Cambridge University Press.

Landau, Idan. 2015. *A two-tiered theory of control.* Cambridge, MA: MIT Press.

Landau, Idan. 2017. Adjunct control depends on voice. In *A pesky set: Papers for David Pesetsky,* ed. by Claire Halpert, Hadas Kotek, and Coppe van Urk, 93–102. Cambridge, MA: MIT, MIT Working Papers in Linguistics.

Landau, Idan. 2020. Nonobligatory control with communication verbs: New evidence and implications. *Linguistic Inquiry* 51, 75–96.

Larson, Richard. 1987. "Missing prepositions" and the analysis of English free relative clauses. *Linguistic Inquiry* 18, 239–266.

Larson, Richard. 1988. On the double object construction. *Linguistic Inquiry* 19, 335–391.

Larson, Richard. 1990. Double objects revisited: Reply to Jackendoff. *Linguistic Inquiry* 21, 589–632.

Larson, Richard. 1991. *Promise* and the theory of control. *Linguistic Inquiry* 22, 103–139.

Larson, Richard. 2004. Sentence-final adverbs and "scope." In *Proceedings of NELS 34,* ed. by Matthew Wolf and Keir Moulton, 23–43. Amherst: University of Massachusetts, Graduate Linguistic Student Association.

Lasnik, Howard. 1988. Subjects and the Theta-Criterion. *Natural Language and Linguistic Theory* 6, 1–17.

Lebeaux, David. 1984. Anaphoric binding and the definition of PRO. In *Proceedings of NELS 14,* ed. by Charles Jones and Peter Sells, 253–274. Amherst: University of Massachusetts, Graduate Linguistic Student Association.

Legendre, Géraldine. 1989. Inversion with certain French experiencer verbs. *Language* 65, 752–782.

Legendre, Géraldine. 1993. Antipassive with French psych-verbs. In *Proceedings of WCCFL 12,* ed. by Erin Dunca, Donka Farkas, and Philip Spaelti, 373–388. Stanford, CA: CSLI Publications.

Legendre, Géraldine, and Tanya Akimova. 1993. Inversion and antipassive in Russian. In *The 2nd Annual Workshop on Formal Approaches to Slavic Linguistics,* ed. by Sergey

Avrutin, Steven Franks, and Ljiljana Progovac, 286–318. Ann Arbor: Michigan Slavic Publications.

Liefke, Kristina, and Markus Werning. 2018. Evidence for single-type semantics—An alternative to *e/t*-based dual-type semantics. *Journal of Semantics* 35, 639–685.

Lobo, Maria. 2002. On the structural position of non-peripheral adjunct clauses. *Journal of Portuguese Linguistics* 1, 83–118.

Lust, Barbara, Larry Solan, Suzanne Flynn, Catherine Cross, and Elaine Schuetz. 1986. A comparison of null and pronoun anaphora in first language acquisition. In *Studies in the acquisition of anaphora, vol. I*, ed. by Barbara Lust, 245–277. Dordrecht: Reidel.

Lyngfelt, Benjamin. 1999. Optimal control: An OT perspective on the interpretation of PRO in Swedish. *Working Papers in Scandinavian Syntax* 63, 75–104.

Lyngfelt, Benjamin. 2000. OT semantics and control. Ms., Göteborg University.

Lyngfelt, Benjamin. 2009a. Control phenomena. In *Grammar, meaning and pragmatics*, ed. by Jan-Ola Östman and Jef Verschueren, 33–49. Amsterdam: John Benjamins.

Lyngfelt, Benjamin. 2009b. Towards a comprehensive Construction Grammar account of control: A case study of Swedish infinitives. *Constructions and Frames* 1, 153–189.

Manetta, Emily. 2013. Copy Theory in *wh*-in-situ languages: Sluicing in Hindi-Urdu. *Journal of South Asian Languages* 6, 3–24.

Manzini, M. Rita. 1983. On control and control theory. *Linguistic Inquiry* 14, 421–446.

Manzini, M. Rita. 1986. On control and binding theory. In *Proceedings of NELS 16*, ed. by Stephen Berman, Jae-Woong Choe, and Joyce McDonough, 322–337. Amherst: University of Massachusetts, Graduate Linguistic Student Association.

Manzini, M. Rita. 2009. PRO, *pro* and NP-trace (raising) are interpretations. In *Explorations of phase theory (2): Features and arguments*, ed. by Kleanthes K. Grohmann, 131–180. Berlin: Mouton de Gruyter.

Manzini, M. Rita, and Anna Roussou. 2000. A Minimalist theory of A-movement and control. *Lingua* 110, 409–447.

McCawley, James D. 1986–1996. Flea circus handouts. Collected by Ronnie Wilbur. https://ling.auf.net/lingbuzz/003698.

McDaniel, Dana, and Helen S. Cairns. 1990. Processing and acquisition of control structures by young children. In *Language processing and language acquisition*, ed. by Lyn Frazier and Jill de Villiers, 311–325. Dordrecht: Kluwer.

McDaniel, Dana, Helen S. Cairns, and Jennifer Ryan Hsu. 1991. Control principles in the grammars of young children. *Language Acquisition* 4, 297–335.

McFadden, Thomas, and Sandhya Sundaresan. 2018. Reducing *pro* and PRO to a single source. *The Linguistic Review* 35, 463–518.

Meinunger, André. 2006. Interface restrictions on verb second. *The Linguistic Review* 23, 127–160.

Merchant, Jason. 2013a. Diagnosing ellipsis. In *Diagnosing syntax*, ed. by Lisa Lai-Shen Cheng and Norbert Corver, 537–542. Oxford: Oxford University Press.

Merchant, Jason. 2013b. Voice and ellipsis. *Linguistic Inquiry* 44, 77–108.

Merchant, Jason. 2018. Roots don't select, categorial heads do: Lexical-selection of PPs may vary by category. Ms., University of Chicago.

Modesto, Marcello. 2000. On the identification of null arguments. PhD dissertation, University of Southern California.

Modesto, Marcello. 2008. Topic prominence and null subjects. In *The limits of syntactic variation*, ed. by Theresa Biberauer, 375–409. Amsterdam: John Benjamins.

Modesto, Marcello. 2011. Finite control: Where movement goes wrong in Brazilian Portuguese. *Journal of Portuguese Linguistics* 10, 3–30.

Mohanan, K. P. 1983. Functional and anaphoric control. *Linguistic Inquiry* 14, 641–674.

Mucha, Anne, Jutta M. Hartmann, and Beata Trawiński. To appear. *Non-canonical control in a cross-linguistic perspective*. Amsterdam: John Benjamins.

Nilsen, Øystein. 2004. Domain for adverbs. *Lingua* 114, 809–847.

Nishigauchi, Taisuke. 1984. Control and the thematic domain. *Language* 60, 215–250.

Nishigauchi, Taisuke. 2014. Reflexive binding: Awareness and empathy from a syntactic point of view. *Journal of East Asian Linguistics* 23, 157–206.

Nissenbaum, Jon. 1998. Derived predicates and the interpretation of parasitic gaps. In *Proceedings of WCCFL 17*, ed. by Kimary Shahin, Susan Blake, and Eun-Sook Kim, 507–521. Stanford, CA: CSLI Publications.

Nissenbaum, Jon. 2000. Covert movement and parasitic gaps. In *Proceedings of NELS 30*, ed. by Masako Hirotani, Andries Coetzee, Nancy Hall, and Ji-Yung Kim. 541–555. Amherst: University of Massachusetts, Graduate Linguistic Student Association.

Nunes, Jairo. 2014. Adjunct control and edge features. In *Minimalism and beyond: Radicalizing the interfaces*, ed. by Peter Kosta, Steven L. Franks, Teodora Radeva-Bork, and Lilia Schürcks, 79–108. Amsterdam: John Benjamins.

Oded, Ilknur. 2011. Recalculating adjunct control. PhD dissertation, University of Maryland.

Parker, Dan, Sol Lago, and Colin Phillips. 2015. Interference in the processing of adjunct control. *Frontiers in Psychology*, 8 September 2015. https://doi.org/10.3389/fpsyg.2015.01346.

Paz, Justin. 2019. Revising the distribution of control: Evidence from Spanish. Handout of a talk presented at the workshop "Crosslinguistic Variation in Control Phenomena," DGFS 41, University of Bremen.

Pearson, Matthew. 2005. The Malagasy subject as an Ā-element. *Natural Language and Linguistic Theory* 23, 381–457.

Perlmutter, David M. 1984. Working 1s and inversion in Italian, Japanese and Quechua. In *Studies in Relational Grammar 2*, ed. by David M. Perlmutter and Carol G. Rosen, 292–330. Chicago: University of Chicago Press.

Petter, Marga. 1998. *Getting PRO under control*. LOT International Series, Vol. 8. The Hague: HIL, Holland Academic Graphics.

Pires, Acrisio. 2007. The derivation of clausal gerunds. *Syntax* 10, 165–203.

Pitteroff, Marcel, and Florian Schäfer. 2019. Implicit control cross-linguistically. *Language* 95, 136–184.

Poole, Ethan. 2015. An argument for implicit arguments. Ms., University of Massachusetts, Amherst.

Postal, Paul M. 1974. *On raising.* Cambridge, MA: MIT Press.

Postal, Paul M. 2004. *Skeptical linguistics essays.* Oxford: Oxford University Press.

Potts, Christopher. 2002. The lexical semantics of parenthetical-*as* and appositive-*which. Syntax* 5, 55–88.

Preminger, Omer. 2014. *Agreement and its failures.* Cambridge, MA: MIT Press.

Quirk, Randolph, Sidney Greenbaum, Geoffrey Leach, and Jan Svartvik. 1985. *A comprehensive grammar of the English language.* London: Longman.

Radford, Andrew. 1996. Towards a structure-building model of acquisition. In *Generative perspectives on language acquisition,* ed. by Harald Clahsen, 43–90. Amsterdam: John Benjamins.

Ramchand, Gillian. 2008. *Verb meaning and the lexicon: A first phase syntax.* Cambridge: Cambridge University Press.

Reed, Lisa. 2012. A semantic constraint on tenseless clausal complementation. *Studia Linguistica* 66, 286–321.

Reed, Lisa. 2014. *Strengthening the PRO Hypothesis.* Berlin: de Gruyter.

Reinhart, Tanya. 1983. *Anaphora and semantic interpretation.* London: Croom Helm.

Reinhart, Tanya. 1998. *Wh*-in-situ in the framework of the Minimalist Program. *Natural Language Semantics* 6, 29–56.

Reinhart, Tanya. 2000. Strategies of anaphora resolution. In *Interface strategies,* ed. by Hans Bennis, Martin Everaert, and Eric J. Reuland, 295–325. Amsterdam: Royal Academy of Arts and Sciences.

Reinhart, Tanya. 2006. *Interface strategies: Optimal and costly computations.* Cambridge, MA: MIT Press.

Reinhart, Tanya, and Eric Reuland. 1993. Reflexivity. *Linguistic Inquiry* 24, 657–720.

Reuland, Eric J. 1983. Governing -*ing. Linguistic Inquiry* 14, 101–136.

Richards, Norvin. 2000. Another look at Tagalog subjects. In *Formal issues in Austronesian linguistics,* ed. by Ileana Paul, Vivianne Phillips, and Lisa Travis, 105–116. Dordrecht: Kluwer.

Richardson, John F. 1986. Super-Equi and anaphoric control. In *Proceedings of the 22nd Meeting of the Chicago Linguistic Society,* ed. by Anne M. Farley, Peter T. Farley, and Karl-Erik McCullough, 248–261. Chicago: University of Chicago, Chicago Linguistic Society.

Rigau, Gemma. 1998. On temporal and causal infinitive constructions in Catalan dialects. *Catalan Working Papers in Linguistics* 6, 95–114.

Ritter, Elisabeth, and Sara T. Rosen. 1998. Delimiting events in syntax. In *The projection of arguments: Lexical and compositional factors,* ed. by Miriam Butt and Wilhelm Geuder, 135–164. Stanford, CA: CSLI Publications.

Rizzi, Luigi. 1986. Null objects in Italian and the theory of *pro. Linguistic Inquiry* 17, 501–557.

Rizzi, Luigi. 2000. Remarks on early null subjects. In *The acquisition of syntax*, ed. by Marc-Ariel Friedeman and Luigi Rizzi, 269–292. London: Longman.

Rochette, Anne. 1988. Semantic and syntactic aspects of Romance sentential complementation. PhD dissertation, MIT.

Rodrigues, Cilene. 2004. Impoverished morphology and A-movement out of Case domains. PhD dissertation, University of Maryland.

Roeper, Thomas. 1987. Implicit arguments and the head-complement relation. *Linguistic Inquiry* 18, 267–310.

Roeper, Tom, and Jill de Villiers. 1995. Barriers, binding, and acquisition of the DP-NP distinction. *Language Acquisition* 4, 73–104.

Roeper, Tom, and Bernard Rohrbacher. 2000. Null subjects in early child English and the theory of economy of projection. In *The acquisition of scrambling and cliticization*, ed. by Susan M. Powers and Cornelia Hamann, 345–396. Dordrecht: Kluwer.

Rosenbaum, Peter. 1967. *The grammar of English predicate complement constructions*. Cambridge, MA: MIT Press.

Růžička, Rudolph. 1999. *Control in grammar and pragmatics: A cross-linguistic study*. Amsterdam: John Benjamins.

Safir, Ken. 1985. *Syntactic chains*. Cambridge: Cambridge University Press.

Safir, Ken. 1993. Perception, selection, and structural economy. *Natural Language Semantics* 2, 47–70.

Sag, Ivan, and Carl Pollard. 1991. An integrated theory of complement control. *Language* 67, 63–113.

Salzmann, Martin. 2017. Prolepsis. In *The Wiley Blackwell companion to syntax, second edition*, ed. by Martin Everaert and Henk C. van Riemsdijk. Oxford: Wiley-Blackwell.

Schachter, Paul. 1976. The subject in Philippine languages: Topic, actor, actor-topic, or none of the above. In *Subject and topic*, ed. by Charles N. Li, 491–518. New York: Academic Press.

Schaeffer, Jeannette. 2000. *The acquisition of direct object scrambling and clitic placement: Syntax and pragmatics*. Amsterdam: John Benjamins.

Schaeffer, Jeannette, and Lisa Matthewson. 2005. Grammar and pragmatics in the acquisition of article systems. *Natural Language and Linguistic Theory* 23, 53–101.

Sellar, Melanie. 1999. The acquisition of temporal connectives from a Reichenbachian perspective. MA thesis, University of Ottawa.

Sells, Peter. 1987. Aspects of logophoricity. *Linguistic Inquiry* 18, 445–480.

Sharvit, Yael. 2003. Trying to be progressive: The extensionality of *try*. *Journal of Semantics* 20, 403–445.

Sigurðsson, Halldór Ármann. 2011. Conditions on argument drop. *Linguistic Inquiry* 42, 267–304.

Sigurjónsdóttir, Sigríður. 2013. The acquisition of reflexives and pronouns by Faroese children. In *Generative linguistics and acquisition: Studies in honor of Nina M.*

Hyams, ed. by Misha Becker, John Grinstead, and Jason Rothman, 129–156. Amsterdam: John Benjamins.

Sigurjónsdóttir, Sigríður, and Nina Hyams. 1992. Reflexivization and logophoricity: Evidence from the acquisition of Icelandic. *Language Acquisition* 2, 359–413.

Song, Jae Jung. 2001. *Linguistic typology: Morphology and syntax*. London: Pearson Education.

Spadine, Carolyn. 2018. Control in illocutionary adjuncts as a diagnostic for discourse arguments. Poster presented at NELS 49, Cornell University.

Speas, Margaret. 2006. Economy, agreement, and the representation of null arguments. In *Arguments and agreement*, ed. by Peter Ackema, Patrick Brandt, Maaike Schoorlemmer, and Fred Weerman, 35–75. Oxford: Oxford University Press.

Stassen, Leon. 1985. *Comparison and Universal Grammar*. Oxford: Blackwell.

Steedman, Mark. 1987. Combinatory grammars and parasitic gaps. *Natural Language and Linguistic Theory* 5, 403–439.

Steedman, Mark. 1988. Combinations and grammars. In *Categorial grammars and natural language structures*, ed. by Richard T. Oehrle, Emmon Bach, and Deirdre Wheeler, 417–442. Dordrecht: Springer.

Stromdahl, Larson. 2018. The control of infinitival adjuncts and ditransitive constructions. Poster presented at the 92nd annual meeting of the Linguistic Society of America, Salt Lake City, UT.

Stump, Gregory T. 1985. *The semantic variability of absolute constructions*. Dordrecht: Reidel.

Su, Yi-ching. 2017. Logophoric *ziji* in Mandarin child language. In *Studies in Chinese and Japanese language acquisition: In honor of Stephen Crain*, ed. by Mineharu Nakayama, Yi-ching Su, and Aijun Huang, 65–84. Amsterdam: John Benjamins.

Sundaresan, Sandhya. 2014. Making sense of silence: Finiteness and the (OC) PRO vs. *pro* distinction. *Natural Language and Linguistic Theory* 32, 59–85.

Sundaresan, Sandhya. 2018a. An alternative model of indexical shift: Variation and selection without context-overwriting. Ms., Universität Leipzig.

Sundaresan, Sandhya. 2018b. Perspective is syntactic: Evidence from anaphora. *Glossa* 3(1), 128.

Sundaresan, Sandhya, and Thomas McFadden. 2009. Subject distribution in Tamil and other languages: Selection vs. Case. *Journal of South Asian Linguistics* 2, 5–34.

Swierskia, Anna. 2004. *Person*. Cambridge: Cambridge University Press.

Szabolcsi, Anna. 1983. ECP in Categorial Grammar. Ms., Max Planck Institute, Nijmegen.

Szabolcsi, Anna. 1989. Bound variables in syntax (Are there any?). In *Semantics and contextual expression*, ed. by Renate Bartsch, Johan van Benthem, and Peter van Emde Boas, 295–319. Dordrecht: Foris.

Thornton, Rosalind, and Graciela Tesan. 2013. Sentential negation in early child English. *Journal of Linguistics* 49, 367–411.

Thornton, Rosalind, and Kenneth Wexler. 1999. *Principle B, VP ellipsis, and interpretation in child grammar*. Cambridge, MA: MIT Press.

Thráinsson, Höskuldur. 1996. On the (non)universality of functional categories. In *Minimalist ideas: Syntactic studies in the Minimalist framework*, ed. by Werner Abraham, Samuel David Epstein, Höskuldur Thráinsson, and C. Jan-Wouter Zwart, 253–282. Amsterdam: John Benjamins.

Truswell, Robert. 2011. *Events, phrases, and questions*. Oxford: Oxford University Press.

Valian, Virginia. 2016. Null subjects. In *The Oxford handbook of developmental linguistics*, ed. by Jeffrey L. Lidz, William Snyder, and Joe Pater, chapter 17. Oxford: Oxford University Press.

Vanden Wyngaerd, Guido J. 1994. *PRO-legomena*. Berlin: Mouton de Gruyter.

VanDyne, Katie. 2020. Adjunct control by object clitics in Spanish: An argument against control as movement. Paper presented at the 50th meeting of the Linguistic Symposium on Romance Languages (LSRL), University of Texas, Austin.

Vinet, Marie-Thérèse. 1987. Implicit arguments and control in middles and passives. In *Advances in Romance linguistics*, ed. by David Birdsong and Jean-Pierre Montreuil, 427–437. Dordrecht: Foris.

Wexler, Kenneth. 1992. Some issues in the growth of control. In *Control and grammar*, ed. by Richard Larson, Sabine Iatridou, Utpal Lahiri, and James Higginbotham, 253–295. Dordrecht: Kluwer.

Whelpton, Matthew. 2001. Elucidation of a telic infinitive. *Journal of Linguistics* 37, 313–337.

Whelpton, Matthew. 2002. Locality and control with infinitives of result. *Natural Language Semantics* 10, 167–210.

Williams, Alexander. 2015. *Arguments in synax and semantics*. Cambridge: Cambridge University Press.

Williams, Alexander, and Jeffrey Green. 2017. Why control of PRO in rationale clauses is not a relation between arguments. In *Proceedings of NELS 47*, ed. by Andrew Lamont and Katerina Tetzloff, 233–246. Amherst: University of Massachusetts, Graduate Linguistic Student Association.

Williams, Edwin. 1980. Predication. *Linguistic Inquiry* 11, 203–238.

Williams, Edwin. 1985. PRO and subject of NP. *Natural Language and Linguistic Theory* 3, 297–315.

Williams, Edwin. 1992. Adjunct control. In *Control and grammar*, ed. by Richard Larson, Sabine Iatridou, Utpal Lahiri, and James Higginbotham, 297–322. Dordrecht: Kluwer.

Williams, Edwin. 1994. *Thematic structure in syntax*. Cambridge, MA: MIT Press.

Witkoś, Jacek, and Sylwiusz Żychliński. 2014. Solving adjunct control through tiered attachment sites plus smuggling. In *Proceedings of FASL 22*, ed. by Cassandra Chapman, Olena Kit, and Ivona Kučerová, 423–443. Ann Arbor: Michigan Slavic Publications.

Woods, Rebecca. 2014. The syntax of orientation shifting: Evidence from English high adverbs. In *Proceedings of ConSOLE 22*, ed. by Martin Kohlberger, Kate Bellamy, and Eleanor Dutton, 205–230. Leiden: Leiden University Centre for Linguistics.

Wurmbrand, Susi. 2002. Semantic vs. syntactic control. In *Proceedings of the 15th Workshop on Comparative Germanic Syntax*, ed. by C. Jan-Wouter Zwart and Werner Abraham, 93–127. Amsterdam: John Benjamins.

Wurmbrand, Susi. 2003. *Infinitives: Restructuring and clause structure*. New York: Mouton de Gruyter.

Wurmbrand, Susi. 2004. Two types of restructuring—Lexical vs. functional. *Lingua* 114, 991–1014.

Wurmbrand, Susi, and Magdalena Lohninger. To appear. An implicational universal in complementation—Theoretical insights and empirical progress. In *Propositional arguments in crosslinguistic research: Theoretical and empirical issues*, ed. by Jutta Hartmann and Angelika Wölkstein. Tübingen: Gunter Narr Verlag.

Zeijlstra, Hedde. 2007. Doubling: The semantic driving force behind functional categories. In *Logic, language and computation*, ed. by Balder ten Cate and Henk Zeevat, 260–280. Berlin: Springer.

Zeijlstra, Hedde. 2020. Labeling, selection, and feature checking. In *Agree to agree: Agreement in the Minimalist Programme*, ed. by Peter W. Smith, Katharina Hartmann, and Johannes Mursell, 31–70. Berlin: Language Science Press.

Zobel, Sarah. 2018. An analysis of the semantic variability of weak adjuncts and its problems. In *Proceedings of Sinn und Bedeutung 22*, ed. by Uli Sauerland and Stephanie Solt, 2:499–516. Berlin: ZAS.

Zobel, Sarah. 2019. Accounting for the "causal link" between free adjuncts and their host clauses. In *Proceedings of Sinn und Bedeutung 23*, ed. by M. Teresa Espinal, Elena Castroviejo, Manuel Leonetti, Louise McNally, and Cristina Real-Puigdollers, 491–508. Bellaterra (Cerdanyola del Vallès): Universitat Autònoma de Barcelona.

Zribi-Hertz, Anne. 1989. Anaphor binding and narrative point of view: English reflexive pronouns in sentence and discourse. *Language* 65, 695–727.

Zu, Vera. 2018. Discourse participants and the structural representation of context. PhD dissertation, New York University.

Index

Linguistic Inquiry Monographs

Samuel Jay Keyser, general editor